Capturing Profit *with* Technical Analysis

Hands-on Rules for Exploiting Candlestick, Indicator, & Money Management Techniques

Sylvain Vervoort

MARKETPLACE BOOKS®
GLENELG, MARYLAND

Publisher: Chris Myers
VP/General Manager: John Boyer
Executive Editor: Jody Costa
Production Editor: Courtney Jenkins
Art Director | Designer: Larry Strauss

This book, along with other books, is available at discounts that make it realistic to provide them as gifts to your customers, clients, and staff. For more information on these long lasting, cost effective premiums, please call us at 800-272-2855 or e-mail us at sales@traderslibrary.com.

Printed in the United States of America.

Library of Congress Cataloging-in-Publication Data

Vervoort, Sylvain.

  Capturing profit with technical analysis : hands-on rules for exploiting candlestick, indicator, and money management techniques / Sylvain Vervoort.

    p. cm.

  Includes bibliographical references.

  ISBN-13: 978-1-59280-375-0 (hbk.)

  ISBN-10: 1-59280-375-X (hbk.)

 1. Technical analysis (Investment analysis) 2. Investment analysis. I. Title.

  HG4529.V47 2009

  332.63'2042--dc22

                          2009028904

CONTENTS

FOREWORD

The following is my weak attempt to glorify a book that I have fallen in love with.

This decade has been resounding proof that the philosophy of "buy and hold" doesn't work and certainly doesn't reduce risk. In the late '90s, advisors were illustrating returns above 12 percent because that is what they experienced from the market in the 10 years prior. Now, after two recessions in one decade where many lost half their portfolios two different times, I believe there is a new awareness about risk in the asset allocation methodology. We are told time and again from investment representatives that return is derived from asset allocation, NOT market timing. I wouldn't want to be the one still selling that!

There is a vast difference between asset allocation and market timing. In between lies an area of opportunity that would shock the average investor who trusts their large firm investment advisor. In this world, investors buy near support levels and sell at resistance levels. They buy when the cycle is low and sell when it is peaking. Each time they buy, they know exactly where it is they would sell if things go wrong. They never lose unacceptable amounts on any single investment position. The result is outperformance of the market with less portfolio volatility. The bottom line is they never experience 50 percent draw downs in their portfolios like their buy and hold counterparts.

The LOCKIT system that Sylvain has outlined in his book is exactly such a system. You don't need to have years of experience in the market to understand this approach. He leads you step-by-step through the decision process of which stocks to buy and when. More importantly, he helps you determine an opportune time to sell.

The robustness of this system is what I like the most. It will work on any type of stock you want to follow. Some like the blue chip names while others look for more growth potential. Simply follow his methodical approach and you will come out ahead of the crowd.

I have been in the investment business since 1992 and have continually worked to improve my investment performance. I have spent countless hours developing quantitative mechanical investment systems and backtesting them. I have taken nearly every formula Sylvain includes in this book and rewrote it to test with my system. I couldn't be more pleased with the results.

There is no doubt in my mind that good technical analysis will beat the market every time. The struggle is going through the maze of technical analysis tools and determining which ones make sense alongside each other. Sylvain has taken the tools that I have liked the most and turned them into a complete system.

John M. Norquay

John M. Norquay has been offering investment advice since 1992. He is the owner of a registered investment advisory service in Madison, Wisconsin, where he utilizes both fundamental and technical analysis for his investment decisions. Mr. Norquay is also the founder of eWatch401k.com, a service which helps individuals keep their 401k accounts invested properly with a quantitative mechanical investment system he designed using technical analysis.

INTRODUCTION

Some 30 years ago, an enthusiastic stock trading colleague at work initiated what has become a lifelong pursuit for me. I can still remember the first technical analysis program running on my first homemade IBM PC. I manually entered the hexadecimal machine code in Read Only Memory for the startup of the machine. This was code that IBM was nice enough to publish in the first IBM PC technical manual.

A couple of years later after the European Options Exchange (EOE), Europe's first option and futures exchange, was founded in Amsterdam, my friend convinced me that this was the place to make a lot of money with only a little starting capital. And so, with a group of colleagues we gathered some 400,000 Belgian Francs (some 10,000 dollars) to start an options investment club. I was going to make the trades based on technical analysis, and everybody would become rich in no time!

A few months later, the money was gone. Luckily, we continued our meetings at the nearby Chinese restaurant, so it wasn't all sad.

Since hitting that bottom, I have been on what seems to be a never-ending quest to find the ideal way of trading the stock market using technical analysis.

After first completing an investment and credit advisor course, I have since conducted many courses and presentations about technical analysis and options. The best thing about presenting a course is that as a teacher you learn even more than your students; so thank you very much to all who have attended my courses!

There are a lot of books about investing and technical analysis. Most of them concentrate on a very specific item, exploring that particular concept in great detail. A book with a real trading system, including all the required basic knowledge, is much more difficult to find.

This trading book is a *complete reference* on how to apply technical analysis for profits. It explains my own trading style—the whole complete story from start to finish. I learned from my mistakes and wrote down some rules to help you avoid making these same mistakes over and over again. You will actually find specific answers to the all-important "where to open" and "when to close" questions in this book. And, to spare your precious time and to speed-up the learning process, I am limiting the text to the bare essentials—what you really need to know. The best part—all of the techniques discussed will be illustrated with an application example.

If you are disappointed with buy-and-hold investing, then medium-term trading based on technical analysis is for you. These days technical analysis is quite extensive and a book with everything you should know about—from the basic bar chart to candlestick patterns and Elliott wave analysis—is not easy to find. Add trading rules, money management, and risk management and you have a book that is virtually impossible to find…. Until now! The goal of my book is to give you all of that information plus my own proprietary indicator SVAPO, a "Short term Volume and Price Oscillator."

All the basics and all the advanced ideas in technical analysis are not worth much if you don't know how to combine and apply them. That is the goal of this book. With the LOCKIT methodology, you can apply the most effective trading techniques to capture consistent results in the markets. This book will teach you to look at the "Long" term trend, when to "Open" a trade, when to "Close" a trade, to look at the "K-factor" for risk and money management, and finally to make sure that you use an "Initial" and a "Trailing" stop—in short, "LOCKIT." What you have in these pages is a step-by-step trading system using technical analysis, including tips on good money and risk management.

You already understand that some trade setups are better than others. That is why you will find trade setups that offer a better chance for success in LOCKIT.

Now and then, I notice advertisements about learning technical analysis in a couple of evenings or a weekend. Do you believe that this is possible? No, of course it's not; you need to invest more time and you must practice as much as possible. The best way to learn technical analysis is to use past price data, advancing day by day to make buy and sell decisions. Only if you are capable of making a profit, should you switch to real time; however, you should still be paper trading. If you are capable of making money at this stage, you can start with real money, but make absolutely sure that by then you have a good set of rules that you will follow without *any* hesitation. The LOCKIT rules will definitely help you to start off on the right foot.

While applying LOCKIT, you will make practical use of all aspects of technical analysis. For that reason, I wrote the part "Technical Analysis Basics," which will give you a detailed description, including examples, of all the technical analysis techniques used by LOCKIT. For most of the techniques, we will show their application within LOCKIT.

LOCKIT introduces you to a number of special indicators and techniques for a more successful application of technical analysis like: zero-lagging moving averages, a Heikin-ashi Bollinger Bands %b indicator, SVAPO "Short term Volume and Price Oscillator," trailing stop methods, and more. And let's not forget, I've also included a very good money management method and a number of examples for good risk management.

I am fully convinced that trading based upon technical analysis (as proposed in this book) and following the LOCKIT rules will help you to make better and more profitable trading decisions.

To simplify the decision-making process, there is a set of LOCKIT trading rules for a number of different circumstances: long and short trading with a trend reversal or after a correction in an ongoing trend.

Please note that I will continue to contribute articles about technical analysis in *Technical Analysis of Stocks & Commodities* magazine. Here, my new ideas and findings (as well as other writers) will keep you up-to-date.

I am sure that this book with all the technical analysis techniques, money management, risk management, and high probability entries will be a turning point for your own technical trading.

I wish you lots of success and happy trading!

– Sylvain Vervoort

Capturing Profit *with* Technical Analysis

PART I
LOCKIT TECHNICAL ANALYSIS TOOLS

LOCKIT

LOCKIT is a stock-trading method based on applying technical analysis and money and risk management techniques.

LOCKIT is an acronym that stands for:

L **"Long term"** What is the Long-term trend?

O **"Open"** The rules for Opening a position.

C **"Close"** The rules for Closing a position.

K **"K-ratio"** Keep risk under control and manage your money.

I **"Initial stop"** Set an Initial stop loss.

T **"Trailing stop"** Set a Trailing stop loss.

Please note that special indicators used within LOCKIT are available in MetaStock® code. I have included a disc in the back of this book that has all of these codes ready for upload. If, however, you don't use Metastock, the Appendix gives you a list of other programs that have all or most of the used code available for their application.

Chapter 7 will give you an overview of the entire LOCKIT system in a step-by-step process; however, you need a working knowledge of the basic technical analysis tools first.

Chapter 1 | Technical Analysis Basics

echnical analysis starts with the graphical representation of stock prices in a chart. Let's have a look at the different charts and which type provides the most information. For some of you, this information may seem too basic; however, I would *highly recommend* giving it a quick read as a review before you continue on to the more advanced topics. You will need a complete understanding of all the technical analysis tools found in this Part in order to fully utilize the LOCKIT trading indicators and rules found in Parts II, III, and IV.

CHARTS

Although there are many charts, the ones listed below are those used most often, and the candle chart is our preference in LOCKIT because it provides the most information.

Line Chart

A line chart is not used much anymore. It was the basic chart used prior to the advent of the personal computer. Stock price data was registered manually, and only closing prices were registered.

The line chart was created connecting the closing prices (figure 1.1).

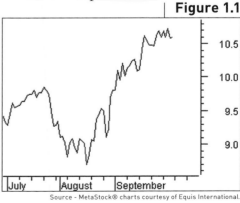

Figure 1.1

Source - MetaStock® charts courtesy of Equis International.

Figure 1.2

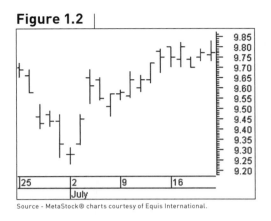

Bar Chart

The highest and the lowest prices in the given period (minutes, hours, days, weeks, and months) are connected with a vertical bar.

In figure 1.2, the opening price is represented by the tick mark at the left side; the closing price is represented by the tick mark at the right side. The bottom and the top of the vertical bar represent the lowest and highest prices of the period, respectively. The bar chart is used mostly in Western technical analysis.

Candle Chart

The candle chart has its roots in the Far East. It is believed that Mr. Homma, a Japanese rice merchant, used candle charts for the first time around the year 1750. Steve Nison introduced the candle chart to the Western world in his book, *Japanese Candlestick Charting Techniques* (Nison, 1991).

Figure 1.3

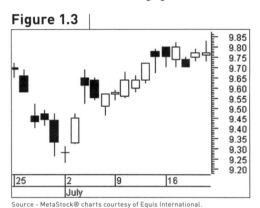

Candle charts clearly depict price development in a trading period. The body of the candle in figure 1.3 represents the move between the opening and closing prices. If the price closes above the opening price, the candle body is blank (white). If the stock price closes below the opening price, the candle body is filled (black).

A candle can be either a body or a body with long or short wicks, called shadows that reach to the highest and lowest prices in the trading period.

The recognition of candlestick patterns is a study unto itself. We will discuss most of these patterns in chapter 3.

LOCKIT

In LOCKIT, candle patterns are a vital part of our decision-making process and are most commonly used on the daily charts. We will on occasion use bar charts in our examples when looking at longer-term trends.

LINEAR OR LOGARITHMIC SCALING

If you are using a division of five points on a linear scale, a price change from $20 to $40 comprises four divisions, whereas a price change from $40 to $80 comprises eight divisions.

This means that the distance on the vertical axis in figure 1.4 from $40 to $80 is twice as large as the one from $20 to $40. On the other hand, a price change from $20 to $40 or from $40 to $80 equals the same 100% price increase.

A price moving from $5 to $10 or from $100 to $105 is also the same distance on a linear scale. Clearly, this does not provide a good visual impression of what the price movement really represents. Moving from $5 to $10 equals a 100% price increase, but moving from $100 to $105 equals only a 5% increase.

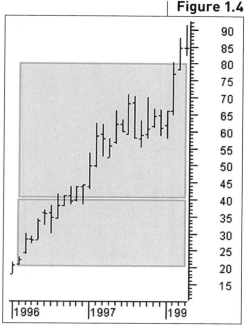

Source - MetaStock® charts courtesy of Equis International.

Figure 1.4

Semi-logarithmic Scaling

To have the same distance on the vertical scale representing equal percent changes, you can use logarithmic scaling.

We use the expression "semi-logarithmic scaling" because there is a linear time scale on the horizontal axis and a logarithmic price scale on the vertical axis (figure 1.5). This means that the distance on the vertical axis from $40 to $80 is now the same as the one from $20 to $40, namely a 100% price increase.

This gives a much better visual impression on charts with large price moves.

For a chart with small overall price changes up to 50% or more, the difference between a linear and a logarithmic scale will be hardly visible on the screen.

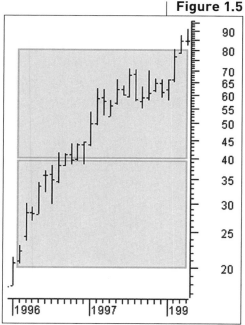

Source - MetaStock® charts courtesy of Equis International.

Figure 1.5

Using Linear or Logarithmic Scaling on the Price Axis

When there are large price moves, applying a linear scale can be a disadvantage.

Figure 1.6

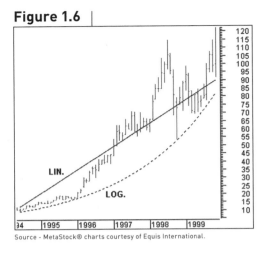

LIN.

LOG.

Source - MetaStock® charts courtesy of Equis International.

Figure 1.7

Source - MetaStock® charts courtesy of Equis International.

Figure 1.8

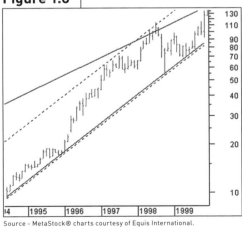

Source - MetaStock® charts courtesy of Equis International.

As you can see in figure 1.6, it is simply not possible to draw a trend line under the up-move from 1996 through 2000.

When you use a logarithmic trend line (the dotted line), the price finds support on this trend line.

Compare this to the linear line that is drawn between the same start and endpoint as the logarithmic curve.

In figure 1.7, you see the same chart, but this time it's using a logarithmic scale on the vertical axis. It is no longer a problem to have a linear trend line under the monthly price move from 1996 through 2000. The dotted logarithmic curve is now a straight line because the logarithmic scale on the vertical axis compensates the logarithmic curve of this trend line.

The correct choice is to use a logarithmic scale on the charts. This gives you the ability to use linear trend lines without a problem.

There is, however, a serious disadvantage. In the chart in figure 1.8, both the linear and logarithmic trend lines were moved up to see if they can form a trend channel. This works well with the logarithmic trend line because it is compensated at every level by the logarithmic vertical axis scaling.

But this is not the case for the linear trend line. Moving the linear trend line will change the inclination of that line because it is moving into a different price range. So the correct thing to do is to use a logarithmic trend line on a logarithmic price chart.

Nevertheless, most people will use linear scaling on daily price charts, which is fine as long as the price moves within limits. More often, logarithmic scaling is applied to longer-term charts, such as weekly or monthly charts, mainly because the price moves are much more significant.

The right solution is to use logarithmic price charts with logarithmic trend lines all the time.

In the chart in figure 1.14, notice the first reversal with a hammer pattern and the next two reversals with engulfing bullish patterns.

Application Example

In figure 1.15, after the price tops in April, it falls back to $11.70.

The price bounces up, but it falls back on June 13 at the support of the previous low point. Support is confirmed by a hammer in the candlestick chart. This is an ideal situation for opening a long position.

Buying here allows keeping a close stop at $11.70. If the closing price drops below this level, the support is no longer valid, and it will be better to sell with a small loss. The possible profit-to-loss ratio is very good. "Buy now" is the message!

And a good buy it was!

Look also at the intermediate support levels during the six months' up-move (figure 1.16). It received some support from price turning points and some from window support.

Don't forget: There is always the possibility that the price will move the other way. Then you will have to sell as soon as the closing price falls below the support level.

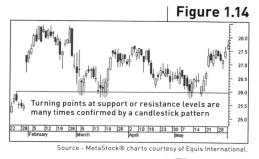

Figure 1.14

Turning points at support or resistance levels are many times confirmed by a candlestick pattern

Source - MetaStock® charts courtesy of Equis International.

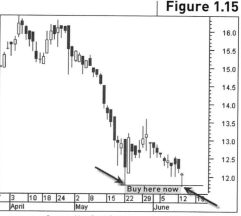

Figure 1.15

Buy here now

Source - MetaStock® charts courtesy of Equis International.

Figure 1.16

A good buy!

Source - MetaStock® charts courtesy of Equis International.

Support and resistance levels are a very important part of the decision-making process in LOCKIT and are used on all time frames. Confirmed support or resistance has great influence on the buying decision, while breaking support or resistance will trigger selling signals.

LOCKIT

TREND LINES

Technical analysis is built on the assumption that prices trend. A trend line is a straight line that connects two or more price points and then extends into the future to act as a line of support or resistance.

Figure 1.17 |

Figure 1.18 |

Figure 1.19 |

An uptrend line (figure 1.17) has a positive slope and is formed by connecting two or more low points. Uptrend lines act as support. As long as closing prices remain above the trend line, the uptrend is intact.

A break below the uptrend line indicates a change in trend for the period being considered. In LOCKIT, a stock price closing below the uptrend line is a selling signal.

A downtrend line (figure 1.17) has a negative slope and is formed by connecting two or more high points. Downtrend lines act as resistance. As long as closing prices remain below the downtrend line, LOCKIT considers the downtrend intact.

A break above the downtrend line indicates a change of trend for the period being considered. A price closing above the downtrend line is a LOCKIT buying signal.

One or more large up or down bars at a reversal point (figure 1.18 & 1.19) may be the reason that it is difficult to draw a new trend line from the highest or lowest point.

In the chart, you will see a sharp V-pattern or, at least, that the last up- or down-move was very large, eventually with a larger window (figure 1.19).

Ninety-nine percent of the time, the move that follows will not be as steep as the new trend start. In these circumstances, the new downtrend or uptrend line will have to start with one of the previous or following bars, or at some previous support or resistance level. A 20-period exponential moving average or a last pitchfork is generally a good indication for the expected trend line inclination.

Trend Line Application

A long-term investor using a monthly chart could act upon a number of trend lines.

Figure 1.20 shows all the trend lines used. We assume trading both long and short:

1. At the end of 1992, the closing price breaks above the downtrend line. This is a buy signal.

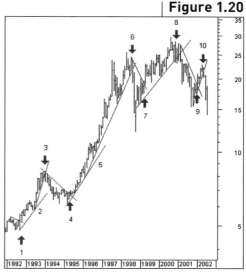

| **Figure 1.20**

Source - MetaStock® charts courtesy of Equis International.

2. After a first reaction, the price moves up again during the second half of 1993. This is a clear second pivot point for drawing a longer-term uptrend line. Note that from this point on, the price is accelerating and, in time, moving farther away from the uptrend line. The best thing to do when this kind of move develops is to follow the new move with a new, sharper trend line.

3. Beginning in 1994, the price drops below the uptrend line. It's time to close the long position and open a short one. The idea is to buy the stock back at a later date at a lower price to make a profit.

4. In the second quarter of 1995, the price rises above the downtrend line. This is a signal to close the short position and open a new long one.

5. Note that at a certain point in time, the price moves farther away from the trend line again. You can start a new, sharper uptrend line.

6. In the third quarter of 1998, the price drops below the uptrend line. You must sell the stock and open a new short position. In just two months, the price drops dramatically. When you see this kind of move-ment, it is a good idea to change from a monthly chart to a weekly or even a daily chart. With this kind of move, you must take the short-term profit. As soon as there is a trend line break on the weekly or daily chart, just take the profit. You would then wait for the long-term downtrend line to be broken before taking any new action.

7. The downtrend line is broken in the second quarter of 1999. If you haven't done so already, you should close your short position and buy the stock again for a new long position. After a big move down in a short time period, it usually will be difficult to draw a new trend line from the lowest point reached. The new uptrend line will have to start with one of the following bars or previous bars.

8. Beginning in 2001, the price falls through the uptrend line. This means that you close your long position and open a new, short posi-tion. Again, the accelerating down-move means that you have to draw a faster, declining downtrend line.

9. The price moves above the downtrend line in the beginning of 2002, so you close the short position and open a new long position.

10. The uptrend line is broken in the second quarter of 2002. You sell the stock and open a new short position. Again, the price drop is large and fast, which means that you have to go for the short-term profit.

Trading Result

The following table displays the result of trading long and short positions each time the trend line is broken at the end of the month. A starting equity of $25,000 would have become $249,855 after about 10 years. This is 10 times the starting capital, or a composite interest rate of more than 25% per year, which is not a bad result for looking at just one chart, once a month.

Transaction date	Position	Opening price	Closing date	Closing price	Qty	Opening amount	Closing amount	Value
								25000
09/30/1992	Long	5.50	01/31/1994	8.18	4545	24997.5	37148.1	37151
01/31/1994	Short	8.18	05/31/1995	6.78	4541	37145.4	30758.0	43538
05/31/1995	Long	6.78	08/31/1998	20.42	6421	43534.4	131086.8	131090
08/31/1998	Short	20.42	03/31/1999	19.30	6419	131076.0	123856.7	138310
03/31/1999	Long	19.30	02/28/2001	23.32	7166	138303.8	167081.1	167087
02/28/2001	Short	23.32	01/31/2002	20.13	7164	167064.5	144181.3	189970
01/31/2002	Long	20.13	05/31/2002	20.69	9437	189966.8	195221.5	195225
05/31/2002	Short	20.13	07/31/2002	14.50	9698	195220.7	140591.0	249855

Trend Line Evolution

A medium to longer-term uptrend or downtrend does not always evolve in the same way. Looking at different charts and periods, we noticed that from the start of a new price move, the trend shows three possible scenarios before reaching the end of that trend:

1. No change; the price continues to move along the trend line until it breaks the trend line.

2. The price accelerates and moves far away from the trend line; you need to draw a new, steeper trend line.

3. The price decelerates and breaks the trend moderately and continues, temporarily, less steep or even flat.

4. Then, of course, in some longer-term price moves, you will find all three possibilities combined in one trend.

No Change

If there's no change (figure 1.21), the trend line stays intact during the whole up- or down-move.

When the trend line is broken, it is the start of a new trend in that specific time period. It is rather uncommon that there is no change. Medium- and long-term moves will show (most of the time) a change in trend acceleration.

Price Acceleration

Price acceleration is often a three-step process (figure 1.22). The trend is broken after the third change in acceleration, when it has become a very sharp move.

Later when we talk about price chart patterns, you will see that these changes in acceleration often are announced by a price continuation pattern.

Price Deceleration

A longer-term uptrend starting with a sharp up-move will generally slow down.

In figure 1.23, you can see how short-term reactions against the main trend will slow down the up-move. A longer-term, flatter price channel is formed.

The S&P 500 Index in figure 1.23 gives a buy signal at the end of October 2004 when the closing price moves above the downtrend line. The price takes off with high acceleration. It is clear that this cannot be sustained for a long period of time.

The price continues to move higher, but not at the beginning speed. When this sharp trend line is broken, do we have to close the position?

Because of the previously high acceleration, you should leave enough room for the price to slow down. For example, you can use a support line or a trailing stop level to allow this process. Most of the time, the trailing stop will not be broken if the price continues to move higher. After some time, you can draw a flatter trend line followed by a steeper trend line, as is the case here.

Figure 1.21

Source - MetaStock® charts courtesy of Equis International.

Figure 1.22

Source - MetaStock® charts courtesy of Equis International.

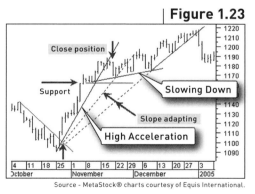

Figure 1.23

Source - MetaStock® charts courtesy of Equis International.

You can, of course, also adapt the slope from the start (dotted trend lines) to represent the new longer-term trend line.

LOCKIT

> We keep a close eye on trend line evolution to find entry and exit points as part of the LOCKIT set of rules. Additionally, we use a number of special trend lines described in the following paragraphs to help with our analysis.

Special Trend Lines

Inverse Trend Line

Sometimes, it may seem difficult to start drawing a normal trend line.

In figure 1.24, the move starts with a sharp trend line up. Next, the prices slow down for a short time; then subsequently continue with high acceleration. In such a scenario, it is difficult to draw a trend line or price channel that would help to estimate future price targets.

This is where the inverse trend line comes in handy. The last price high in September and a previous end of July high pivot are good reference points for drawing the inverse (thick) trend line in figure 1.24. In an ascending trend, the inverse trend line is drawn from price tops. In a descending trend, the inverse trend line is drawn from price bottoms.

From the lowest bottom in August, you now can draw a parallel line with the inverse trend line, creating the other side of what probably will become a future price channel.

Figure 1.25 shows the further price evolution perfectly in line with the trend channel created on the base of the inverse trend line.

Sometimes you will see a normal downtrend line and an inverse trend line that have different slopes.

As you can see in figure 1.26, the prices touch both the inverse trend line and the parallel line. The parallel line with the inverse trend line from the start of

Figure 1.24

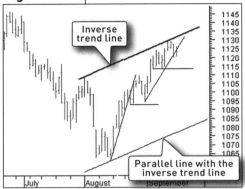

Source - MetaStock® charts courtesy of Equis International.

Figure 1.25

Source - MetaStock® charts courtesy of Equis International.

Figure 1.26

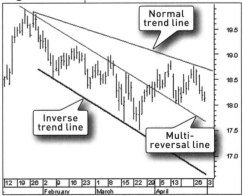

Source - MetaStock® charts courtesy of Equis International.

the downtrend forms a multi-reversal line that alternates between resistance and support. It also looks as if the downtrend channel is widening.

Looking at the further price development in figure 1.27, it is fun to see how each of the trend lines does the job. The inverse trend line gives support, just like the multi-reversal line does, while the normal downtrend line is now resisting.

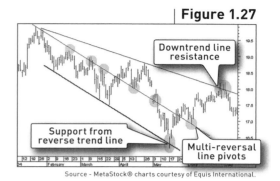

Figure 1.27

Downtrend line resistance

Support from reverse trend line

Multi-reversal line pivots

Source - MetaStock® charts courtesy of Equis International.

> The inverse trend line is a good LOCKIT tool to find medium and longer-term trends when it is not possible to draw a normal trend line in the early stages of a new trend development.

LOCKIT

Centerline

The centerline is drawn between a bottom pivot point and a top pivot point or visa versa. This kind of trend line can be used as a reference for action-reaction lines.

In figure 1.28, a parallel line with the centerline through a previous high or low point is the action reference. Preferably, the action line and the price data should show a similar slope.

From here on, you can create a second parallel line; this is the reaction line projected into the future. The distance from the centerline is equal to the distance between the centerline and the action line.

Note how the prices turn at the reaction line and how they start moving up again with approximately the same slope as the original top–bottom centerline.

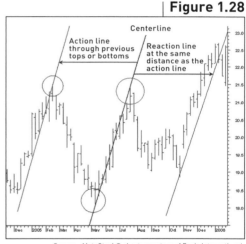

Figure 1.28

Centerline

Action line through previous tops or bottoms

Reaction line at the same distance as the action line

Source - MetaStock® charts courtesy of Equis International.

Multi-reversal Line

A multi-reversal line touches the bottoms as well as the tops of the price bars. Multi-reversal lines mostly are used as a reference for action/reaction lines but are also used for future support or resistance in relation with future price projections.

In figure 1.29, look at how multi-reversal lines show support and resistance to future price movement. Multi-reversal lines complement price targets because

Figure 1.29

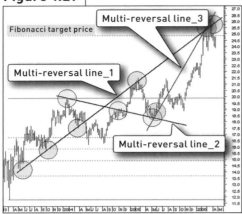

Source - MetaStock® charts courtesy of Equis International.

they can be used as references for future price support and resistance.

Note how all multi-reversal lines are close to the $25 target given by a Fibonacci projection (dashed horizontal line). This gives a good time estimate as to when this first Fibonacci target can be reached.

LOCKIT

The centerline and multi-reversal line are most useful for LOCKIT when you want to find targets that are both price and time related.

TREND CHANNELS

Trend channels are parallel lines containing a smaller or larger price move. The unparallel lines of a triangle formation also are a trend channel. Trend channels represent support and resistance and can be used within LOCKIT to find price targets.

Parallel Trend Channels

Let's look at the trend channels in figure 1.30, a chart with weekly price data.

Figure 1.30

Source - MetaStock® charts courtesy of Equis International.

- A trend line A is formed by a range of higher low points. A parallel line B to the upper part of the prices is the start of what will become the upper side of a long-term trend channel.

- The price falls through trend line A and consolidates in a horizontal to slightly decreasing trend channel D.

- The consolidation period finishes with a price jump out of channel D and forms a strong rising channel E. This uptrend finishes at the resistance of the upper side of the long-term trend channel B.

- The parallel line C with the long-term trend line B at the bottom of channel D creates the lower part of the broad channel BC. Falling through this trend line in the future will probably be the start of a larger, long-term correction.

- The price falling out of channel E makes up the lower part of channel F, a narrower trend channel within the large trend channel of the same slope.

- Leaving channel F, we get an accelerating, rising channel G, a fraction beyond the upper part of the broad channel, but returning back fast inside the long-term channel.

- What follows is an equally fast move down with channel H, until reaching the lower part of the long-term broad channel BC.

As long as a channel is valid, the price is moving between the extremes of that channel. The price reaching the upper part or the lower part of a trend channel is, therefore, not only a buying or selling signal, but also a good indication of what price level can be reached in the future.

Triangle Trend Channel

We also consider a triangle formation as a trend channel.

In figure 1.31, there is an uptrend line between March and April. The resistance line from the top at the beginning of March is broken in April with a rising window, but the price falls back below this resistance line, turning it into a support line by the end of April. A couple of days later, the resistance line is broken again.

Figure 1.31

Source - MetaStock® charts courtesy of Equis International.

The price develops lower tops and higher bottoms; and, the result is a symmetrical triangle formation.

A triangle formation is a continuation pattern, but it also can be a reversal pattern. The direction of the price will be clear only after the price breaks out of the pattern, either to the upper or the lower side of the triangle. Most of the time, the triangle is a continuation pattern, and the price will continue to move in the direction of the previous trend.

Price Targets

Price targets in LOCKIT can not only be estimated based on support lines and resistance lines, but also using trend channels.

The primary price targets in trend channels are logically the lower part and upper part of the channel. A smaller trend channel within a larger trend channel is a good indication of where the price is expected to go within the larger price channel.

LOCKIT

> Note that support lines, resistance lines, trend lines, trend channels, pitchforks, action/reaction lines, Fibonacci ratios, and Elliott wave analysis all provide important contributions to LOCKIT for estimating future price targets.

Figure 1.32

Source - MetaStock® charts courtesy of Equis International.

In the weekly chart in figure 1.32, we use a logarithmic price scale because of the larger price move. It is difficult to draw an uptrend line. The inclination is constantly changing.

A reference that seems to do well is the up-line between a previous bottom and a top in the present up-move. This line breaks the previous downward correction approximately in half and has a slope in line with the price inclination.

We create a parallel line with this reference line through the start of the uptrend. Notice how the two low prices at the start have the same inclination as the trend line. Drawing a parallel line with the reference line through the previous top of the down-move apparently also touches a previous bottom. Visually, this channel looks good; the price itself is giving confirmation.

Figure 1.33

Source - MetaStock® charts courtesy of Equis International.

The price now reaches the lower part of this upward trend channel and breaks through the short-term downtrend line.

Time to buy! We set a stop at the low of the trend channel.

A few weeks later (figure 1.33), there is a new higher bottom usable for drawing a new sharper uptrend line. A parallel line through a previous top is confirmed by a previous bottom. We have a new, smaller and sharper rising channel within the bigger channel.

Figure 1.34

Source - MetaStock® charts courtesy of Equis International.

In figure 1.34, a first price target is reached at the junction of the upper side of the small channel with the reference line of the big channel. A second target is reached at the crossing of the upper side of the small channel with the upper side of the big channel. A correction follows, and a new falling trend channel gives direction to the move toward the lower side of the big channel.

> Price channels within price channels are a very nice tool within LOCKIT to find price targets related to time.

MOVING AVERAGES

Moving averages are used to smooth short-term swings to get a better indication of the price trend. Averages are trend-following indicators. A moving average of daily prices is the average price of a share over a chosen period, displayed day by day.

- For calculating the average, you have to choose a time period.

- The choice of a time period is always a reflection upon more or less lag in relation to price compared to a greater or smaller smoothing of the price data.

> Within LOCKIT, we use price averages as a trend-following indicator and mainly as a reference for price support and resistance. In general, we use averages in all kinds of LOCKIT formulas to smooth data.

Simple Moving Average

A simple moving average is calculated by adding all prices within the chosen time period, divided by that time period. This way, each data value has the same weight in the average result.

The thick, black curve in the chart of figure 1.35 is a 20-day simple moving average.

Exponential Moving Average

An exponential moving average gives more weight, percentage-wise, to the individual prices in a range, based on the following formula:

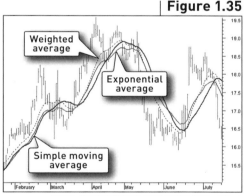

Figure 1.35

Source - MetaStock® charts courtesy of Equis International.

EMA = (price * EMA %) + (previous EMA * (1 – EMA %))

Most investors do not feel comfortable with an expression related to percentage in the exponential moving average; rather, they feel better using a time period.

If you want to know the percentage in which to work using a period, this formula gives you the conversion:

$$\text{EMA Percentage}(\%) = \frac{2}{\text{Time period} + 1}$$

A time period of three days corresponds to an exponential percentage of:

$$\text{EMA} = \frac{2}{3+1} = 0.5 = 50\%$$

The thin, black curve in figure 1.35 is a 20-day exponential moving average.

Weighted Moving Average

A weighted moving average puts more weight on recent data and less weight on older data.

A weighted moving average is calculated by multiplying the datum with a factor from day "1" until day "n" for the oldest to the most recent data; the result is divided by the total of all multiplying factors.

In a 10-day weighted moving average, there is 10 times more weight for the price today in proportion to the price 10 days ago. Likewise, the price of yesterday gets nine times more weight, and so on.

The thin, black-dashed curve in figure 1.35 is a 20-day weighted moving average.

Simple, Exponential, or Weighted?

If we compare these three basic averages, we see that the simple average has the most smoothing, but generally the biggest lag after price reversals.

The exponential average lies closer to the price and will react faster to price swings. But shorter period corrections also are visible in this average because of less smoothing.

Finally, the weighted average follows the price movement even more closely.

Determining which of these averages to use depends on your objective. If you want a trend indicator with better smoothing and only little reaction for shorter movements, the simple average is best.

If you want a smoothing where you can still see the short period swings, then either the exponential or weighted moving average is the better choice.

Importance of the 20-, 50-, and 200-day Simple Averages

The 20-, 50-, and 200-day simple moving averages were mostly used in the past before the advent of personal computers. A simple average was used because the calculation was simple; longer periods were used because the movements in those days took time to take off and to complete.

This tradition is still alive today in the sense that investors still watch these averages. That is the reason why prices generally experience support and resistance at the level of these averages.

In figure 1.36, note how the 20-day average gives direction to the shorter period price move and often runs parallel with a trend line.

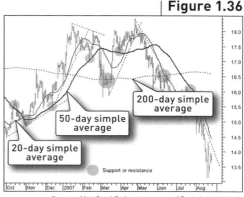

Figure 1.36

Source - MetaStock® charts courtesy of Equis International.

The 50-day moving average gives direction to the medium time period. If the price is moving above this average, it is good to have this share in your portfolio. If the price, however, moves below the 50-day average, it is better not to have this share in possession.

The 200-day moving average is important for a look at the long-term trend.

Around the 50- and the 200-day averages, you will almost always notice some form of support or resistance.

> In LOCKIT, we pay special attention to support and resistance of the 20-, 50-, and 200-day simple moving averages. Additionally, the 20-day simple moving average is a nice tool to help you estimate the inclination of the shorter-term trend line.

LOCKIT

TEMA Average

The TEMA, or Triple Exponential Moving Average, was introduced by Patrick Mulloy in *Technical Analysis of Stocks & Commodities* magazine, February 1994.

TEMA is not simply a triple exponential moving average, as you probably would assume from the name. The intention of TEMA is to limit the typical lag of an average.

An 'n' day exponential average (EMA) has a smoothing factor alpha of:

$$\alpha = \frac{2}{n+1} \quad \text{and a delay of} \quad \frac{n+1}{2}$$

The larger the average period "n," the better the smoothing; but, unfortunately, you'll experience a larger delay. TEMA uses a technique of John Wilder Tukey's to compensate for the delay. The data is sent several times through the same filter and combined afterward:

TEMA = (3*EMA – 3*EMA(EMA)) + EMA(EMA(EMA))

Figure 1.37

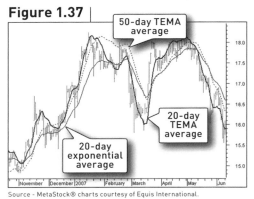

Source - MetaStock® charts courtesy of Equis International.

The application of the TEMA average makes most sense if we want to smooth larger data periods, whereas the delay must remain as small as possible.

Compare in figure 1.37 the 50-day TEMA average with the 20-day exponential average. You can see that the much longer TEMA average is at least as fast at the reversal points as the exponential average.

LOCKIT

> The TEMA average is generally not used directly on a chart within LOCKIT. This average is, however, used in many of the formulas to smooth longer periods of data with only a small amount of lag.

Figure 1.38

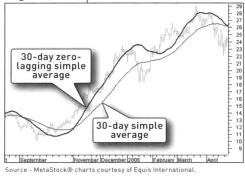

Source - MetaStock® charts courtesy of Equis International.

Limiting the Lag

It is important to our LOCKIT rules to use a technique to limit (as much as possible) the lagging nature of an average. We make use of this technique in all kinds of LOCKIT formulas and applications in order to have enough smoothing without the side effect of too much lag.

Principles for limiting the lag (zero-lagging) of an average were introduced by Dr. Joe Sharp in *Technical Analysis of Stocks & Commodities* magazine, January 2000.

The zero-lagging principle in figure 1.38 clearly shows less lag compared to the standard simple moving average. The reversals are faster, but the zero-lagging average more closely follows the price move, so there is less smoothing.

An application in MetaStock® formula language for a zero-lagging simple moving average on the closing prices is as follows:

```
Period:= Input('Which period?',1,250,10);
SMA1:= Mov(CLOSE,Period,S);
SMA2:= Mov(SMA1,Period,S);
Difference:= SMA1 - SMA2;
ZeroLagSMA:= SMA1 + Difference;
ZeroLagSMA
```

 Please utilize the disc in the back of the book for instant access to these codes. You may also download them from www.traderslibrary.com/tlecorner.

CHART PATTERNS

Chart patterns are part of the buying and selling rules within LOCKIT. Most of the time there will already be an open position at the appearance of a price chart pattern. The point is that the pattern will give you an important confirmation for your decision. Some patterns can help to calculate future price targets; however, we won't use this capacity within LOCKIT.

Medium- and long-term trend reversals are often gradual. The art is to distinguish between whether you are dealing with a continuation pattern, after which the price will continue its previous trend, or a reversal pattern, which will lead to a trend reversal.

REVERSAL PATTERNS

Head and Shoulders Formation

With an accuracy of about 90%, the head and shoulders formation can be named as one of the most reliable reversal patterns.

Head and Shoulders Top Reversal Pattern

The price moves in an uptrend. Only after the pattern has formed will you recognize A as the left shoulder (figure 1.39). The price drops back to the support B of the up-going trend line. From here, the price makes a last move up to C often with lower volume compared to the A move. This will be the head of the pattern. The turning point at B will be part of the neck line.

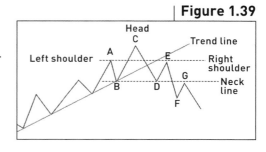

Figure 1.39

Next, the price drops through the up-going trend line and falls back to the level of the neck line D. After that, the price will move up again to E to form the right shoulder. From here, the price will drop below the neck line, making lower lows.

The shoulders (A-E) and the neck line (B-D) in the head and shoulders formation should be at about the same price level and at about the same distance in time from the head.

The head and shoulders pattern is confirmed when the price falls below an up-trending neck line or after the right shoulder in case of a down-trending neck line.

ATTENTION! In approximately half of the cases, there is a bounce back up to the neck line G, or even up to between the neck line and the right shoulder.

Figure 1.40

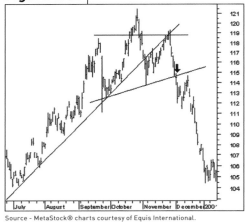

Source - MetaStock® charts courtesy of Equis International.

Figure 1.41

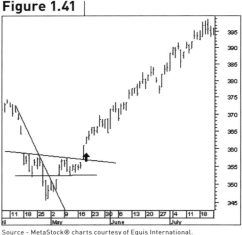

Source - MetaStock® charts courtesy of Equis International.

Figure 1.40 shows an example of a head and shoulders top reversal pattern in the Euro-dollar currency pair.

Head and Shoulders Bottom Reversal Pattern

Mirroring the head and shoulders top reversal pattern gives a head and shoulders bottom reversal pattern. Shoulder bottoms should be at around the same price level and at about the same distance from the head.

The head and shoulders bottom reversal pattern is confirmed when the price moves above a descending neck line or after the right shoulder with an ascending neck line.

ATTENTION! In approximately half of the cases, there is a bounce back down to the neck line or even down to between the neck line and the right shoulder.

Look at figure 1.41 for an example of a head and shoulders bottom reversal.

Complex Head and Shoulders Top Reversal Pattern

In a complex head and shoulders reversal pattern, you will see more shoulders or more heads, but rarely both. In more than half of the cases, you will see a retracement to the neck line.

The shoulder tops are around the same price level and at approximately the same distance from the head. The neck line has a moderate slope most of the time.

The complex head and shoulders pattern is confirmed when the price falls below an up-trending neck line (figure 1.42) or after the right shoulder in the case of a down-trending neck line.

If you can recognize an internal head and shoulders pattern within the complex head and shoulders pattern, you can, of course, take a position based on the internal head and shoulders pattern.

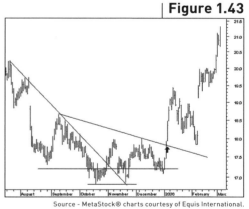

Figure 1.42

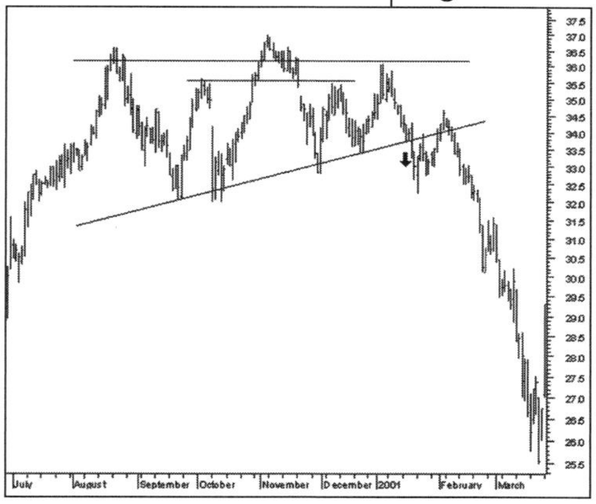

Source - MetaStock® charts courtesy of Equis International.

Complex Head and Shoulders Bottom Reversal Pattern

In a complex head and shoulders bottom reversal pattern, you will see more shoulders or more heads, but rarely both. In more than half of the cases, you will see a retracement to the neck line.

The shoulder bottoms are around the same price level and at approximately the same distance from the head. The neck line has a moderate slope most of the time.

The complex head and shoulders bottom pattern is confirmed when the price rises above a down-trending neck line (figure 1.43) or after the right shoulder in the case of an up-trending neck line.

If you can recognize an internal head and shoulders pattern within the complex head and shoulders pattern, you can, of course, take a position based on the internal head and shoulders pattern.

Triple Tops and Bottoms

Triple tops and bottoms are a variation on the head and shoulders theme. The difference is that tops or bottoms are at approximately the same level.

Triple tops and bottoms offer a reliable pattern with an accuracy of about 80%.

A triple top is confirmed when the price falls below the lowest valley, as in figure 1.44.

Figure 1.43

Source - MetaStock® charts courtesy of Equis International.

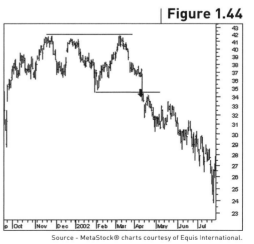

Figure 1.44

Source - MetaStock® charts courtesy of Equis International.

Figure 1.45

Source - MetaStock® charts courtesy of Equis International.

Figure 1.46

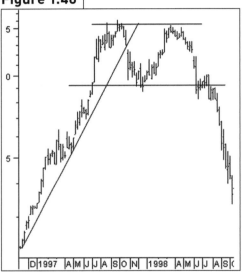

Source - MetaStock® charts courtesy of Equis International.

Figure 1.47

Source - MetaStock® charts courtesy of Equis International.

A triple bottom formation is confirmed when the price rises above the highest top of the pattern, as in figure 1.45. Triple tops or bottoms are rather rare.

Double Tops and Bottoms

Double Top

A double top reversal pattern is formed with a large demand during the formation of the first top and a lack of demand with the second top.

With daily price bars (figure 1.46), tops are separated by about four to eight weeks and should only have a small difference in price level. The in-between reaction should have a price drop of about 10% measured from the first top. The pattern is confirmed when the price falls below the level of the middle reaction.

With an accuracy of 80%, this pattern is very reliable.

Double Bottom

For a double bottom, the reasoning is analogous to that of a double top. The trend is down, and a double bottom pattern is formed as an indication that the trend probably will reverse.

With daily price bars, bottoms are separated by about four to eight weeks (figure 1.47) and should only have a small difference in price level. The in-between reaction should have a price rise of about 10% measured from the first bottom. The pattern is confirmed when the price rises above the level of the middle reaction.

With 80% reversals, this pattern is also very reliable.

Rounding Bottoms

A rounding bottom pattern (rounded bowl shape) appears on daily and weekly bar charts. This pattern takes time to complete. The price can peak halfway through the pattern, but usually it retraces most of it quickly. Rounding bottoms are becoming rare because of the high volatility of the markets, somewhat as a result of our information society.

Currently, rounding bottoms lead to a price reversal 90% of the time.

Like in figure 1.48, a rounding bottom starts with a steep falling trend line that, with time, becomes increasingly flat. The opposite is true in most of the other patterns; that is, you start with a flat trend line and finish with a steeper trend line. The pattern confirms when the price closes above the highest peak of the pattern. There may be a saucer lip when the price drops temporarily before continuing the uptrend.

Source - MetaStock® charts courtesy of Equis International.

V-formations

In a V-formation, you are looking for a V-shaped reversal pattern from a range of bars. A bottom reversal creates a V-character; a top reversal creates an inverted V-character. The price at the start of the V-formation will form a one-day reversal, an island reversal, or a spark.

A *one day top reversal* (figure 1.49) arises if the price makes a new high on the same day and reverses and closes below the closing price of the previous day. A one-day top reversal in a candle chart is a black candle and often is part of a candlestick pattern.

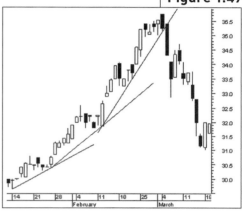
Source - MetaStock® charts courtesy of Equis International.

A one-day bottom reversal (figure 1.50) arises if the price makes a new low on the same day and reverses and closes above the closing price of the previous day.

An *island reversal* occurs when there is a window between the prices of today, the previous day, and the following day(s).

A *spark* is a big, one-day high volatility price move.

A V-formation start can be recognized most of the time when it breaks the last possible steep trend line together with a preceding candlestick reversal pattern and a one-day island or spark reversal.

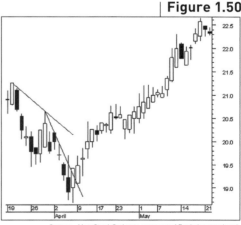
Source - MetaStock® charts courtesy of Equis International.

As I mentioned before, we use reversal patterns within the LOCKIT system only as a confirmation of an already open position.

LOCKIT

CONTINUATION PATTERNS

After a continuation pattern, the price continues in the previous trend. Continuation patterns are part of the LOCKIT rules and are a very good indication for entering a trade after a trend reaction.

Figure 1.51

Source - MetaStock® charts courtesy of Equis International.

Figure 1.52

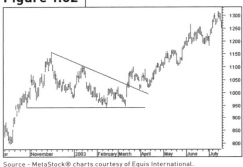

Source - MetaStock® charts courtesy of Equis International.

Figure 1.53

Source - MetaStock® charts courtesy of Equis International.

Triangles

Triangle formations appear as symmetrical triangles, ascending triangles, and descending triangles. The triangle is a correction pattern for the previous price move.

A triangle formation takes a minimum of 30 bars. Shorter-period triangle formations are classified as pennants.

Triangles in an Uptrend

In the weekly price chart in figure 1.51, you can see higher bottoms and lower tops; this creates a symmetrical triangle. A breakout in the direction of the previous trend confirms the continuation pattern.

In the daily chart in figure 1.52, lower tops are made in an uptrend. Next, the price drops back to horizontal support levels, and a descending triangle is created. A breakout in the direction of the previous trend confirms the continuation pattern.

Triangles in a Downtrend

Higher bottoms are appearing in a reaction to the falling price trend, but the tops that follow are lower. This creates the symmetrical triangle in figure 1.53.

Breaking out of this triangle formation on the lower side confirms the continuation pattern and continues the previous downtrend.

Look out for the very rare triangle pattern at **the end** of an uptrend or a downtrend! In this case, you will get a breakout against the previous trend direction and thus, a reversal, not a continuation of the trend.

The Rectangle

The rectangle is a relatively rare pattern, appearing almost always as a continuation pattern, although it can exist as a reversal pattern. The price moves between two horizontal trend lines and touches each line a minimum of two times.

Rectangle in an Uptrend

Figure 1.54 shows a rectangle continuation pattern in an uptrend.

Rectangle in a Downtrend

Figure 1.55 shows a rectangle continuation pattern in a downtrend.

Flags and Pennants

With a continuation of the previous trend happening 90% of the time, flags and pennants are reliable short-term continuation patterns. They create a pause from 5 up to 25 bars in the current trend before movement continues in the direction of the previous trend. Most of the flags and pennants take up 10 to 15 bars. Generally, the volume goes down during this phase.

Flags in an Uptrend

Figure 1.56 shows flags in an uptrend.

Flags in a Downtrend

Figure 1.57 shows flags in a downtrend.

Pennants in an Uptrend

Figure 1.58 shows pennants in an uptrend.

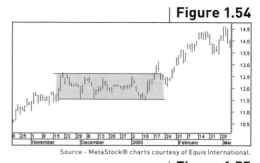

Figure 1.54

Source - MetaStock® charts courtesy of Equis International.

Figure 1.55

Source - MetaStock® charts courtesy of Equis International.

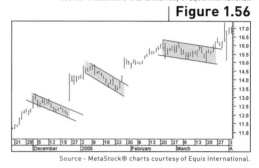

Figure 1.56

Source - MetaStock® charts courtesy of Equis International.

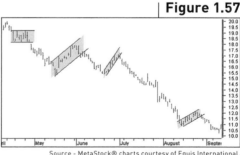

Figure 1.57

Source - MetaStock® charts courtesy of Equis International.

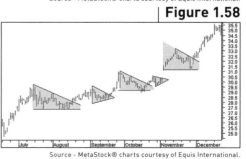

Figure 1.58

Source - MetaStock® charts courtesy of Equis International.

Figure 1.59

Source - MetaStock® charts courtesy of Equis International.

Figure 1.60

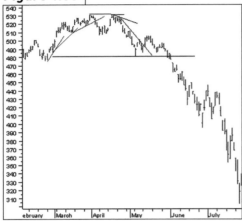

Source - MetaStock® charts courtesy of Equis International.

Figure 1.61

Source - MetaStock® charts courtesy of Equis International.

Pennants in a Downtrend

Figure 1.59 shows pennants in a downtrend.

REVERSAL OR CONTINUATION PATTERNS

Some of the patterns we consider in LOCKIT can appear as a reversal or as a continuation pattern.

Rounding Top as a Reversal Pattern

A rounding top pattern (inverse rounded bowl shape) appears on daily and weekly bar charts.

A rounding top starts with a steep rising trend line (figure 1.60), which, with time, becomes increasingly flat. Rounding tops as a reversing pattern break to the down side and lead to a farther move down 90% of the time.

The pattern confirms when the price closes below the left-hand border or with a saucer lip when breaking the right-hand side of the border.

Rounding Top as a Continuation Pattern

A break to the upper side of the saucer gives, on average, less profit than a break to the lower side. This is simply because, as a continuation pattern, part of the up-move already has been completed.

A rounding top as a continuation pattern is confirmed when the price moves above the highest point of the rounding top (figure 1.61).

Diamond Formation

The diamond formation is a combination of two triangles. The left is an inverted, broadening triangle; the right side is a symmetrical triangle. Together they make up a diamond formation.

This pattern is most common as a continuation pattern, but it can be a top or bottom reversal pattern as well.

Diamond Formation as a Continuation Pattern

Figure 1.62 shows a diamond continuation pattern.

Diamond Formation as a Reversal Pattern

Figure 1.63 shows a diamond top reversal pattern.

Figure 1.64 shows a bottom reversal diamond pattern followed by another continuation diamond pattern.

Wedge Formations

Wedge formations in LOCKIT are not only interesting as reversal or continuation patterns, but they are also good for recognizing an Elliott beginning or ending wedge impulse wave. Therefore, they will help you to make a correct Elliott wave count in generally difficult circumstances. Both applications are part of the LOCKIT rules.

Falling Wedge Reversal Pattern

The falling wedge exists as a reversal pattern in a falling trend and as a continuation pattern in a rising trend. The duration of the wedge should be a minimum of 20 bars; with fewer than 20 bars, it is considered a flag.

Breaking out of a falling wedge is generally a bullish signal (figure 1.65 on page 35). Rarely will you see the price breaking a falling wedge to the lower side.

Falling Wedge Continuation Pattern

A falling wedge continuation pattern in a rising trend is a price reaction in the upward move.

The chance for a big profit is less than for a falling wedge reversal pattern because part of the up-move is already history (figure 1.66 on page 35).

Pay attention to the rare falling wedge after the top of an uptrend.

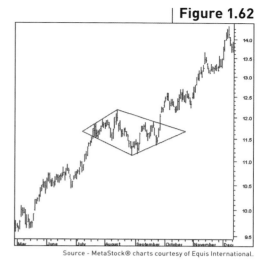

Figure 1.62

Source - MetaStock® charts courtesy of Equis International.

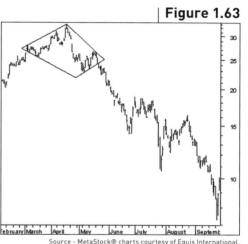

Figure 1.63

Source - MetaStock® charts courtesy of Equis International.

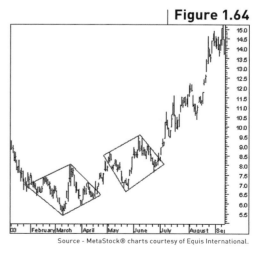

Figure 1.64

Source - MetaStock® charts courtesy of Equis International.

In figure 1.67, the falling wedge from the top is the first reaction after a longer-term uptrend. As a result, the breakout to the upside is more likely a temporary reaction against the new, longer-term down-move.

Rising Wedge Reversal Pattern

The rising wedge exists as a reversal pattern in a rising trend and as a continuation pattern in a falling trend.

The duration of the wedge should be a minimum of 20 bars; with fewer than 20 bars, it is considered a pennant. Breaking out of a rising wedge is generally a bearish signal (figure 1.68).

It is rare for the price to break to the upper side of the rising wedge, although it can happen.

Rising Wedge Continuation Pattern

A rising wedge continuation pattern in a falling trend is a price reaction to the down-move.

The chance for a big profit is less for a rising wedge continuation pattern than for a rising wedge reversal pattern because part of the down-move is already history (figure 1.69).

Pay attention to the rare rising wedge after the bottom of a downtrend, as in figure 1.70.

Here the rising wedge probably is the first reaction after a longer-term downtrend. The breakout to the lower side is most likely a temporary reaction against the new, longer-term up-move.

WINDOWS

An up window in a bar chart appears when the low price of the current bar is higher than the high price of the previous bar. A down window in a bar chart appears when the high price of the current bar is lower than the low price of the previous bar.

We consider four window types: a common window, a breakaway window, a continuation window, and an exhaustion window. A window is closed, and support or resistance has no further meaning, when the price turns around and completely covers the window.

As long as a window is not closed, the whole area of a window represents support or resistance for future price moves. A breakaway window, a continu-

Figure 1.65

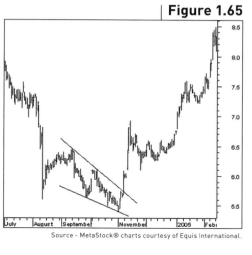

Figure 1.66

Figure 1.67

Figure 1.68

Figure 1.69

Figure 1.70

ation window, or an exhaustion window represent a much more important support or resistance level compared to a common window.

The support or resistance of a window is only broken when it is penetrated with the closing price.

LOCKIT

> Windows in LOCKIT are part of support and resistance and can be used for initial stops (because of their support) as well as for price targets (because of their resistance). Additionally, by understanding the type of window, we can expect to be at a trend reversal, a trend continuation, or near a trend conclusion.

Figure 1.71

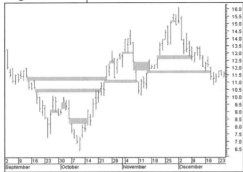

Source - MetaStock® charts courtesy of Equis International.

Figure 1.72

Source - MetaStock® charts courtesy of Equis International.

Common Windows

A common window is so-called because it is common in the normal price evolution. Most of the common windows can be found during periods of price consolidation when the price is moving sideways.

In figure 1.71, you can see that a common window does not give any indication about an expected price move. Generally, it only can be used as a support and resistance level for the short term. On a daily chart, common windows will be closed most of the time within a couple of weeks.

Breakaway Windows

A breakaway window will appear with a change in the medium- to longer-term price trend.

Rising Breakaway Window

About three-quarters of the rising breakaway windows (figure 1.72) on a daily chart are closed within a year. Only about 2% will be closed within a week.

Usually the breakaway window is created with high volume or gradually higher volume on a number of bars before the breakaway.

Falling Breakaway Window

About 60% of the falling breakaway windows (figure 1.73) on a daily chart are closed within a year. Only about 2% will be closed within a week. Usually the breakaway window is created with high volume or gradually higher volume on a number of bars before the breakaway.

Continuation Windows

A continuation window will be found halfway through a running trend, often after a short consolidation pattern like a flag or a pennant, or a bigger correction pattern like a triangle or a rectangle.

Rising Continuation Window

Almost all of the rising continuation windows (figure 1.74) on a daily chart are closed within a year. Only about 5% will be closed within a week. Usually the continuation window is created with high volume or gradually higher volume on a number of bars before the continuation window.

Falling Continuation Window

Almost all of the falling continuation windows (figure 1.75) on a daily chart are closed within a year. Only about 5% will be closed within a week. Usually the continuation window is created with high volume or gradually higher volume on a number of bars before the continuation window.

Exhaustion Window

The exhaustion window can be found near the end of the running trend. Often, you will see a bigger window with highly volatile price moves.

Rising Exhaustion Window

Almost all of the rising exhaustion windows (figure 1.76) on a daily chart are closed within a year. As many as half of them will be closed within a week. Usually, the exhaustion window is created with high volume or gradually higher volume on a number of bars before the exhaustion window.

Falling Exhaustion Window

Almost all of the falling exhaustion windows (figure 1.77) on a daily chart are closed within a year. As

Figure 1.73

Source - MetaStock® charts courtesy of Equis International.

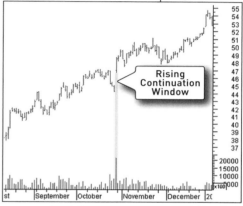

Figure 1.74

Source - MetaStock® charts courtesy of Equis International.

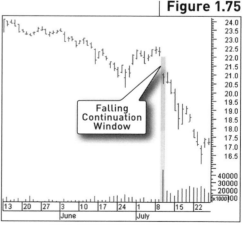

Figure 1.75

Source - MetaStock® charts courtesy of Equis International.

Figure 1.76 |

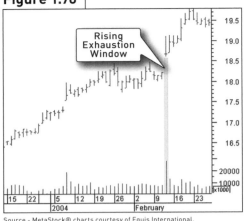

Source - MetaStock® charts courtesy of Equis International.

Figure 1.77 |

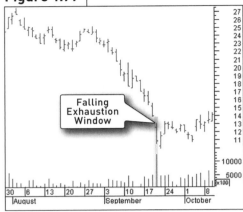

Source - MetaStock® charts courtesy of Equis International.

many as half of them will be closed within a week. Usually, the exhaustion window is created with high volume or gradually higher volume on a number of bars before the exhaustion window.

Breakaway, Continuation, and Exhaustion Windows

Figure 1.78 |

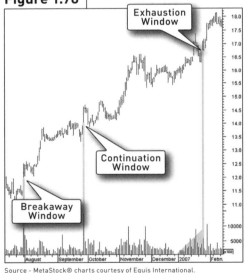

Source - MetaStock® charts courtesy of Equis International.

Most of the time, breakaway, continuation, and exhaustion windows are created with high volume or gradually higher volume on a number of bars before the breakaway.

Regularly, you will notice chart price patterns before these windows.

LOCKIT

> Support and resistance, trend lines, trend channels, moving averages, price patterns, and windows are basic LOCKIT tools used both for buying and selling decisions and for price projections. Next, we will have a look at indicators used within the LOCKIT system.

 For a closer look at the charts in this chapter, go to www.traderslibrary.com/TLEcorner.

TEST YOUR CHAPTER 1 KNOWLEDGE

1. Which is the preferred chart type in LOCKIT?

_____

_____

_____

_____

_____

2. When do we have to use a semi-logarithmic scaling on the price chart?

_____

_____

_____

_____

_____

3. How does volume normally relate to price?

_____

_____

_____

_____

_____

4. Where do you find price resistance or support and how does a resistance line change to a support line?

_____

_____

_____

_____

_____

5. In LOCKIT we use trend lines and we consider three sorts of trend line evolution, can you describe them?

_____

_____

_____

_____

6. What is and why do we use an inverse trend line in LOCKIT?

_____

_____

_____

_____

7. What do we use a centerline for in LOCKIT?

_____

_____

_____

_____

8. What is the use of the multi-reversal line in LOCKIT?

_____

_____

_____

_____

9. What is the use of trend channels in LOCKIT??

_____

_____

_____

_____

10. Why do we look specifically at the 20-, 50-, and 200-day simple averages in LOCKIT?

_____

_____

_____

_____

11. What does zero-lagging mean?

_____

_____

_____

_____

12. When is a head and shoulders bottom reversal pattern confirmed?

_____

_____

_____

_____

13. In LOCKIT, what are the three types of V-formation patterns we look for?

_____

_____

_____

_____

14. Triangles are most of the time what kind of pattern?

_____

_____

_____

_____

15. Flags and pennants are what kind of price patterns?

_____

_____

_____

_____

16. What do you know about falling and rising wedge patterns?

_____

_____

_____

_____

17. What type of windows do you know?

_____

_____

_____

_____

 For answers, please visit the Traders' Library Education Corner at www.traderslibrary.com/tlecorner.

Indicators

These days, there are hundreds, and probably thousands, of indicators and oscillators, especially if you count the many indicators that have been developed solely for personal use. We will strictly limit the discussion here to indicators used within the **LOCKIT** system.

A special indicator used in LOCKIT is SVAPO. SVAPO (or Short term Volume And Price Oscillator) is my own indicator and will be discussed in detail in Part II, Chapter 5.

SVAPO is the first indicator below the price chart of the standard LOCKIT chart template.

LOCKIT

RSI (RELATIVE STRENGTH INDEX)

The Relative Strength Index (RSI) indicator is used in LOCKIT as part of the decision process to open or close a position. Divergence signals between price and RSI offer a trade confirmation when other buy or sell signals are present. On the other hand, an overbought or oversold RSI can help you to hold on to the position when selling signals appear, that way you can avoid unnecessarily closing the position.

RSI is a popular momentum oscillator. Momentum refers to the speed of change; oscillator means that the value of the RSI moves (oscillates) between two values (0 and 100). The RSI was introduced by J. Welles Wilder in *New Concepts in Technical Trading Systems* (Wilder, 1978).

The term "relative strength" might sound a little confusing because it does not compare the relative strength between stocks; rather, it compares the actual price with past prices.

LOCKIT

> For the application and estimation of price evolution in LOCKIT, we primarily look at divergences between the RSI and the price bars. We will use a standard RSI with a dynamic reference level.

THE FORMULA

$$RSI = 100 - \left[\frac{100}{1 + \left(\frac{U}{D}\right)}\right]$$

Definitions:
U = Averaged sum of the prices when the closing price was higher (compared to the previous bar) in the period used.

D = Averaged sum of the prices when the closing price was lower (compared to the previous bar) in the period used.

Within the time period used, RSI measures the relationship between the price bars with a higher closing price compared to the previous bar, and between the bars with a lower closing price compared to the previous price bar.

Originally, Wilder used a 14-day period on daily charts; this remains the standard and most widely used value today. The RSI is a leading indicator. Tops and bottoms will be visible in the RSI before they show on the price chart.

The standard 14-period RSI makes tops above 70, which is called the overbought area; when it bottoms below 30, it is called the oversold area (figure 2.1). These tops and bottoms show up in the RSI before there are tops or bottoms visible on the price chart; however, a continuing uptrend or downtrend will keep the RSI in the overbought or oversold zone.

Convergence and Divergence

When tops or bottoms of a stock price and an oscillator move in the same direction, it's known as convergence. When price and oscillator tops or bottoms move in opposite directions, it's known as a divergence.

Figure 2.1: RSI divergences and overbought and oversold areas

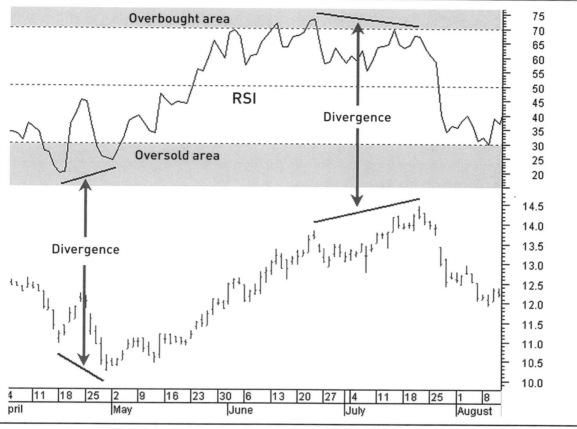

Source - MetaStock® charts courtesy of Equis International.

In looking at the lows of the oscillator and comparing them with the lows in price, we can define three different situations (see figure 2.2):

- When the price and oscillator make higher or equal bottoms, they converge. Until there is no other indication, the most probable price move is a continuation of the uptrend.

- When the oscillator creates a higher bottom while the price makes a lower bottom, they diverge. This is mostly found at the end of a downtrend, indicating an uptrend reversal.

- When the oscillator has a lower bottom while the price sets a higher bottom, they diverge. This is mostly found in a price uptrend after a price correction, indicating a continuation of the uptrend.

Figure 2.2: Basic bottom convergence and divergence

Up move convergence		Condition	Expectation
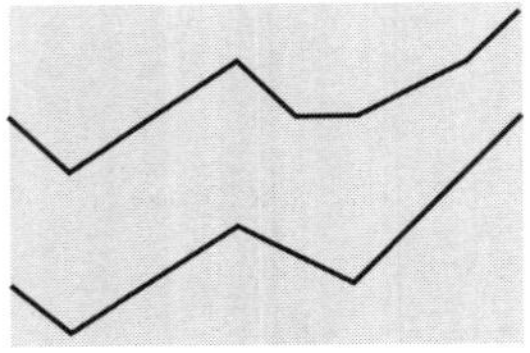	Price	Higher bottom	Uptrend continuation
	Oscillator	Higher bottom	
Oscillator higher bottom divergence			
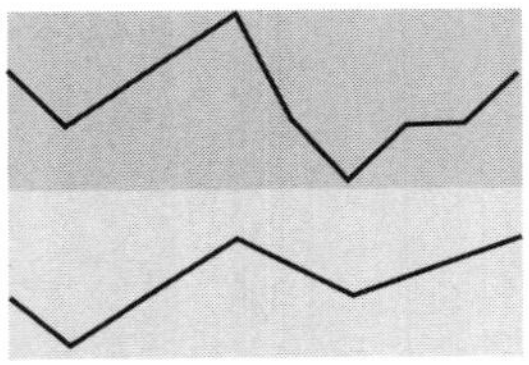	Price	Lower bottom	Uptrend reversal
	Oscillator	Higher bottom	
Oscillator lower bottom divergence			
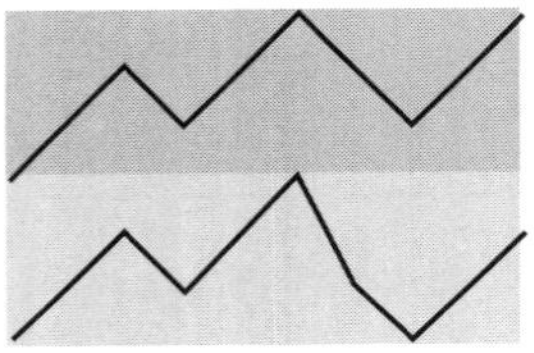	Price	Higher bottom	Uptrend continuation
	Oscillator	Lower bottom	

Simply looking at bottoms, we can say that the price is going to move up if there is a divergence between the price and the oscillator, or if the price and the oscillator bottoms converge in an uptrend.

Looking at the highs of the oscillator and comparing them with highs in price, we can define three other situations (see figure 2.3):

- When the price and the oscillator make equal or lower tops, they converge. Until there is no other indication, the most probable price move is a continuation of the downtrend.

Figure 2.3: Basic bottom convergence and divergence

Down move convergence		Condition	Expectation
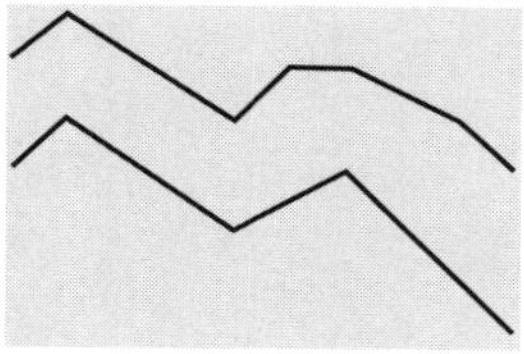	Price	Lower top	Downtrend continuation
	Oscillator	Lower top	
Oscillator lower top divergence			
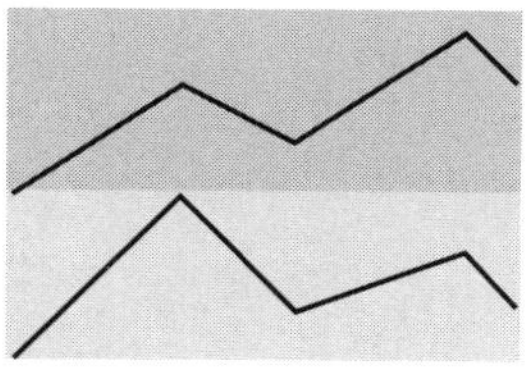	Price	Higher top	Downtrend reversal
	Oscillator	Lower top	
Oscillator higher top divergence			
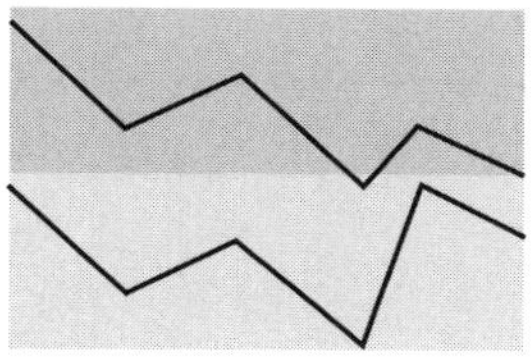	Price	Lower top	Downtrend continuation
	Oscillator	Higher top	

- When the oscillator makes a lower top while price makes a higher top, they diverge. This is mostly found at the end of an uptrend, indicating a downtrend reversal.

- When the oscillator makes a higher top while price makes a lower top, they diverge. This is usually found in a price downtrend after a price up correction, indicating a continuation of the downtrend.

Just by looking at the tops, you can say that the price will move down if there is a divergence between the price and the oscillator, or if the price and the oscillator tops converge in a downtrend.

Figure 2.4: Inverse divergence with a higher top in the RSI and a lower top in price

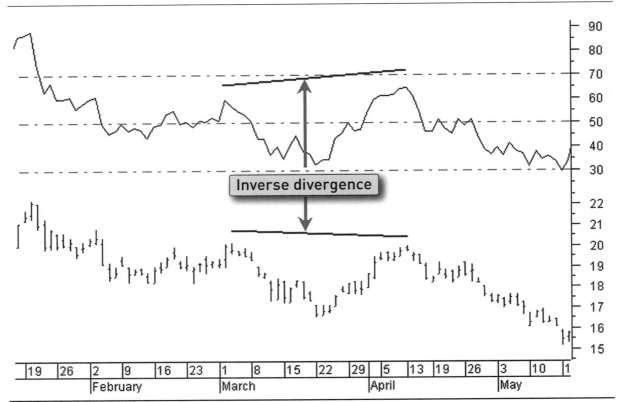

Source - MetaStock® charts courtesy of Equis International.

To summarize, a divergence with a higher bottom in the RSI indicator and a lower bottom on the price chart indicates an uptrend reversal. On the other hand, a divergence with a higher top in the price chart and a lower top in the RSI indicator points to a downtrend reversal (figure 2.1).

LOCKIT

> Divergences are reliable LOCKIT tools for predicting trend reversals.

Figure 2.4 is an inverse divergence with a higher top in the RSI and a lower top in price. This is most common in a downtrend when there is a temporary up-correction. The price makes a lower top while the RSI makes a higher top. This is an indication that the price is reversing and will continue the previous downtrend.

Figure 2.5: Inverse divergence with a lower RSI bottom and a higher or equal price bottom

Inverse divergence

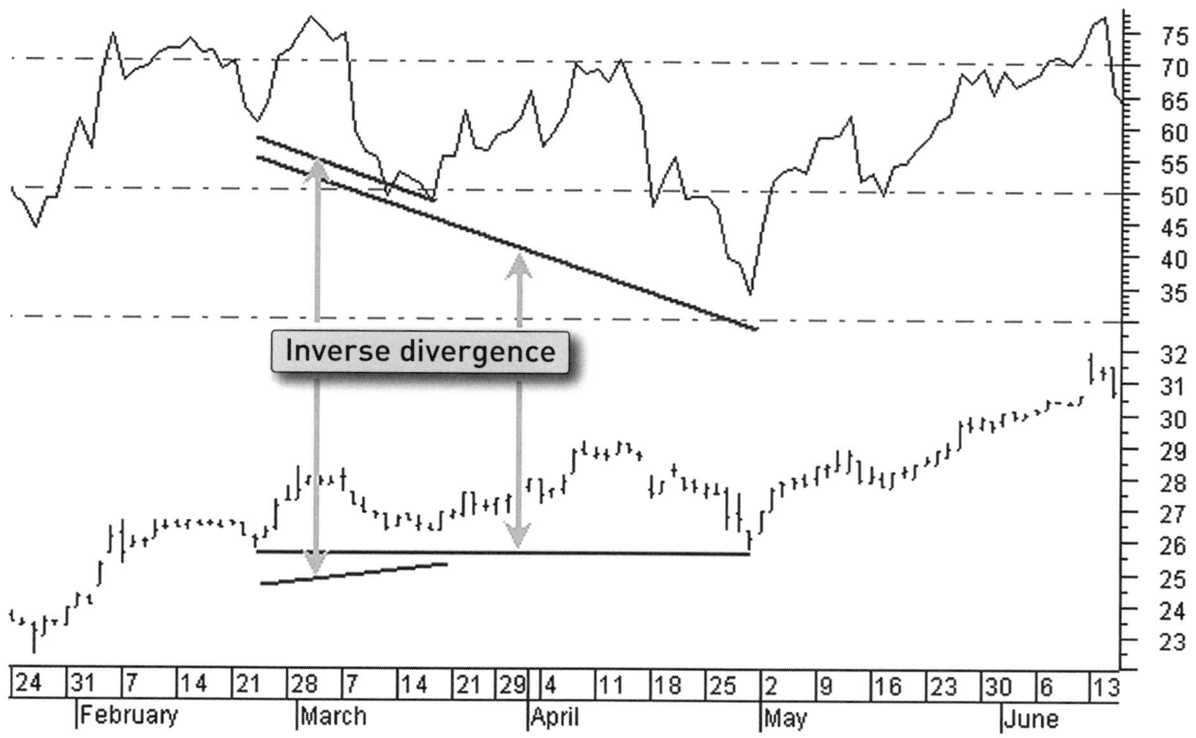

Source - MetaStock® charts courtesy of Equis International.

Figure 2.5 shows an inverse divergence with a lower RSI bottom and a higher or equal price bottom. It is more common in an uptrend when temporary downward corrections end with a higher price bottom while having a lower bottom in the RSI. This is a signal that the price is reversing and will continue the previous uptrend.

Figure 2.6: Using an RSI 30 bars average

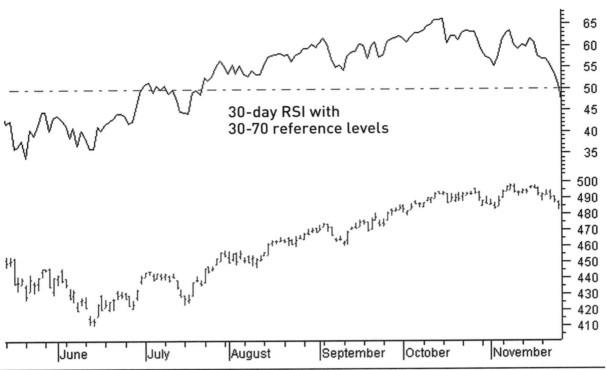

30-day RSI with
30-70 reference levels

Reference Level

The 30–70 fixed reference level used in the standard RSI is a disadvantage if you are using time periods other than the standard 14 bars.

If you used a 30-bar reference, as shown in figure 2.6, you would notice that the 30–70 levels are not reached anymore. We can solve this by using a variable reference level.

Figure 2.7: RSI with a standard deviation reference level

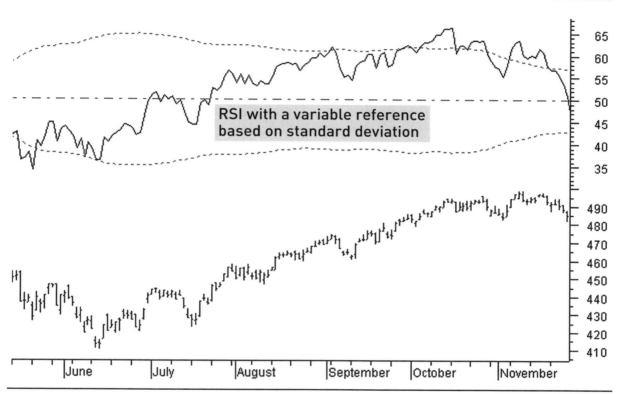

RSI with a variable reference based on standard deviation

Source - MetaStock® charts courtesy of Equis International.

In figure 2.7, you see a simple way of achieving this by using a standard deviation value referenced to the RSI 50 level in a predefined look-back period.

Figure 2.8: Lower and upper reference set to 1.5 times standard deviation for a 5-period RSI

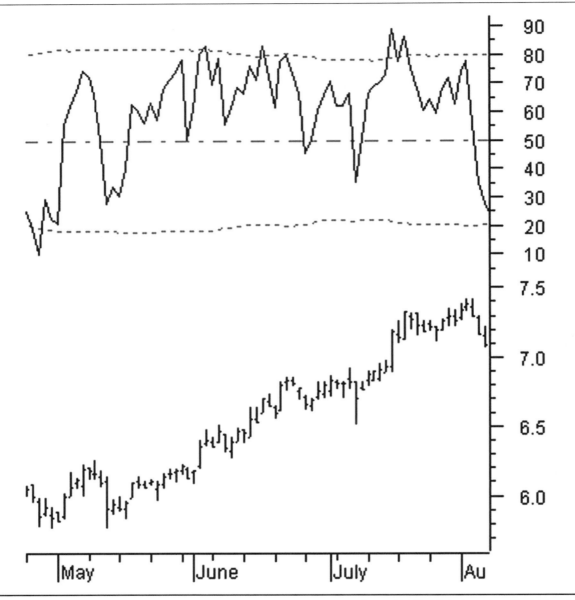

Source - MetaStock® charts courtesy of Equis International.

We set the upper standard deviation to a value of 50 plus 1.5 times the standard deviation over a 100-day look-back period. This is demonstrated in figure 2.8 with a 5-bar RSI.

For bigger RSI time periods, the reference level moves closer to the 50 level, whereas for smaller periods, like our 5-day RSI example, reference levels move farther away to the 20 and 80 levels.

The RSI custom formula with the variable standard deviation lines is as follows:

{SVE_RSI_StDev}

period:= Input("RSI period?",1,100,14);

afwh:= Input("Standard deviation high side",0.1,5,1.5);

afwl:= Input("Standard deviation Low side",0.1,5,1.5);

afwper:= Input("Standard deviation period ",1,200,100);

SVERSIStDev:=RSI(C,period);

50+afwh*Stdev(SVERSIStDev,afwper);

50-afwl*Stdev(SVERSIStDev,afwper);

SVERSIStDev

 Please utilize the disc in the back of the book for instant access to these codes. You may also download them from www.traderslibrary.com/tlecorner.

The RSI is the second indicator below the price chart in the standard LOCKIT chart template.

LOCKIT

Figure 2.9: Small M- and W-shaped patterns give short-term reversal signals

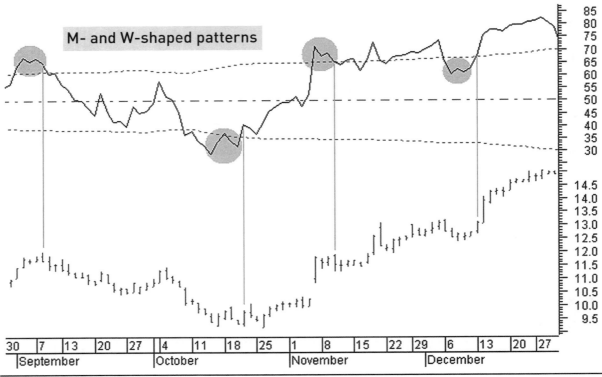

Source - MetaStock® charts courtesy of Equis International.

M- and W-shaped Patterns

M- and W-shaped patterns are short-term patterns visible in the overbought or oversold areas of the RSI indicator.

Figure 2.9 shows small M-shaped patterns at the top and small W-shaped patterns at the bottom that give reliable short-term price reversal signals. Preferably, they'll incline in the direction of the reversal.

The second leg of the M-shaped pattern does not move above the first leg. The second leg of the W-shaped pattern does not move below the first leg. M and W patterns are unrelated to convergences or divergences between the price and RSI indicator.

They are more useful when there is a convergence because they are, at that particular moment in time, the only visible indicators of (at least) a short-term reversal.

HEIKIN ASHI PRICE BARS

Heikin ashi, Japanese for "average bar," is a technique used to better visualize price trends by recalculating candlesticks (Dan Valcu, 2004).

To calculate the new candle:

> **HaClose = (Open+High+Low+Close)/4**
> **= the average price of the current bar**
>
> **HaOpen = [HaOpen(previous bar) + Close(previous bar)]/2**
> **= the midpoint of the previous bar**
>
> **HaHigh = Max(High, HaOpen, HaClose)**
> **= the highest value in the range**
>
> **HaLow = Min(Low, HaOpen, HaClose)**
> **= the lowest value in the range**

Heikin Ashi Chart

The heikin ashi chart is a candle chart based on the recalculated values for open, high, low, and closing prices, but with a different interpretation.

At the top of figure 2.10 is the standard candle chart, based on the real open, high, low, and closing prices. Below is the heikin ashi candle chart, based on the re-calculated prices for open, high, low, and closing prices.

Interpretation of heikin ashi candles:			
Scenario	**Trend behavior**	**Actual trend**	
		Uptrend	**Downtrend**
1	Normal trend	Up-moving white bodies	Down-moving black bodies
2	Strong trend	Up-moving white bodies without a lower shadow	Down-moving black bodies without an upper shadow
3	Weakening trend	Bodies are getting smaller; lower shadows are appearing	Bodies are getting smaller; upper shadows are appearing
4	Consolidation	Small bodies with upper and lower shadows	Small bodies with upper and lower shadows
5	Trend reversal	Small bodies with large upper and lower shadows (not always reliable)	Small bodies with large upper and lower shadows (not always reliable)

Figure 2.10: Standard candle chart and heikin ashi candle chart

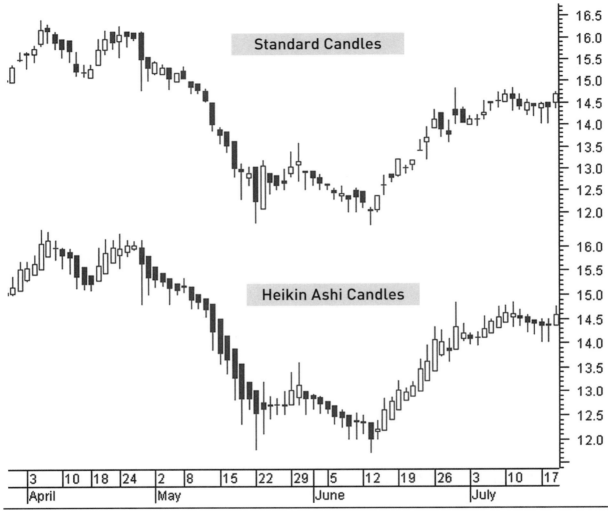

Source - MetaStock® charts courtesy of Equis International.

Heikin Ashi Candles in MetaStock®

In MetaStock®, it is not possible to create an indicator that will result in more than one data item displayed on a single bar. For heikin ashi candles, however, you need four data items displayed on the same bar.

If you really want to use heikin ashi candle charts, it is best to buy conversion software that can automatically convert the data and then create a mirror of the data in heikin ashi format.

Figure 2.11: Good smoothing effect of the heikin ashi closing price average

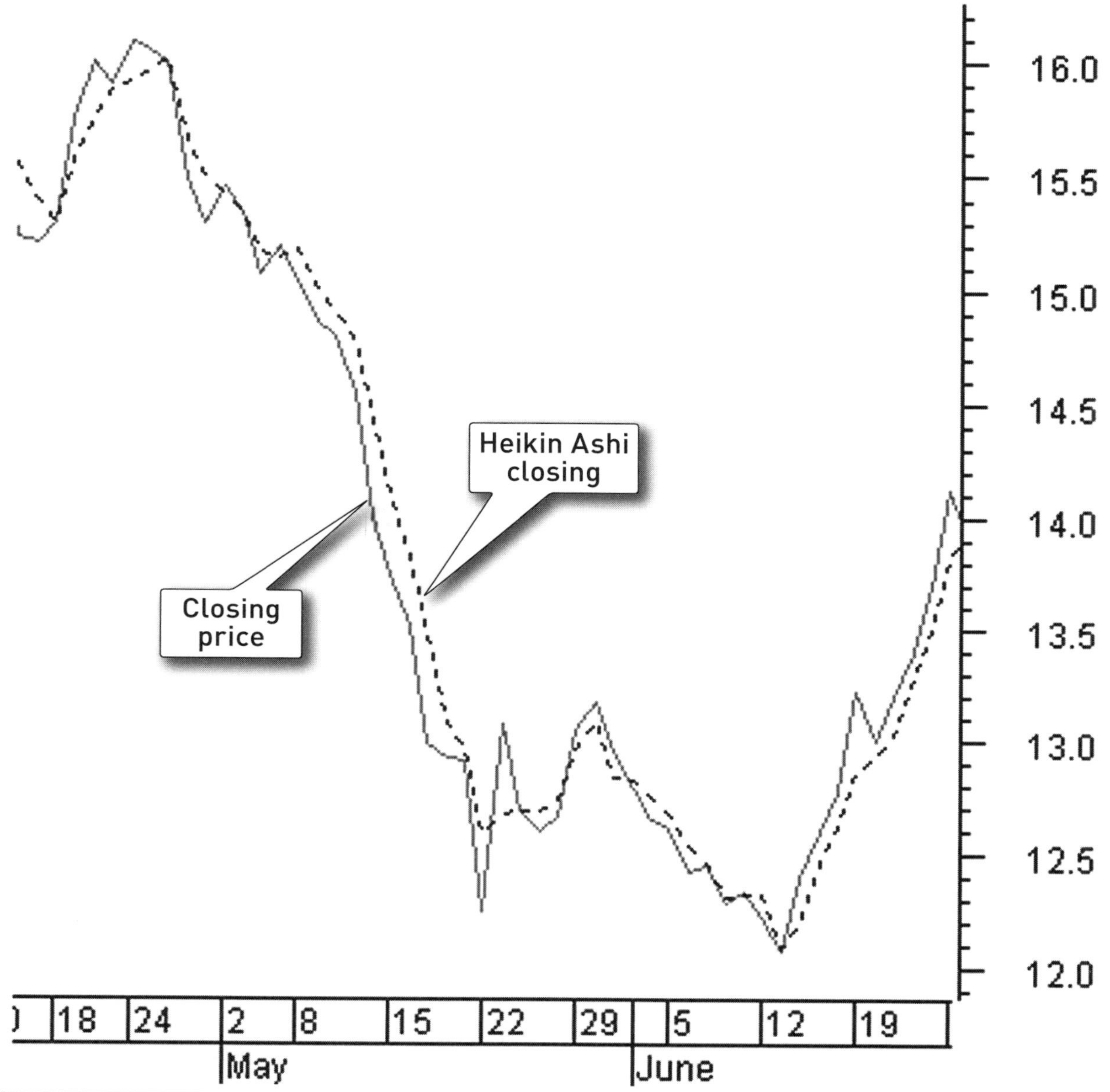

Source - MetaStock® charts courtesy of Equis International.

"HeikinAshi4MetaStock" is a shareware program that does this; it is easy to find on the Internet.

In our LOCKIT application, we only use the average of the heikin ashi closing price because it has a very good smoothing effect without lag, as you can see in figure 2.11.

HA_C Calculation formula for the average heikin ashi closing price in MetaStock®:

{haC}

haOpen:=(Ref((O+H+L+C)/4,-1) + PREV)/2;

haC:=((O+H+L+C)/4+haOpen+Max(H,haOpen)+Min(L,haOpen))/4;

haC

 Please utilize the disc in the back of the book for instant access to these codes. You may also download them from www.traderslibrary.com/tlecorner.

Figure 2.12: S&P 500 Index with zero-lag TEMA crossover

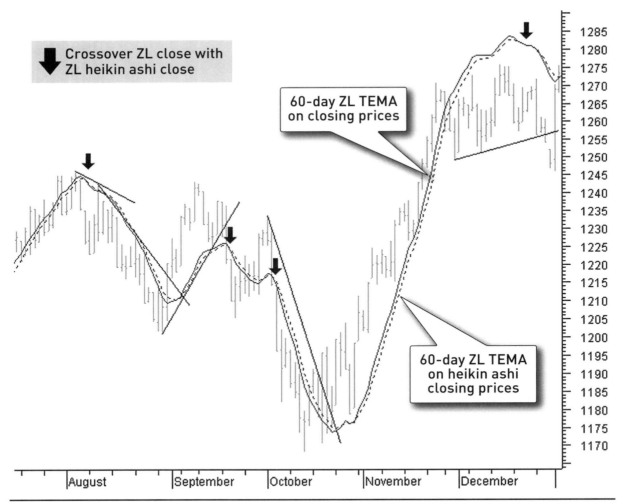

Source - MetaStock® charts courtesy of Equis International.

Application: Heikin Ashi with Zero-lag TEMA Average

Using a longer-period, zero-lagging TEMA average on the heikin ashi closing prices gives a smooth average with limited lag.

In the chart of the S&P 500 Index (figure 2.12), we applied the same zero-lag TEMA principle on the normal closing prices. Putting both averages on the price chart, you can see crossovers between the averages, which are very useful medium-term selling signals to close a long position. I have found that a 60-day period for the TEMA average gives the most useful results.

The Formulas Used

ZLTMACL MetaStock® formula for a zero lagging TEMA average on the closing prices:

```
{ZLTMACL}

Periode:= Input("Zero-lagging CL TEMA Average ",1,100,60);
TMA1:= Tema(CLOSE,Periode);
TMA2:= Tema(TMA1,Periode);
Difference:= TMA1 - TMA2;
ZLTMACL:= TMA1 + Difference;
ZLTMACL
```

ZLTMAHA MetaStock® formula for a zero-lagging heikin ashi TEMA average:

```
{ZLTMAHA}

avg := Input("Zero-lagging HA TEMA average ",1,100,60);

haOpen:=(Ref((O+H+L+C)/4,-1) + PREV)/2;

haC:=((O+H+L+C)/4+haOpen+Max(H,haOpen)+Min(L,haOpen))/4;

TMA1:= Tema(haC,avg);

TMA2:= Tema(TMA1,avg);

Diff:= TMA1 - TMA2;

ZLTMAHA:= TMA1 + Diff;

ZLTMAHA
```

 Please utilize the disc in the back of the book for instant access to these codes. You may also download them from www.traderslibrary.com/tlecorner.

I will also present the crossings of the ZLTMACL and the ZLTMAHA as a complementary technique in Chapter 9, "The Quest for Profitable Cross-overs," for creating automatic buy and sell signals.

<u>LOCKIT</u> — We use the heikin ashi closing average in a number of formulas in the LOCKIT system, but we do not use the graphical display of heikin ashi candles in LOCKIT.

BOLLINGER %b OSCILLATOR

Bollinger Bands were created by John Bollinger and are mentioned in his book *"Bollinger on Bollinger Bands"* (Bollinger, 2001).

The Bollinger Bands in figure 2.13 consist of a set of three curves drawn in relation to price data. The middle band usually is a simple 20-bar moving average, which serves as the base for the upper and lower bands.

Figure 2.13: Bollinger Bands consist of three curves drawn in relation to price data

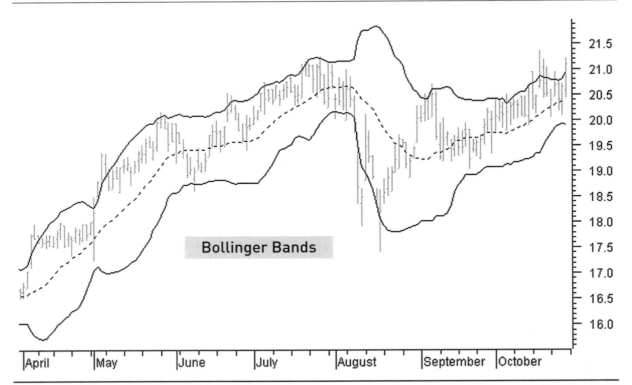

Bollinger Bands

Source - MetaStock® charts courtesy of Equis International.

Middle Bollinger Band = 20-period simple moving average
Upper Bollinger Band = Middle Bollinger Band + 2 * 20-period
    standard deviation
Lower Bollinger Band = Middle Bollinger Band - 2 * 20-period
    standard deviation

The use of standard deviation bands is a method to measure price volatility. With trending prices, the bands will be wider as a result of the higher volatility in price, whereas consolidation-period bands will be narrower as a result of smaller price moves.

> **In LOCKIT, we will not use Bollinger Bands; instead, we will use %b, a measure of where the last price is in relation to the bands.**

LOCKIT

Bandwidth is used for volatility-based trading opportunities; %b is strongly influenced by volatility, and we use it as an oscillator to show overbought and oversold situations, preferably by looking at divergences.

We do not get the best %b indicator by using closing prices, but by using heikin ashi average closing prices. We also are not using a simple moving average, but a weighted moving average for a faster short-term response.

This is the MetaStock® formula for the heikin ashi Bollinger Bands %b indicator:

We call this function SVE_BB%b_HA:

{SVE_BB%b_HA}

peri:=Input("Average period: ",2,100,18);

haOpen:=(Ref((O+H+L+C)/4,-1) + PREV)/2;

haC:=((O+H+L+C)/4+haOpen+Max(H,haOpen)+Min(L,haOpen))/4;

SVEBB%bHA:=((haC+2*Stdev(haC,peri)-Mov(haC,peri,W))/
(4*Stdev(haC,peri)))*100;

SVEBB%bHA

 Please utilize the disc in the back of the book for instant access to these codes. You may also download them from www.traderslibrary.com/tlecorner.

Figure 2.14: SVE_BB%b_HA leading indicator

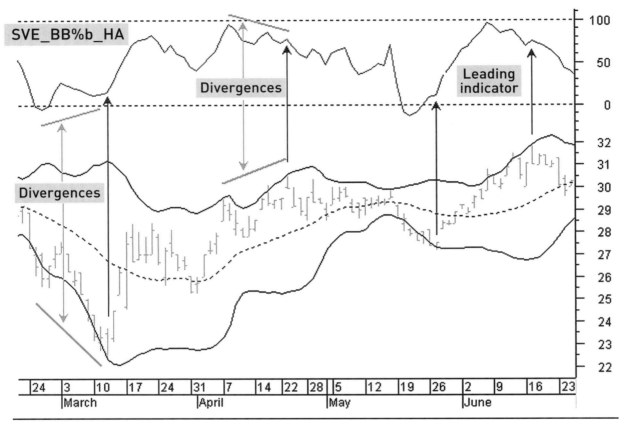

SVE_BB%b_HA

Divergences

Leading indicator

Divergences

Divergences

We use as a standard an 18-bar SVE_BB%b_HA.

LOCKIT

> SVE_BB%b_HA is the third indicator below the price chart in the standard LOCKIT chart template.

As you can see in figure 2.14, the indicator is leading most of the time, showing high levels, low levels, and divergences prior to turning points in price movement. It is a fast and useful indicator and is used in combination with the other indicators within the LOCKIT system.

Remember the first indicator in the LOCKIT chart template is the SVAPO oscillator. Because this is the oscillator I developed, we will look at it in detail in Chapter 5.

The next chapter is dedicated to candle chart patterns.

→ For a closer look at the charts in this chapter, go to www.traderslibrary.com/TLEcorner.

TEST YOUR CHAPTER 2 KNOWLEDGE

1. How do you recognize an RSI bottom divergence?

_____

_____

_____

2. How do you recognize an RSI top divergence?

_____

_____

_____

3. How would you describe RSI inverse or hidden divergences?

_____

_____

_____

4. What do you know about RSI M- and W-shaped patterns?

_____

_____

_____

5. The Bollinger bands %b indicator is a measure of?

_____

_____

_____

 For answers, please visit the Traders' Library Education Corner at www.traderslibrary.com/tlecorner.

Chapter 3

Candlestick Charts

Candlestick charts are the preferred chart type used in LOCKIT. LOCKIT uses candle chart patterns as part of the buying and selling process to find short-term price turning points and additionally uses these patterns for support and resistance.

If you are new to candlestick charts, then it will not be that easy learning and recognizing all the patterns. I would like to suggest that you read through the chapter and that you start by recognizing at least the following patterns.

- For a bottom reversal: hammer, engulfing bullish, bullish harami (cross), piercing line, and morning star patterns.

- For a top reversal: hanging man, engulfing bearish, bearish harami (cross), dark cloud cover, and evening star patterns.

Make sure you apply the rules for bottom or top reversals correctly and that you completely understand the paragraphs "To doji or not?" and "Trading in the context of price history."

INTRODUCTION

Around 1750 a legendary Japanese rice trader named Homma used trading techniques that eventually evolved into the candlestick techniques that technical analysts on the Japanese stock market used later on. Steve Nison introduced these techniques to the Western world in his first book, *Japanese Candlestick Charting Techniques* (Nison, 1991).

The advantage of using candles on charts is that single or multiple candle patterns give earlier and more reliable reversal signals. Every candle shows the activity for the referenced period in hourly, daily, or weekly charts, for example.

Figure 3.1

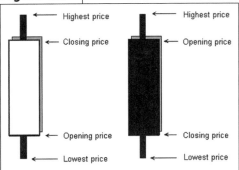

In figure 3.1, the horizontal reference points of the candle represent the opening price, the highest price, the lowest price, and the closing price of the considered period. The rectangular portion of the candle, or the body, represents the range between the opening and the closing prices. If the closing price is higher than the opening price, the body is white (not filled). If the closing price is lower than the opening price, the body is black (filled).

A candle consists of either just a body or a body with an upper and/or a lower shadow. A candle with an opening and closing price at almost the same price level is called a doji (figure 3.2). The candlewicks are called shadows, and they extend up to the highest price and down to the lowest price of the related period. Candlestick charts can be used in any time frame, including minutes, hours, days, weeks, or months.

Candlestick chart patterns are formed by one or more candles; they indicate a short-term trend reversal or a trend continuation. You must always take into account the previous trend when interpreting candlestick patterns.

Candlestick patterns do NOT give price targets!

Format, Naming, and Meaning

Please see figure 3.3 and the chart below for an overview of the candlesticks' formats.

Figure 3.2

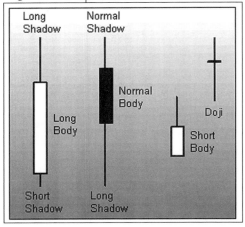

Figure 3.3

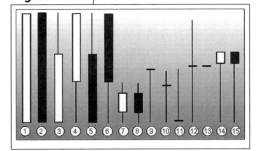

Format Description		
Nr.	**Name**	**Interpretation**
1	Big white body (White Marubozu)	Very positive
2	Big black body (Black Marubozu)	Very negative
3	White opening Marubozu	Quite positive
4	White closing Marubozu	Positive
5	Black closing Marubozu	Negative
6	Black opening Marubozu	Quite negative
7	White candle	No direction
8	Black candle	No direction
9	Dragonfly doji	Reversal?
10	Doji star	Reversal?
11	Gravestone doji	Stable/Reversal
12	Long-legged doji	Reversal?
13	Four price doji	Reversal?
14	Hammer (white) Hanging man	Bottom reversal Top reversal
15	Hammer (black) Hanging man	Bottom reversal Top reversal

Psychological Background

The candlesticks in figures 3.4 and 3.5 demonstrate the psychological trading that takes place during the period represented by a single candle. Study these charts carefully!

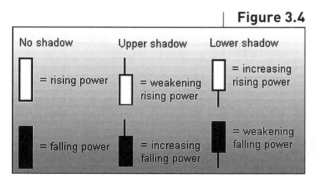

Figure 3.4

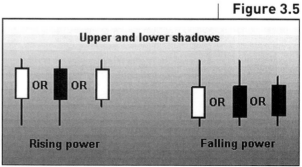

Figure 3.5

Figure 3.6

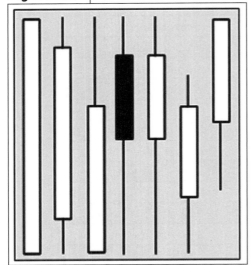

Figure 3.6 shows some rising power candles.

Figure 3.7

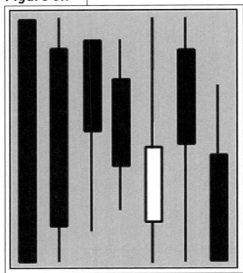

Figure 3.7 shows some candles with falling power.

Figure 3.8 shows candles with reversal power.

Figure 3.8

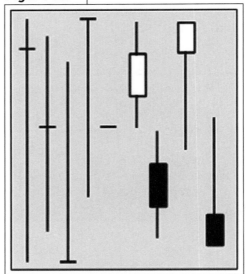

To review:

- A big white body means buyers are in power, and the trend is up.

- A big black body means sellers are in power, and the trend is down.

- A small body means that buyers and sellers are trying to take power.

- A big shadow below is a positive sign and indicates strength.

- A big shadow above is a negative sign and indicates weakness.

- A doji is a candle with opening and closing prices that are close together.

- A doji means that price acceleration is slowing down and that bulls and bears are in balance.

- A doji at a top or bottom often is the first signal of a price reversal.

Combination Technique

You can use a candlestick combination technique to better understand the meaning of a series of candles.

Figure 3.9 shows how the price reached a top and then consolidated in a rectangular formation.

A rectangle can be a reversal pattern or a continuation pattern.

We can apply the combination technique as follows. From the start of the formation, we take the opening price. This will be the opening price for the combined candle. From the last candlestick, we take the closing price; this will be the closing price for the combined candle. Finally, we take the highest and the lowest prices in the formation to find the high and low prices of the combined candle.

Here, the result of the combination is a black hanging man pattern. This is a top reversal pattern, so the price moved down (figure 3.10).

Candlesticks Reveal More

When comparing the commonly used bar charts in Western technical analysis to the Eastern candle charts, it is evident that candle charts have a bigger visual impact.

Figure 3.9

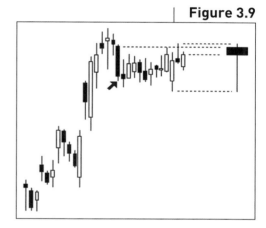

Figure 3.10

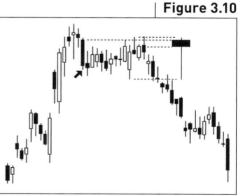

Figure 3.11

Figure 3.12

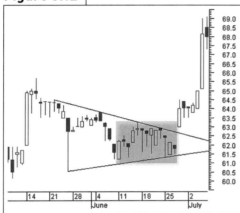

Note the triangle formation in the bar chart of figure 3.11. A triangle formation often is a continuation pattern, but sometimes it can be a reversal pattern. The bar chart does not give any clue about which side of the triangle pattern will be broken.

But in the candle chart in figure 3.12, we see only candles with rising power in the last couple of weeks. The break to the upper side was, therefore, no big surprise, and we got a continuation of the uptrend.

FOUR RULES OF CANDLESTICKS
Size

Bigger candles are more important than smaller ones. When you notice an increasing number of bigger candles, it means that the trend is accelerating and there is accumulation of the stock. But when you see an increasing number of smaller candles, it means that the trend is decelerating and distribution is ongoing.

The marubozu candles are very important. These are big white or big black candles without shadows. A white marubozu means that the bulls were in charge during the whole of the trading period. A black marubozu means the bears were in action from the beginning until the end of the session.

Shape

The shape of a candle or pattern gives information about the possible direction of the price trend. Shape and size work together; a small-sized, rising pattern indicates the potential for the price to move in the direction of the pattern, but, because the pattern is small, it means that the move is not yet accelerating.

Shadows give important information about the on-going session. Candlesticks with small shadows indicate that the price moved mainly between the opening and closing prices during the whole of the session. Big shadows mean that there was trading far above or below the opening or closing prices.

Candles with a long shadow at the top and a small shadow below indicate high bid prices during the session; however, in a later stage, prices had to move down under the selling pressure of the bears.

Candles with a long shadow at the bottom and a small shadow at the top indicate lower asking prices during the session; however, in a later stage, the prices had to move up under the buying pressure of the bulls.

Candles with a small body and upper and lower shadows (spinning tops or big waves with big shadows) are a sign of indecision. It means that the bulls and bears were both very active, but that there was no winner.

When this happens after an uptrend or a big white candle, it means that the bulls are losing power, and the price may reverse. But if this happens after a downtrend or a big black candle, the bears are losing control, and the price may turn up.

Position

The place in the chart where a pattern appears indicates whether it is a usable signal. A reversal pattern after an up-move is a strong reversal signal.

The same pattern in a sideways price move has only limited meaning as a support or resistance level. Most patterns within a sideways move have no meaning at all.

Volume

A reversal pattern with higher-than-average volume on the reversal day offers extra confirmation for a reversal.

BASIC PATTERNS

Different basic patterns offer an indication about what kind of price evolution can be expected.

White Body

A white body is when the closing price closed higher than the opening price. The white body has a normal average size compared to recent prices.

It is a *rising* pattern.

Black Body

A candle is black when the closing price closed below the opening price. The black body has a normal average size compared to recent prices.

It is a *falling* pattern.

Big White Candle

Rare. This is a long white body with little or no shadows compared to recent prices. High price and closing price are close together, and low price and opening price are also close together.

A stronger rising pattern. If there is no other support nearby, you can use the mid-point of the white body as a support level.

Big Black Candle

Rare. This is a long black body with little or no shadows compared to recent prices. High price and opening price are close together, and low price and closing price are also close together.

A stronger falling pattern. If there is no other resistance nearby, you can use the mid-point of the black body as a resistance level.

Doji

A doji is when the opening price and closing price are very close together with upper and lower shadows.

Dojis are part of many candlestick patterns. Dojis with bigger shadows are more important.

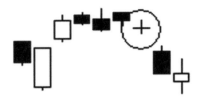

- A doji in an up-move with a closing price below the previous closing price is a strong reversal indication.

- A doji in an up-move with a closing price above the previous closing price needs confirmation for a reversal.

- A doji or any other reversal pattern followed by a candle with a window is a sure reversal indication.

- There is extra pressure on the market when more dojis appear together.

- A doji in a downtrend has much less value than a doji in an uptrend. A doji in a downtrend always needs confirmation as a reversal signal.

- A doji during a flat, neutral trading period has no meaning.

- A doji or any other candle pattern confirms existing support or resistance.

Long-legged Doji

A doji with big upper and lower shadows is also called a big wave doji.

A warning signal for a reversal. This is an indication of big uncertainty in the market.

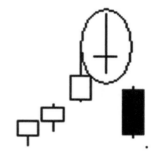

Doji Star

A doji star is a doji above a white candle in an up-move or below a black candle in a down-move.

A reversal signal, to be confirmed by the next candle to become an evening doji star or a morning doji star.

Spinning Tops and Bottoms

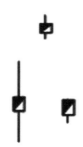

Spinning tops and bottoms are very common in a consolidation phase at a price top or bottom. The most important characteristic of a spinning top or bottom is the small body. The body can be black or white and can have no shadow up to big shadows. As such, this candle is neutral, and the market does not know which way to go. Nevertheless, just like a doji, this might be the first indication of a possible price reversal.

Tweezer Tops and Bottoms

Tweezer tops and bottoms are two or more candles with tops or bottoms at the same price level indicating resistance or support. The first candle is preferably the bigger candle; the second is the smaller one. The shared price level does not have to be the high or low price. A combination with a closing or an opening price is also acceptable. Tweezer tops and bottoms are reliable reversal patterns.

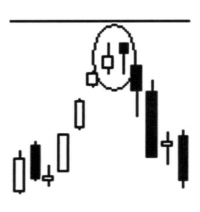

Figure 3.13

TO DOJI OR NOT?

A strong indication of a price reversal is a doji after a price move up and with a closing price below the previous closing price. (figure 3.13).

| **Figure 3.14**

A doji after a price move up and with a closing price above the previous closing price needs confirmation for a price reversal. Figure 3.14 shows an example without confirmation; the price continues in the uptrend.

| **Figure 3.15**

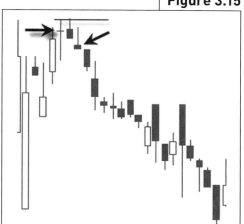

Figure 3.15 is an example with confirmation resulting in a price reversal.

| **Figure 3.16**

A doji or any other candle reversal pattern followed by a candle with a window is a reliable reversal signal (figure 3.16).

Figure 3.17

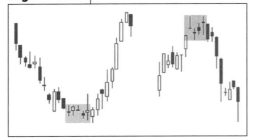

There is extra pressure on the market when more dojis appear together (figure 3.17).

Figure 3.18

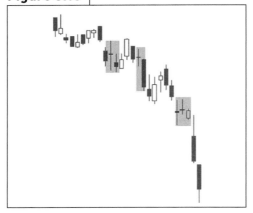

A doji within a downtrend (figure 3.18) has much less value than a doji in an uptrend.

Figure 3.19

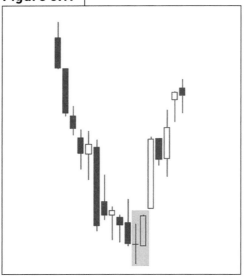

A doji in a downtrend always needs confirmation for a reversal signal (figure 3.19).

Figure 3.20

A doji within a flat, neutral price zone has no meaning (figure 3.20).

| **Figure 3.21**

A doji or any other candle pattern confirms existing support or resistance (figure 3.21).

REVERSAL PATTERNS

Reversal patterns are candlestick patterns that announce a trend reversal.

Bottom Reversals

The following rules are applicable for a bottom reversal:

- A bottom reversal is only possible AFTER a downtrend.

- Most of the patterns need a confirmation.

- A confirmation must appear one up to three candles after the pattern.

- Confirmation is a big white candle, high volume with the new up-move, a rising window, or a break of resistance.

- A reversal pattern during a price reaction must be considered a continuation pattern.

- For the best result, you must combine candlestick patterns with Western technical analysis.

- An unconfirmed pattern has no further meaning.

Let's look at a few of the common bottom reversal patterns.

Engulfing Bullish

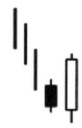

In a downtrend, there is a small black body, not a doji, followed and enclosed by a bigger white body.

Though not necessary, it is better when the white body also encloses the short shadows of the black candle.

An exceptional occurrence at the end of a downtrend is a white body followed by a bigger black body; this is called a last engulfing pattern.

Piercing Line

In a downtrend, a bigger black body is followed by a white body with a lower opening price than the low of the black body; however, the white candle closes above the midpoint of the black body.

Bullish Counterattack

A bullish counterattack is a bigger black candle in a downtrend, followed by a bigger white candle. Closing prices of both candles are at the same price level.

Confirmation is needed.

Bullish Harami

In a downtrend, a white (but preferably a black) body is followed by a small white or black candle that is completely covered by the first candle body.

This is a bottom reversal signal after confirmation. Black–white and black–black (called homing pigeon) combinations are the most common.

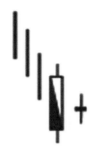

Bullish Harami Cross

In a downtrend, a white (but preferably a black) body is followed by a doji that is completely covered by the first candle body.

A bullish harami cross pattern needs confirmation.

Morning Star

A morning star is a bigger black body, followed by one or more small black or white bodies below the closing price of the first black body. The white candle that follows ideally has 50% or more of its body within the first black body and has a rising window with the previous candle body.

Morning Doji Star

A morning doji star is a bigger black body, followed by one or more dojis with a falling window below the closing price of the first black body. The white candle that follows ideally has 50% or more of its body within the first black body and has a rising window with the previous doji body.

This is a stronger reversal signal than a morning star.

Bullish Abandoned Baby

An abandoned baby pattern is a morning doji star with a window between the doji and the black and white candle, resulting in an island reversal. The island can have more candles and more than one doji.

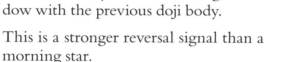

Hammer

A hammer is a small white or black body close to the high price. It has a long shadow below with a minimum size of twice the height of the body. There is a very small shadow or no shadow at the top. A dragonfly doji is a specific version of the hammer pattern.

Confirmation is required. A white body is more positive.

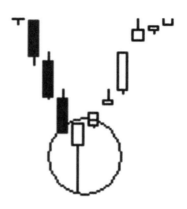

Inverted Hammer

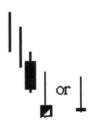

An inverted hammer is a small black (but preferably a small white) body near the low price. It has a long shadow above that is, at minimum, twice the size of the body. It only has a very small shadow or no shadow below. A gravestone doji is a specific version of the inverted hammer.

This is a bottom reversal only after confirmation.

Tweezer Bottoms

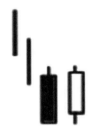

Tweezer bottoms are two or more candles making lows together. Preferably, the lows are made with low prices, but they also can be combinations of any of the other prices. Size and color are not important. This is a reversal pattern that, most of the time, is part of another pattern.

Fry Pan Bottom

The fry pan bottom is formed with a number of smaller candles. After this bottoming pattern, the price usually makes an up-move with a rising window.

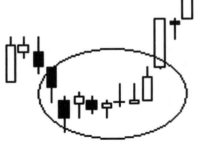

A fry pan bottom is a powerful reversal pattern.

Three River Bottom

During a downtrend, there is a bigger black candle on the first day of this pattern. The second day starts with a higher opening price; then makes a new lower low and closes the day below the opening price. The third day opens lower and forms a small white body with a closing price below the closing price of the second day.

A rare bottom reversal pattern, confirmation is required.

Three White Soldiers

Three white sodiers are three white candlesticks with each bar having higher closing prices, close to the high of the bar. Opening prices of candles two and three are within the body of the previous candles.

Many times, there will be a small reaction before the new uptrend is resumed.

Top Reversals

The following rules are applicable for a top reversal:

- A top reversal is only possible AFTER an uptrend.

- Most patterns need a confirmation.

- A confirmation must appear one up to three candles after the pattern.

- Confirmation is a big black candle, high volume with the new down move, a falling window, or a break of support.

- A reversal pattern during a price reaction must be considered a continuation pattern.

- For best results, you must combine candlestick patterns with Western technical analysis.

- An unconfirmed pattern has no further meaning.

Let's take a look at some of the common top reversal patterns.

Engulfing Bearish

In an uptrend, there is a small white body, not a doji, followed and enclosed by a bigger black body. Though not necessary, it is better when the black body also encloses the short shadows of the white candle.

An exceptional occurrence at the end of an uptrend is a black body followed by a bigger white body, which is called a last engulfing pattern.

Dark Cloud Cover

In an uptrend, a bigger white body is followed by a black body with a higher opening price than the high of the white body; however, the black candle closes below the mid-point of the white body.

Confirmation is required.

Bearish Counterattack

A bearish counterattack is a bigger white candle in an uptrend, followed by a bigger black candle. Closing prices of both candles are at the same price level.

Confirmation is a must.

Bearish Harami

In an uptrend, a black (but preferably a white) body is followed by a small white or black candle that is completely covered by the first candle body.

It is a top reversal signal after confirmation. White-black and white-white combinations are the most common.

Bearish Harami Cross

In an uptrend, a black (but preferably a white) body is followed by a doji that is completely covered by the first candle body.

A bearish harami cross pattern needs confirmation.

Evening Star

An evening star is a bigger white body, followed by one or more small black or white bodies with a rising window above the closing price of the first white body. The black candle that follows ideally sits 50% or more within the first white body and has a falling window with the previous candle body.

Evening Doji Star

An evening doji star is a bigger white body, followed by one or more dojis with a rising window above the closing price of the first white body. The black candle that follows is ideally 50% or more within the first white body and has a falling window with the previous candle body.

This is a stronger reversal pattern than the evening star.

Bearish Abandoned Baby

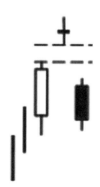

An abandoned baby pattern is an evening doji star with a window between the doji and the white and black candle, resulting in an island reversal. The island can have more candles and more than one doji.

Hanging Man

A hanging man is a small white or black body close to the high price. It has a long shadow below, with a minimum size of twice the height of the body. There is a very small shadow or no shadow at the top. A dragonfly doji is a specific version of the hanging man pattern. Confirmation is required.

Bearish Shooting Star

A bearish shooting star is a small white (but preferably a small black) body near the low price. It has a long shadow above, which is, at minimum, twice the size of the body. It has a very small shadow or no shadow below. There is a gap between the bodies of the bearish shooting star and the previous candle.

A top reversal only after confirmation.

Bearish Gravestone Doji

A bearish gravestone doji is a bearish shooting star where the opening, closing, and low prices are all about the same. It has a long shadow above and no shadow below. There is a gap between the bodies of the doji and the previous candle.

A top reversal only after confirmation.

Tweezer Tops

Tweezer tops are two or more candles making highs together. Preferably, the highs are made with high prices, but they also can be combinations of any of the other prices. Size and color are not important. This is a reversal pattern that, most of the time, is part of another pattern.

Three Black Crows

Three black candlesticks with each subsequent bar having lower closing prices, close to the low of the bar are three black crows. Opening prices of candles two and three are within the body of the previous candles.

Many times, there will be a small reaction before the new downtrend is resumed.

Bearish Dumpling Top

The bearish dumpling top is formed with a number of smaller candles. After this top formation pattern, the price usually makes a down-move with a falling window.

A bearish dumpling top is a powerful reversal pattern.

Upside Gap Two Crows

A white candle in an uptrend is followed by a smaller black candle with a gap above the closing price of the white candle. The body of the next black bar completely covers the previous black bar. This bar also has a gap with the closing price of the white candle.

A very rare pattern.

Two Crows

A white candle in an uptrend is followed by a smaller black candle with a gap above the closing price of the white candle. The body of the next black bar has an opening price within the body of the first black bar and a closing price within the body of the white candle.

Confirmation is needed.

TRADING IN THE CONTEXT OF PRICE HISTORY

Would you be confident opening a short position with the bearish engulfing pattern, as shown in figure 3.22?

YES! Despite the fact that there is no confirmation yet, you should not have any doubt about opening a short position here. The doji and the bearish engulf-

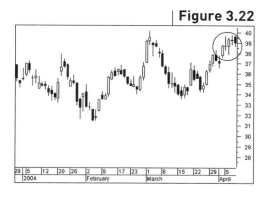

Figure 3.22

Figure 3.23

Figure 3.24

Figure 3.25

Figure 3.26

Figure 3.27

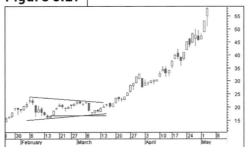

ing pattern confirm the resistance of a previous evening star top from the beginning of March; therefore, a price reversal is almost certain. Additionally, you can open the position with a favorable risk-to-reward ratio, placing a stop at the top of the bearish engulfing or at the level of the previous top, which is almost the same.

And the confidence was rewarded (figure 3.23)!

In the chart shown in figure 3.24, the prices moved down considerably. The last two days make up a bullish harami cross. Is this a good buying moment?

NO! Right above the bullish harami cross, there is resistance from a falling window. If this resistance prevents an up-move now, the risk-to-reward ratio is not good. So, it will be much better to wait for the window to be broken before taking a position.

Further price evolution confirmed that it was better to wait (figure 3.25).

The last three candles in figure 3.26 are a morning doji star. Should you buy here?

YES! It does not look like an ideal morning doji star, but the third candle reaches just within the first candle and is very important for future resistance; the window between the first and second candles of the morning doji star is already closed by the third candle, so this window has no more meaning. The middle small hammer in the morning doji star confirms a previous window support from half of February; furthermore, you can see a symmetrical triangle price pattern, which mostly is a continuation pattern. Opening a position now, with a stop at the low side of the support window, and a primary price target calculated from the height of the start of the triangle and added to a breakout of the triangle, gives a very good risk-to-reward ratio. These are good reasons to open a position now!

Again, a good decision (figure 3.27)!

CONTINUATION PATTERNS

A continuation pattern suggests that, despite any temporary deviations, the trend will continue in its original direction.

Bullish Continuation Patterns

Bullish Three-line Strike

In an uptrend, there are three or more days of higher prices, followed by a big black candle covering most of the previous bars' up-move.

Wait for a confirmation.

Rising Three

In an uptrend, a big white candle is followed by a number of small, mostly black bodies. The pattern ends with a big white candle with a new high price.

Mat Hold

This is a variation of the rising three. In an uptrend, a big white candle is followed by a small candle with a rising window and a lower closing price, forming an evening star pattern. Next, there are a number of small, mostly black candles. The pattern ends with a big white candle with a new high price.

Separating Lines

In an uptrend, a black body is followed by a white body with the same opening price.

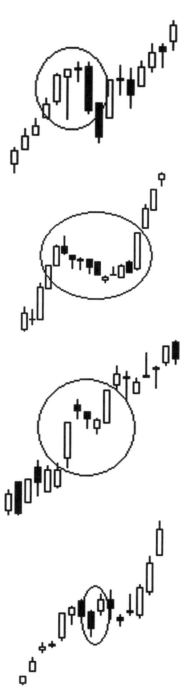

Bearish Continuation Patterns

Bearish Three-line Strike

In a downtrend, there are three or more days of lower prices, followed by a big white candle covering most of the previous bars' down-move.

Wait for a confirmation.

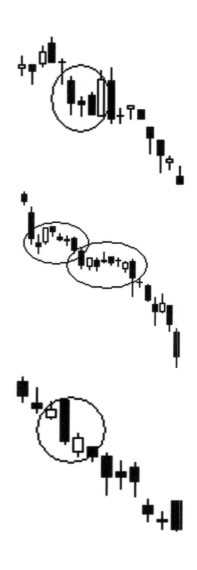

Falling Three

In a downtrend, a big black candle is followed by a number of small, mostly white bodies. The pattern ends with a big black candle with a new low price.

In-neck Line, On-neck Line

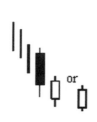

In a downtrend, a relatively big black body is followed by a white body with a lower opening price than the black candle's closing price. With the in-neck line, the white body closes just within the black body. With the on-neck line, the white body closes within the lower shadow of the black body.

Confirmation is required.

Thrusting Line

In a downtrend, a relatively big black body is followed by a white body with a lower opening price than the black candle's closing price. The white body closes below the mid-point of the black body, and does not form a piercing line.

Confirmation is required.

Separating Lines

In a downtrend, a white body is followed by a black body with the same opening price.

In the next chapter we will learn more about applying Elliott wave analysis in the LOCKIT system.

 For a closer look at the charts in this chapter, go to www.traderslibrary.com/TLEcorner.

TEST YOUR CHAPTER 3 KNOWLEDGE

1. Is this candle pattern a bottom or top reversal pattern? What is it called?

_____

_____

_____

_____

_____

2. Is this candle pattern a bottom or top reversal pattern? What is it called?

_____

_____

_____

_____

_____

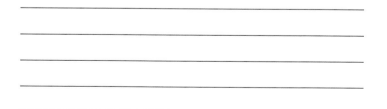

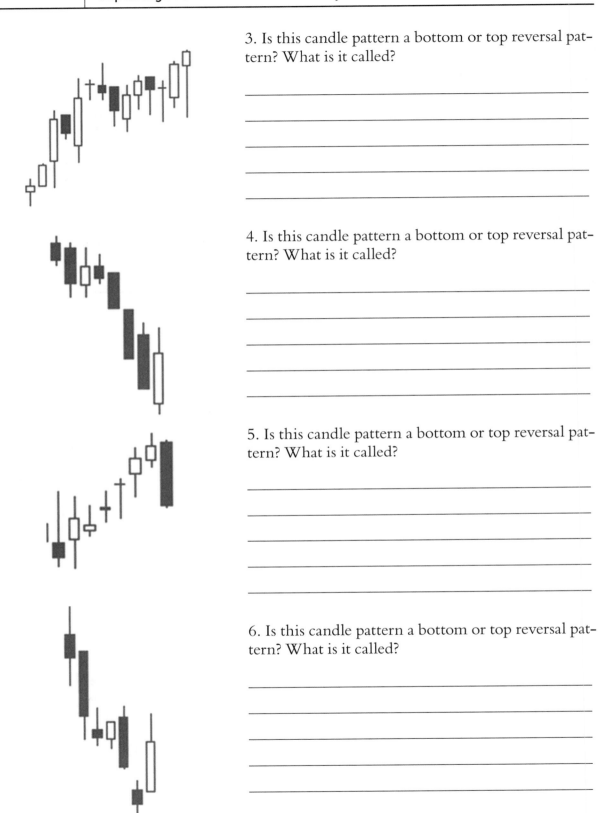

3. Is this candle pattern a bottom or top reversal pattern? What is it called?

_____

_____

_____

_____

_____

4. Is this candle pattern a bottom or top reversal pattern? What is it called?

_____

_____

_____

_____

_____

5. Is this candle pattern a bottom or top reversal pattern? What is it called?

_____

_____

_____

_____

_____

6. Is this candle pattern a bottom or top reversal pattern? What is it called?

_____

_____

_____

_____

_____

7. Is this candle pattern a bottom or top reversal pattern? What is it called?

_____

_____

_____

_____

_____

8. Is this candle pattern a bottom or top reversal pattern? What is it called?

_____

_____

_____

_____

9. Is this candle pattern a bottom or top reversal pattern? What is it called?

_____

_____

_____

_____

10. Is this candle pattern a bottom or top reversal pattern? What is it called?

_____

_____

_____

_____

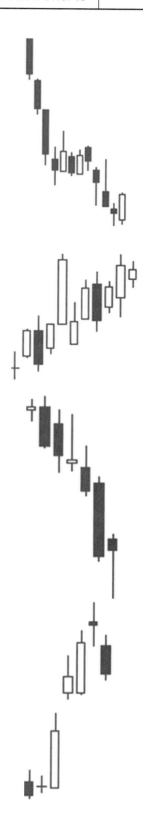

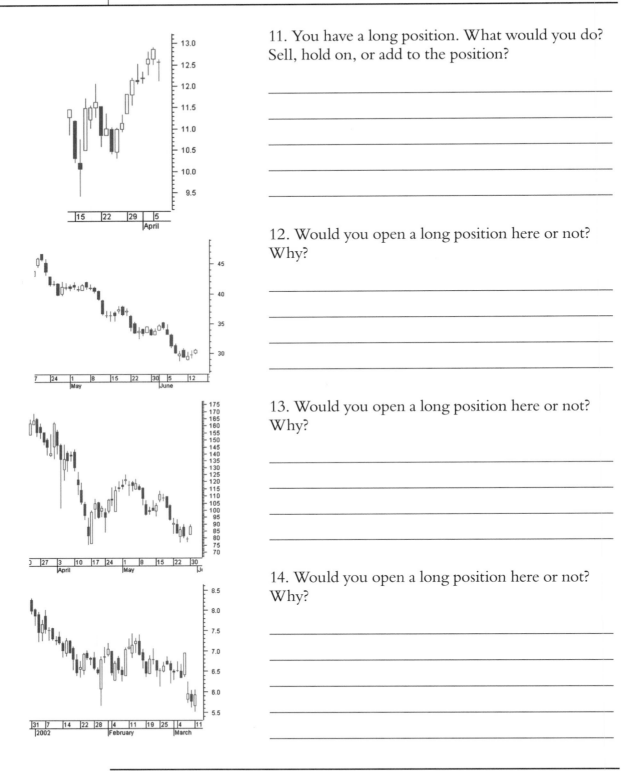

11. You have a long position. What would you do? Sell, hold on, or add to the position?

_____

_____

_____

_____

_____

12. Would you open a long position here or not? Why?

_____

_____

_____

_____

13. Would you open a long position here or not? Why?

_____

_____

_____

_____

14. Would you open a long position here or not? Why?

_____

_____

_____

_____

_____

 For answers, please visit the Traders' Library Education Corner at www.traderslibrary.com/tlecorner.

Chapter

4

Elliott Waves

I n LOCKIT, one of the only tools that can give you an idea as to which direction the stock price will move next is Elliott wave analysis. With short, medium, and long-term Elliott wave trend analysis, we can have a pretty good indication if price has a better chance of going up or going down in those different time periods. As an added bonus, Elliott waves can give us price targets too.

Your Elliott wave count does not have to be perfect.

You will have to review counts regularly. What is important, though, is that price moves in the direction you expect. At the end of the theoretical part about Elliott waves, I will give you a small tool that will help you to make Elliott wave counts. To finish up this chapter, we will try it out on some examples.

INTRODUCTION

During an illness in the mid–1930s, Ralph Nelson Elliott discovered the correlation between human emotion and trend patterns contained within price charts. Elliott discovered different patterns that repeated themselves in form but not necessarily in size or length of time; these patterns could always be subdivided into smaller waves within the framework of certain rules. He called this phenomenon the "wave principle."

There are two basic waves in Elliott wave theory: a five-wave impulse pattern in the direction of the main trend and a three-wave correction pattern against the main trend.

In a later stage, Elliott used Fibonacci numbers together with the waves to predict target prices.

The Elliott wave principle gained wide attention during the seventies thanks to Frost and Prechter, who published the legendary book, *Elliott Wave Principle: Key to Stock Market Profits* (Prechter, Frost, 1978). During the economic crisis of the seventies, this book forecasted the big bull market of the eighties.

Today, Elliott wave theory is more widely used thanks to computer program applications for automatic wave recognition.

IMPULSE AND CORRECTION WAVES

A trend signals the main direction in which prices are moving; corrections move either against the main trend or sideways.

In Elliott wave terminology, these are called **impulse waves** and **correction waves**.

Figure 4.1: An impulse wave consists of five waves

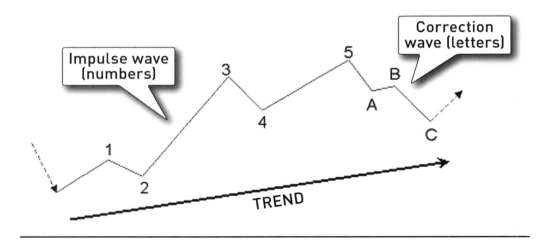

In figure 4.1, you can see that an **impulse wave** consists of five waves: three in the direction of the trend (waves 1, 3, and 5) and two against the trend (waves 2 and 4). The **correction wave** consists of three waves: A, B, and C. Impulse waves are identified by numbers; correction waves are identified by letters.

Figure 4.2: Impulse wave in an uptrend

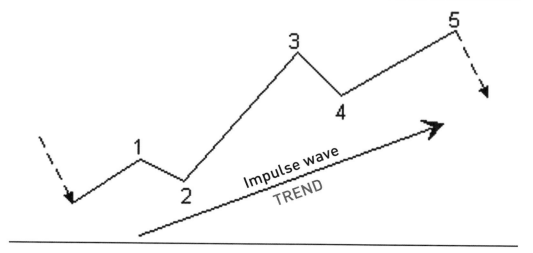

Figure 4.2 is an impulse wave in an uptrend.

Figure 4.3: Impulse wave in a downtrend

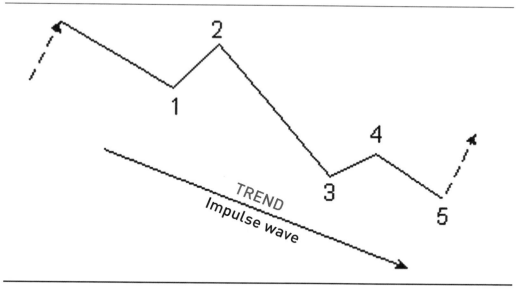

Figure 4.3 is an impulse wave in a downtrend.

Figure 4.4: Waves 1-3-5 in the direction of the trend

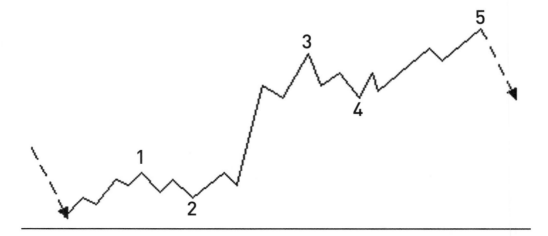

In figure 4.4, waves 1, 3, and 5 moving in the direction of the trend are impulse waves and, therefore, consist of another impulse wave of a lower degree.

Figure 4.5: 3-wave correction waves in an uptrend and downtrend

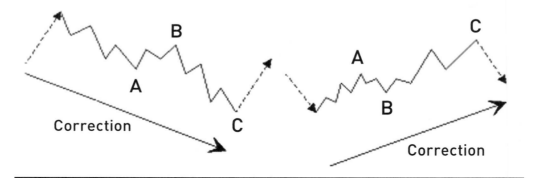

Figure 4.5 shows correction waves in an uptrend and in a downtrend. The correction wave has three waves. Waves A and C point in the direction of the correction; wave B is moving against this direction. Waves 2 and 4 in an impulse wave also are correction waves. Waves A and C in a correction wave move in the direction of the correction trend and are, therefore, impulse waves, again, consisting of five waves.

Figure 4.6: 5-wave triangle corrections in an uptrend and downtrend

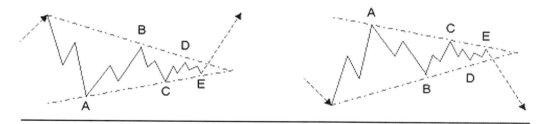

Figure 4.6 shows triangle corrections in an uptrend and in a downtrend. A triangle correction consists of five waves.

IMPORTANT! A triangle correction is part of an ABC correction wave.

Description of a Longer-term Rising Impulse Wave

Top Formation:	
Long-term waves:	Progression and peace last forever; a form of arrogance.
Intermediate waves:	Economic progression; good feeling.
Short-term waves:	Good news.

Figure 4.7: Long-term impulse wave

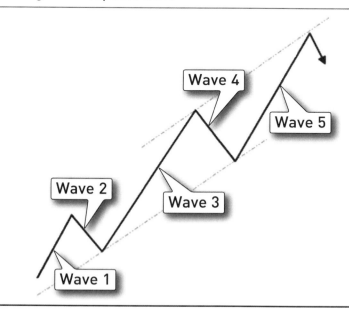

Wave 1

A limited number of people believe that the under-estimated value of stocks is worth buying (figure 4.7); there is a long-term belief in survival.

In about half of the cases, wave 1 is still part of the bottoming pattern of the previous downtrend. As a result, wave 2 will redraw most of wave 1. A lot of investors look at wave 1 as a correction in the downtrend in order to profit from getting a higher price to close positions. They believe the trend will continue farther down. In the other half of the cases, there is a strong belief that the trend will turn up again, in which case wave 2 will usually only make a small correction.

Wave 2

This is a test of the low point of wave 1. There are not yet any visible fundamental changes.

With the start of correction wave 2, believers in an additional downtrend will get confirmation. As a result, and often out of pure panic, call options will drop fast in price. Selling pressure drops with lower volume and lower volatility. Wave 2 never goes below the start of wave 1.

Wave 3

This is a strong up-move based on good economical prospects; there is real improvement in living conditions. This is never the shortest wave.

On its way up, wave 3 will find the resistance of the wave 1 top. This may take some time, but once it is broken, more investors will step in, believing that the trend is really up again. Wave 3 is usually strong because it is supported by big masses. The trend is clear, and there is positive news. Wave 3 makes the biggest move and has intermediate extensions. Almost all stocks take part in this move.

Wave 4

Already reaching the end of the growth cycle? No, just some temporary profit-taking! Wave 4 never reaches the territory of wave 1.

Correction wave 4 is generally predictable in size and pattern. Wave 4 mostly is a limited correction and rather flat. Wave 4 can be used to synchronize the wave.

Wave 5

There are more positive developments, usually not as strong as in wave 3. There is psychological over-estimation.

Those who missed wave 3 believe in a further uptrend. Usually, wave 5 makes a higher top than wave 3 with lower volume from a smaller group of investors. The price acceleration is usually slower than in wave 3. If, however, wave 5 proves to be another extension of wave 3, the acceleration will be stronger.

Description of a Longer-term Correction Wave

Bottom Formation:	
Long-term waves:	Survival, depression, war.
Intermediate waves:	Recession, panic.
Short-term waves:	Bad news.

Figure 4.8: Long-term correction wave

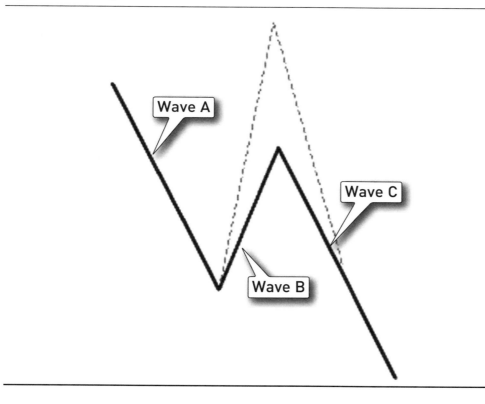

Wave A

Because of the longer-term uptrend (figure 4.8), the technical support levels in between will be an invitation for buying, not selling!

In the first instance, wave A will look like a technical correction related to the previous up-move. Most investors will remain on the buying side. There even are some stocks starting to fall through support levels. If wave A is an impulse wave, there probably will be a zigzag correction. If wave A, on the other hand, is a correction wave, the whole correction probably will be a flat correction.

Wave B

There is only limited support for the up-move. It is selective and, technically, is not well-supported. The economy is weakening, but there is elation and denial.

If you are thinking that there is something wrong with the market, you probably are looking at a B wave. The move up is only supported by a limited number of stocks. There is no confirmation in technical analysis.

Wave C

Complete desperation. Prices keep falling; the economy is a complete disaster.

Wave C is the third wave of the correction and has the same characteristics as an impulse wave 3. The illusion that there was nothing wrong during the development of waves A and B is gone; fear takes over! The correction can be very large.

ELLIOTT WAVES WITH INDIVIDUAL STOCKS

Elliott wave patterns are most clear in market indexes, independent of the stocks within that index. You need a broad market with many investors for a practical application of the Elliott wave rules.

Using Elliott wave analysis with individual stocks can be confusing and impractical. You probably will need to soften the rules for analyzing individual stocks.

On the other hand, we know that 75% of stocks rise when the whole of the market rises, and that 95% fall when the market falls. You should take this into account when looking at clear Elliott wave signals in an individual stock and when making buy or sell decisions.

The Correct Count

Any impulse wave can be interpreted as a correction wave, but it is, of course, wrong to do this because the Elliott wave count will be completely wrong.

Figure 4.9: Correctly counting waves

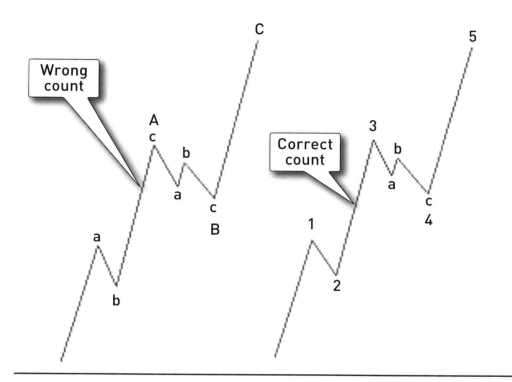

In figure 4.9, a longer 3 wave, followed by a 4 wave with an end-point above the top of wave 1, must be labeled as an impulse wave. When you mark wave 3 as an A wave, consisting of sub-waves abc, you would next expect a flat correction, with a B wave falling back in the neighborhood of the wave A start. This is clearly not the case here. Respecting all of the rules is important.

Figure 4.10: Number of waves in a cycle

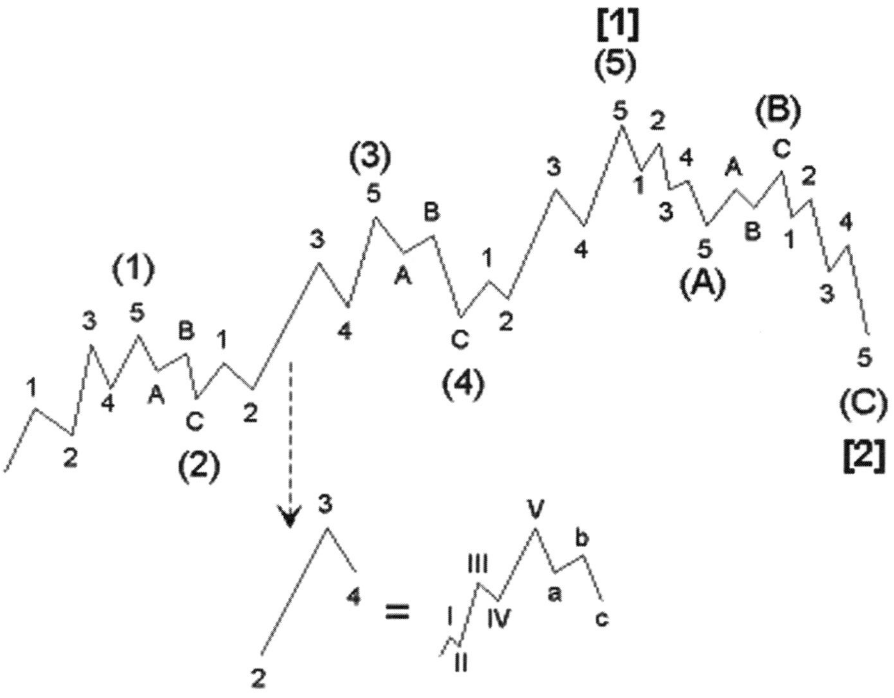

Number of Waves in a Cycle

An **impulse wave** and a **correction wave** together make a **cycle** (figure 4.10).

Biggest wave:	[1] to [2] consist of 1 + 1 = 2 waves
Biggest subdivision:	(1) to (C) consist of 5 + 3 = 8 waves
Next subdivision:	1 to C consist of 21 + 13 = 34 waves
Next subdivision:	I to c consist of 89 + 55 = 144 waves

This subdivision is not limited.

Wave Subdivisions

The basic rule in Elliott wave theory is that wave structures of a higher order are composed of sub-waves of a lower order, which, in turn, are composed of smaller order sub-waves, and so on. They all have, more or less, the same structure as the bigger wave they belong to, impulse or correction.

Elliott used **nine subdivisions**, varying in length from two centuries to one hour. In the next table, we use our own subdivision ordered by time. The timing used gives us an idea about what kind of period we are viewing, but it is not binding.

Subdivision	Time	Impulse	Correction
Grand Super cycle	> 30 years	[I] ... [V]	[A] ... [C]
Super cycle	Decades	(I)...(V)	(A)...(C)
Cycle	Decade	I...V	A...C
Primary	Years	[1]...[5]	[A]... [C]
Intermediate	Months	(1)...(5)	(a)...(c)
Minor	Weeks	1...5	A...C
Minute	Days	i...v	a...c
Minuet	Hours	1...5	a...c
Sub minuet	Minutes	I...V	A...C

IMPULSE PATTERNS

Impulse Wave

Recognizing wave patterns is the most important occupation within Elliott wave analysis. An impulse wave (figure 4.11) is always composed of 5 waves, numbered 1, 2, 3, 4, and 5. Waves 1, 3, and 5 are, again, impulse patterns. Waves 2 and 4 are correction patterns.

Figure 4.11: 5-wave impulse waves in an uptrend and a downtrend

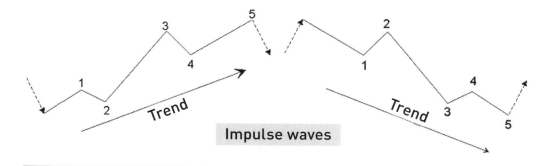

Impulse waves

Rules and Guidelines

The following are the most important rules and guidelines for an impulse pattern.

- Wave 1 is an impulse wave or a starting wedge impulse wave.
- Wave 2 can be any type of correction pattern, except a triangle.
- Wave 2 cannot move beyond the start of wave 1.
- Wave 3 is an impulse wave.
- Wave 3 has a bigger price move than wave 2.
- Wave 3 is never the smallest wave.
- Wave 4 can be any type of correction pattern.
- Waves 2 and 4 are not overlapping.
- Wave 5 is an impulse wave or an ending wedge impulse wave.
- The price move of wave 5 is a minimum 70% of wave 4.
- A wave 5 ending below the top of wave 3 is called a failing wave 5.

Structure

An impulse pattern is composed of 5 waves. The internal structure of these waves is: 5-3-5-3-5. The 5-waves are impulse waves, and the 3-waves are correction waves.

The Correct Count

Look at figure 4.12 for correct interpretation of wave counts.

Figure 4.12: Impulse wave correct count

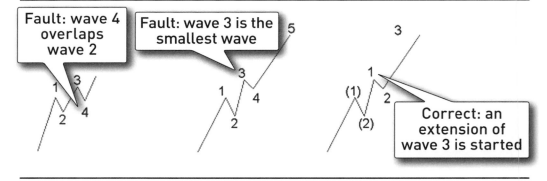

Alternation within Impulse Waves

Sharp corrections are zigzags. Sideways corrections consist of flat corrections, triangles, and double and multiple corrections.

- If wave 2 is a sharp correction, wave 4 will be a sideways correction eight out of ten times.
- If wave 2 is a sideways correction, then there is no alternation; wave 4 will be a sideways correction eight out of ten times.
- It is remarkable that wave 4 makes a sideways correction eight out of ten times.
- Extensions alternate by variation in length of the impulse wave. Wave 1 is short, wave 3 has an extension and is long, and wave 5 is short again.
- Extensions are most common in wave 3, but also in wave 5; this can be considered an alternation.

Price Targets and Fibonacci Levels

Many times, price targets are given by Fibonacci projections. Price retracement during a correction phase often will reach Fibonacci retracement levels.

Looking at wave 1 as an example, you will notice that, in most cases, it will retrace 23.6% up to 38.2% of the complete previous correction wave. Fifty percent retracement or more is rare for wave 1.

Extension of an Impulse Pattern

Waves 1, 3, and 5, and A or C if they are impulse waves, can be extended and, therefore, take much more time than the other waves.

Figure 4.13: Wave extensions are very common in wave 3

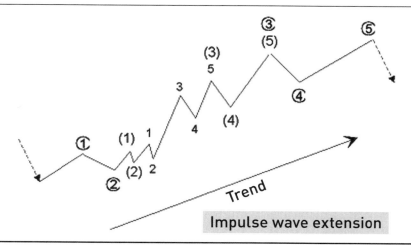

A wave extension is very common (figure 4.13); in most cases, this happens with wave 3.

Waves 1 and 5 incline toward equality. In pattern definitions, we call a wave 1 extension "extension1." This translates to extension3 for a wave 3 extension and extension5 for a wave 5 extension.

A pattern with 1 extension has 9 waves; a pattern with 2 extensions contains 13 waves; and a pattern with 3 extensions contains 17 waves.

The internal structure for 9 waves is 5-3-5-3-5-3-5-3-5. The 3 waves are correction waves.

Figure 4.14: Intermediate Elliott wave analysis of the S&P 500 Index

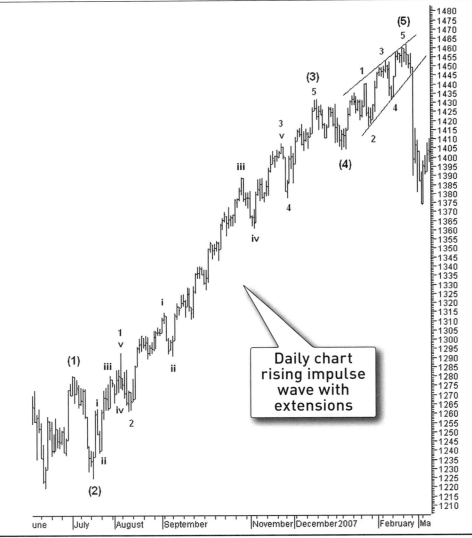

S&P 500 Rising Impulse Wave with Extensions

Figure 4.14 shows an intermediate Elliott wave analysis of the S&P 500 Index. A rising impulse wave with extensions in wave (3) and an ending wedge impulse wave for wave (5).

S&P 500 Falling Impulse Wave with Extensions

Figure 4.15 is an intermediate Elliott wave analysis of the S&P 500 Index on a weekly chart: a falling impulse wave within the bigger first correction wave [A].

Figure 4.15: Intermediate Elliott wave analysis of the S&P 500 Index on a weekly chart

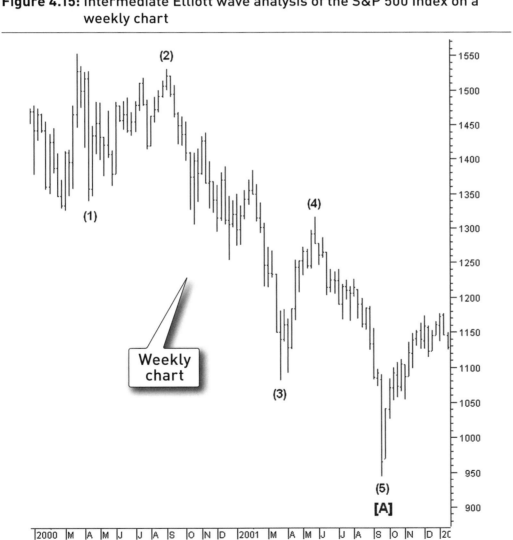

Source - MetaStock® charts courtesy of Equis International.

Starting Wedge Impulse Wave

The starting wedge impulse wave can only appear in waves 1 or A.

Figure 4.16: Starting wedge impulse wave

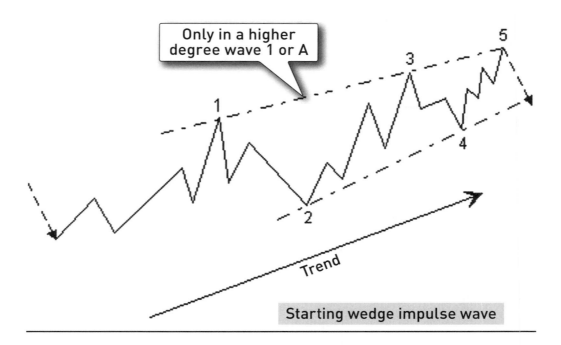

In figure 4.16, there may be, at first, some confusion when waves 3 and 4, within the starting wedge impulse wave, are seen as the start of an extension of waves 1 and 2. You must recognize the starting wedge impulse wave at the start of wave 5 by drawing the wedge pattern.

You know now that the starting wedge impulse wave 5 is really just the top of wave 1 of a higher order wave. The wave that follows is not an extended impulse wave 3, but a correction wave 2.

Rules and Guidelines

- This pattern has five waves.

- The price is moving between two converging lines, a wedge pattern.

- Wave 1 is an impulse wave or a lower order starting wedge impulse wave.

- Wave 2 is any correction pattern, except a triangle.

- Wave 2 is always smaller than wave 1.

- Wave 3 is an impulse pattern.

- Wave 3 is always bigger than wave 2.

- Wave 3 is never the smallest wave.

- Wave 4 can be any correction pattern.

- Waves 4 and 2 are partly overlapping.

- Wave 5 is an impulse pattern or an ending wedge impulse wave.

- Wave 5 is a minimum 50% of the size of wave 4.

The five waves of a starting wedge impulse wave have a 5-3-5-3-5 structure.

Example CXP (Corporate Express)

Figure 4.17 is a wave 1 starting wedge impulse wave, starting a new rising trend.

Figure 4.17: Corporate Express, starting wedge impulse wave example

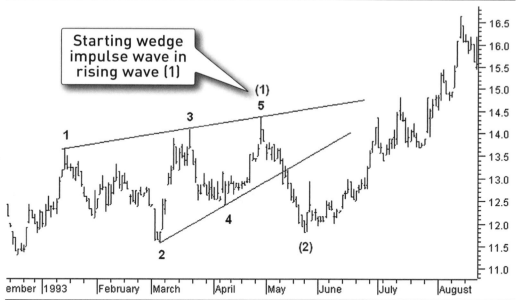

Source - MetaStock® charts courtesy of Equis International.

Ending Wedge Impulse Wave

Ending wedge impulse waves are rare in low order impulse waves. They are found mostly in higher order impulse waves. Because the ending wedge impulse wave is a wave 5 impulse wave or a wave C correction wave, there will be a market reversal upon wave completion.

Figure 4.18: Ending wedge impulse wave

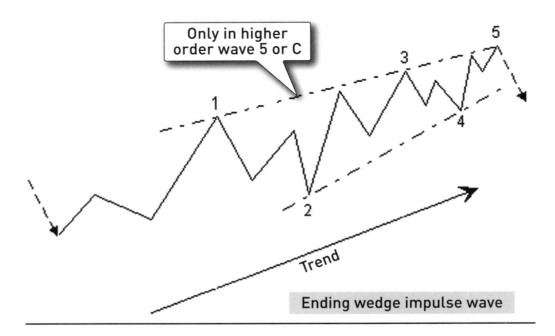

Figure 4.18 shows an ending wedge impulse wave that can be found in impulse wave 5 or correction wave C.

Figure 4.19 shows a descending ending wedge impulse wave.

At first, there may be some confusion when waves 3 and 4, within the ending wedge impulse wave, are seen as the start of extension waves 1 and 2. It is important to recognize the ending wedge impulse wave at the start of wave 5 by drawing the wedge pattern.

You now know that the ending wedge impulse wave 5 is really the end of wave 5 of a higher order wave. The wave that follows is not an extended impulse wave 3, but a bigger correction wave. The ending wedge impulse wave can be easily recognized by the internal 3–3–3–3–3 structure.

Figure 4.19: Descending ending wedge impulse wave

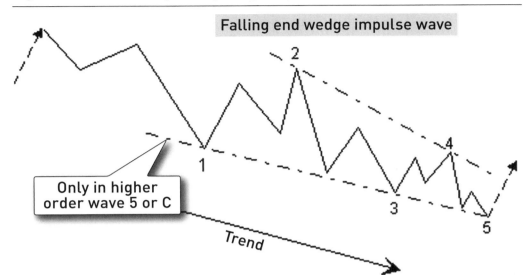

Rules and Guidelines

- This pattern consists of 5 waves.
- The price is moving between two converging lines, creating a wedge pattern.
- Waves 1, 3, and 5 are zigzag patterns.
- Wave 2 is any correction pattern, except a triangle.
- Wave 2 is always smaller than wave 1.
- Wave 3 is always bigger than wave 2.
- Wave 3 is never the smallest wave.
- Wave 4 can be any correction pattern.
- Waves 4 and 2 are partly overlapping.
- Wave 5 is a minimum 50% of the size of wave 4.

The 5 waves of an ending wedge impulse wave have a 3-3-3-3-3 structure.

Figure 4.20: Airtran Holdings Inc., an example of an ascending ending wedge impulse wave

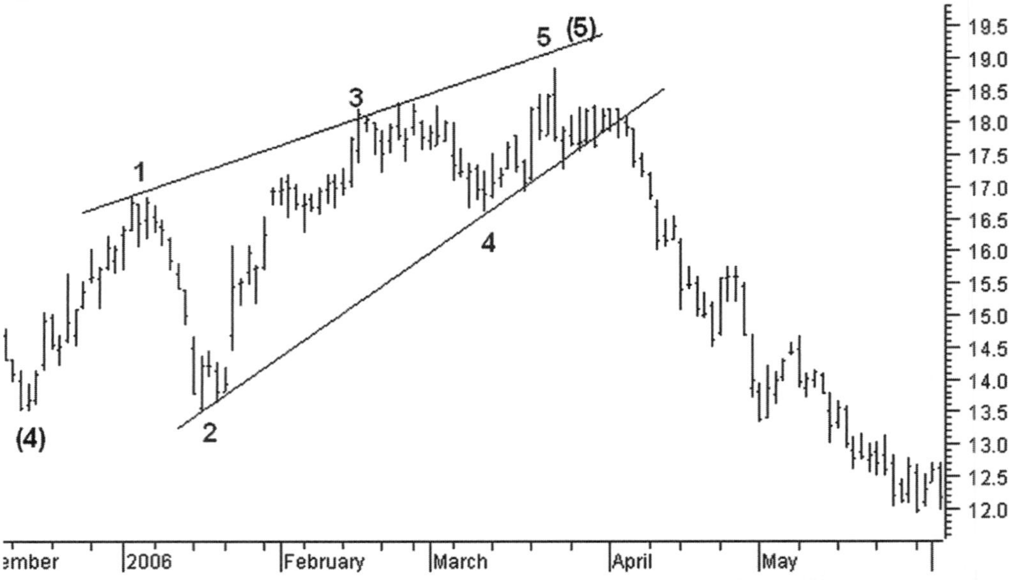

Source - MetaStock® charts courtesy of Equis International.

Example AAI (Airtran Holdings Inc.)

Figure 4.20 is an example of an ascending ending wedge impulse wave.

CORRECTION PATTERNS

Things to keep in mind as we explore correction patterns:

- Recognizing correction waves is more difficult than recognizing impulse waves.
- There are more correction patterns than impulse patterns.
- Correction patterns have the tendency to develop more complex combinations.
- The most important rule is that a correction wave of the same order can never have 5 waves.
- Only impulse waves have 5 waves.
- A correction consisting of a 5 impulse wave can, therefore, never be the end of that correction.

Zigzag

The zigzag pattern shown in figure 4.21 is the most common correction structure.

Figure 4.21: The zigzag pattern

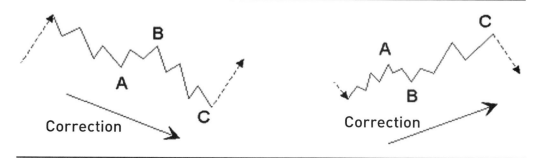

The zigzag belongs to the family of sharp corrections.

Rules and Guidelines

- A zigzag correction has three waves.
- Wave A is an impulse wave or a starting wedge impulse wave.
- Wave B can be any kind of correction pattern.
- Wave B is smaller than wave A.
- Wave C is an impulse wave or an ending wedge impulse wave.
- Wave C is not an ending wedge impulse wave if wave A is a starting wedge impulse wave.

A simple zigzag pattern has three waves. A double zigzag pattern has seven waves, two simple zigzags separated by an X wave. A triple zigzag has 11 waves with two X waves.

The structure of the three waves in a simple zigzag is 5-3-5 and 5-3-5-3-5-3-5 in a double zigzag.

Double and Triple Zigzag Patterns

We use WXY to denote a double zigzag, instead of the standard ABCXABC Elliott notation. For the triple zigzag, this becomes $WXYX^2Z$.

Figure 4.22: Double zigzag pattern using WXY notation

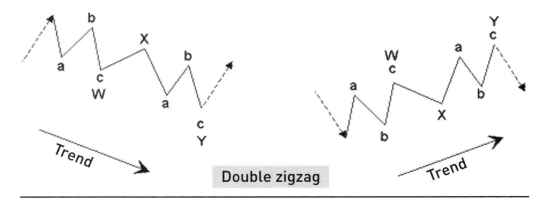

Double zigzag

As you can see in figure 4.22, this is a more consistent way of notation because more zigzags of a lower order (ABC) are connected together by a higher order wave (XYZ).

Rules and Guidelines

- Wave W must be a zigzag pattern.

- Wave X can be any correction pattern, except an inverted broadening triangle.

- Wave X is smaller than wave W.

- Wave Y must be a zigzag pattern.

- Wave Y is, at minimum, equal or bigger than wave X.

- Wave X^2 can be any correction pattern, except an inverted broadening triangle.

- Wave X^2 is smaller than wave Y.

- Wave Z must be a zigzag pattern.

- Wave Z is, at minimum, equal or bigger than wave X^2.

Flat Corrections

Flat corrections are very common.

Note in figure 4.23 that waves A and B of a flat correction are both three-wave correction patterns. Wave C is an impulse pattern and usually does not pass much farther than the end of wave A.

Figure 4.23: Flat corrections

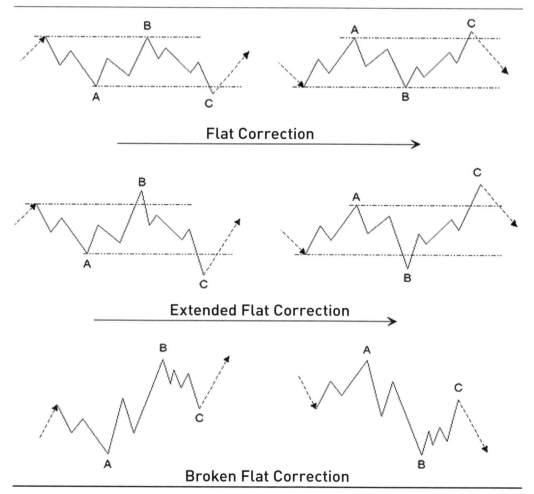

Flat corrections can be found mostly in B waves, but they also appear in waves 2 and 4. In an extended flat correction, waves B and C move past wave A. In a broken flat correction, wave A is passed by wave B, but wave B is still a correction pattern.

Rules and Guidelines

- Wave A can be any correction pattern.
- Wave B can be any kind of correction pattern, except a triangle.
- Wave B takes at least 50% back of wave A.
- Wave B is never more than 200% of wave A.

- Wave C is an impulse wave or an ending wedge impulse pattern.
- Wave C is never more than 300% of wave A.
- Wave C is never more than 200% of waves A and B.
- Wave C moves into the territory of wave A.

Double and Triple Flat Corrections

Just like with the zigzag, in the flat correction, we have variants with a double and a triple flat correction. A double flat correction is quite common, and a triple flat correction is rare.

A double flat correction is composed of two flat corrections connected via a correction pattern. A triple flat correction is composed of three flat corrections connected via correction patterns.

We use WXY to denote a double flat correction, instead of the standard ABCXABC Elliott notation. For the triple flat correction, this becomes $WXYX^2Z$. As before, this is a more consistent way of notation because more flat corrections of a lower order (ABC) are connected together by a higher order wave (XYZ).

Rules and Guidelines

- Wave W is any correction pattern, except a triangle or a double or triple pattern.
- Wave X is any correction pattern, except a triangle or a double or triple pattern.
- Wave X is a minimum 50% of wave W.
- Wave X is a maximum 400% of wave W.
- Wave Y is any correction pattern, except a double or triple pattern.
- Wave Y is bigger than wave X, except with a triangle pattern.
- Wave X^2 is any correction pattern, except a triangle or a double or triple pattern.
- Wave X^2 is a minimum 50% of wave Y.
- Wave X^2 is a maximum 400% of wave Y.
- Wave Z is any correction pattern, except a double or triple pattern.
- Wave Z is not a zigzag if wave Y is a zigzag.
- Wave Z is bigger than wave X^2.

Triangles

A triangle correction pattern has the form of a triangle.

Figure 4.24 shows the different types of triangle correction patterns.

Figure 4.24: Different types of triangle correction patterns

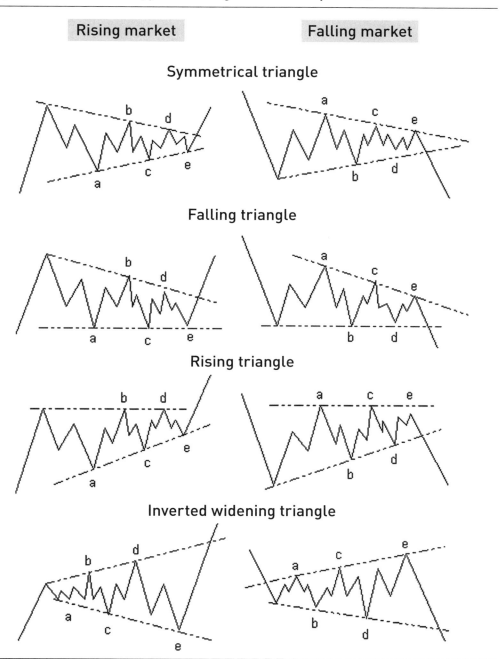

The triangle is a correction pattern consisting of five waves identified with the letters ABCDE. The triangle is drawn between the points AC and BD. It can be a symmetrical triangle or a rising or falling triangle. An inverted widening triangle is rather rare.

Triangles are not found in any type 2 wave, in a flat correction B wave, or in double or triple flat correction waves W, X, and X^2. The inverted widening triangle is never seen in double or triple zigzag waves X or X^2. All waves within a triangle pattern are correction waves.

Wave E will, in some cases, penetrate the AC line.

In the normal triangles we note three types: symmetrical, rising, or falling triangles. The inverted widening triangle only exists in a symmetrical version.

Rules and Guidelines for the Triangle

- Wave A is a simple, double, or triple zigzag pattern, or a flat correction.

- Wave B is a simple, double, or triple zigzag pattern.

- Waves C and D can be any correction pattern, except a triangle.

- Waves A, B, C, and D remain within or close to the triangle channel.

- The triangle is closed after wave E.

- The triangle lines converge; they cannot be parallel lines.

- One of the sides of the triangle can be a horizontal line.

- Wave E is a simple, double, or triple zigzag pattern, or a triangle.

- Wave E has a smaller price move than wave D, but it moves more than 20% of D.

- Either wave A or wave B has the biggest price move.

- Wave E ends in the range of wave A.

- Wave E ends within or close to the BD line.

Rules and Guidelines for the Inverted Widening Triangle

- The five waves have a simple, double, or triple zigzag pattern.

- Wave B is smaller than wave C, but a minimum 40% of wave C.

- Waves A, B, C, and D move within or close to the lines AC and BD.

- Wave C is smaller than wave D, but a minimum 40% of wave D.

- Wave A moves within the line AC.

- Wave A begins after the starting point of the inverted triangle.

- The channel lines of the inverted triangle diverge; they cannot be parallel lines.

- None of the channel lines can move horizontally.

- Wave E is bigger than wave D, but wave D is a minimum 40% of wave E.

- Either wave A or wave B has the smallest price move.

- Wave E ends in the range of wave A.

- Wave E ends within or close to the BD line.

WAVES AND TREND CHANNELS

Trend channels are an important tool to see which waves belong together. Trend channels can be used to project price targets.

Figure 4.25: Wave trend channels

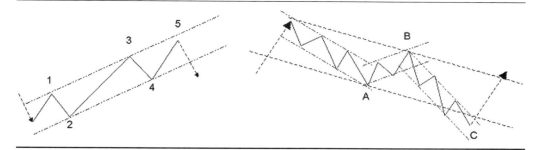

Trend channels are parallel lines that capture the price move of a wave pattern (figure 4.25).

Most of the time Elliott waves of the same order can be isolated using trend channels. This is the case for impulse waves, zigzag correction waves, and triangles. If these patterns are not moving within a trend channel, it is likely that the Elliott count is wrong.

IMPULSE WAVE PRICE TARGETS

Price targets can not only be set based on support and resistance lines, but also by using trend channels and Fibonacci projections. Remember that even the

Elliott wave counts 5+3=8 are all Fibonacci numbers. That is why all further wave subdivisions also are Fibonacci numbers.

Price Target for Wave 1

Figure 4.26: Price target for wave 1

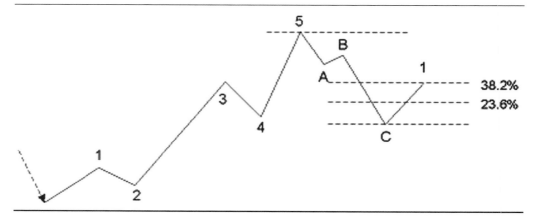

The most common is wave 1, the start of a new impulse wave, which retraces between 23.6% and 38.2% of the complete previous correction wave (figure 4.26). Even 50% is possible, but rare.

Price Target for Wave 2

Figure 4.27: Price target for wave 2

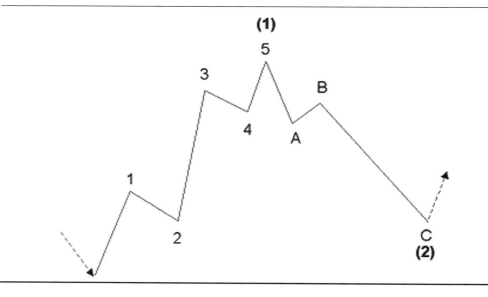

Wave (2) retraces a minimum 38.2% of wave (1) (figure 4.27); however, most of the retracements are between 50% and 61.8%. Even 100% retracement is possible and still complies with the Elliott rules.

Price Target for Wave 3

Figure 4.28: Price target for wave 3

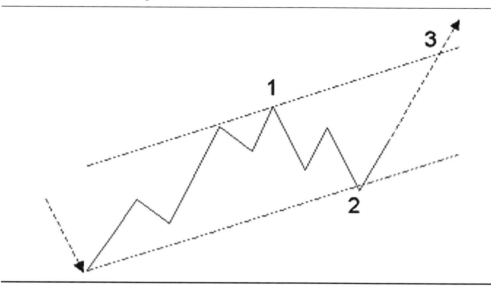

Looking at figure 4.28, once correction wave 2 is completed, you can draw an uptrend line from the start of wave 1 through the end of wave 2.

Next, you draw a parallel line with this trend line through the top of wave 1. Now you have a trend channel. The upper side of this channel is the first price target for wave 3.

If the price does not reach the upper side of this channel anymore, you probably are looking at a wave C, not a wave 3.

You should keep a horizontal support through the endpoint of wave 2. If the price falls through this level, wave 2 is not finished and will become more complex, and wave 3 has not yet started.

Impulse wave 3 often is the wave with the biggest move. So, usually, wave 3 will move up above the trend channel. In a rising impulse wave, it is common for the price to reach 161.8% of wave 1. In a falling impulse wave, wave 1 usually will reach 123.6%.

Price Target for Wave 4

Figure 4.29: Price target for wave 4

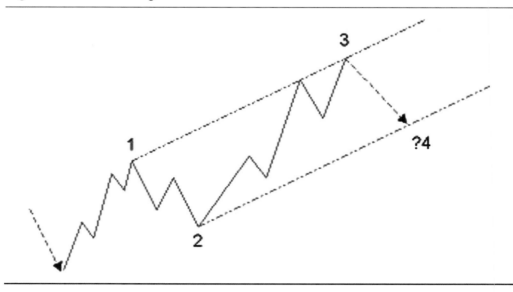

At the end of wave 3 in figure 4.29, you can draw a trend line through the tops of waves 1 and 3. Now draw a parallel line through the bottom of wave 2. You now have a trend channel of which the lower side is the primary target for wave 4. Not reaching the lower side of this channel probably means that there is a strong trend and that you are still in wave 3, or there is only a short wave 5 to be expected.

Looking at Fibonacci levels, wave 4 usually retraces back to 23.6% and to 38.2% of wave 3. Most of the time, this will be in the price area of sub-wave 4 of impulse wave 3.

Price Target for Wave 5

Quite often you will see a wave 5 that is equal to wave 1, or 61.8% to 76.4% of wave 3. If there is a wave 5 extension, then wave 5 is commonly 161% of wave 3, or 161% of the sum of waves 1 and 3.

Looking at trend channels, there are two possible methods you can apply.

Figure 4.30: Price target for wave 5, method 1

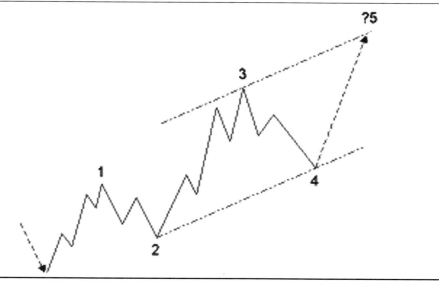

Method 1

At the end of wave 4 in figure 4.30, draw a trend line through the end of wave 2 and wave 4. Draw a parallel line through the top of wave 3. The upper side of this trend channel is the target for wave 5.

Figure 4.31: Price target for wave 5, method 2

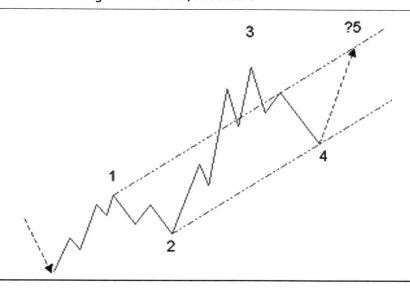

However, most of the time, this target will not be reached by wave 5, except when there are extensions in the making of wave 5, or when wave 3 was weak with just a moderate move.

Method 2

Usually, wave 3 has the highest acceleration compared to waves 1 and 5.

If wave 3 makes a bigger, sharp up-move like in figure 4.31, draw the basic trend line through the end of waves 2 and 4, but draw the parallel line through the top of wave 1.

This line will cross wave 3 and give a more moderate target for wave 5.

CORRECTION WAVE PRICE TARGETS

Price Target for Wave A

Wave A in a zigzag correction will, most of the time, retrace 38.2% and 50% of the previous 5 wave.

Price Target for Wave B

Wave B in a zigzag correction mostly retraces 38.2% of wave A. In a flat correction, this will be 100%. A triangle correction will take back 90% to 100% of wave A. An inverted widening triangle typically retraces 61.8% of wave A.

Price Target for Wave C

Wave C will, many times, equal wave A. Wave C is a minimum 61.8% of wave A. In a double zigzag, this is commonly 138.2% of wave W. In a flat or double flat correction, this often is 138.2% of wave A, or wave Y, respectively. Wave C in a triangle is generally 76.4% of wave B. For an inverted widening triangle, this is usually 123.6% of wave B.

Price Targets for Waves D and E

In figure 4.32, at the end of wave B, draw a trend line through the beginning of wave A and the end of wave B. You now can see a target for wave D, anticipating that a triangle correction is developing.

You will get a confirmation at the end of wave C. At the end of wave C, draw a line through the end of wave A and wave C. You now can see the target for wave E. Many times, wave E will not reach this trend line; conversely, it may pass it very shortly, and then continue the basic trend.

Figure 4.32: Price targets for waves D and E

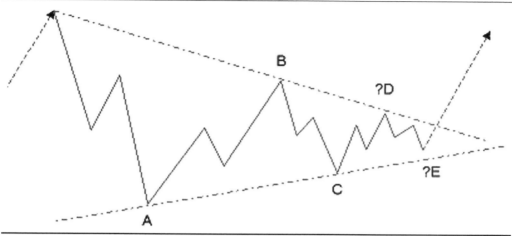

Price Target for Wave X

Wave X of a double zigzag, a double flat correction, or a triple zigzag is, most of the time, 50% of wave W. In a triple flat correction, this will be 76.4% of wave W.

Price Target for a Double Zigzag

When drawing a price trend channel, it is a good idea to distinguish a double zigzag from an impulse wave (figure 4.33). Both have about the same charac-

Figure 4.33: Price target for a double zigzag

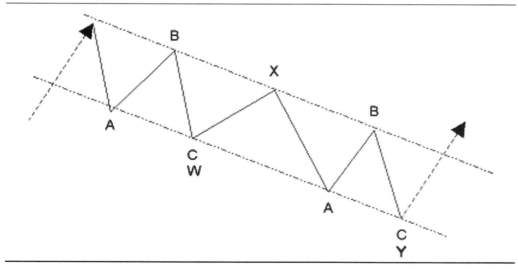

teristics; however, double zigzags fit almost perfect within the price channel. On the other hand, if it is a wave 3, remember that it may break this channel, being the bigger, more accelerating move.

COUNTING WAVES

To count Elliott waves, you can use one of the specific technical analysis programs that specialize in Elliott wave analysis or you can create this type of analysis for your standard TA program.

I actually prefer my own count because, as I mentioned before, it is not important to know exactly which sub-wave of which higher order wave you are in during a specific moment in time. The important thing is to determine where the next move is going: up or down?

Of course, a little Elliott wave technology would be a very useful tool. That is why, within LOCKIT, I use a simple indicator on the price chart to help me make the Elliott wave count.

"SVE_Elliott_Count" is the indicator in MetaStock® code:

```
{SVE_Elliott_Count}
Proc:= Input("ZigZag %?",.01,50,2.4);
haOpen:=(Ref((O+H+L+C)/4,-1) + PREV)/2;
haC:=((O+H+L+C)/4+haOpen+Max(H,haOpen)+Min(L,haOpen))/4;
Zig(haC,Proc,%)
```

 Please utilize the disc in the back of the book for instant access to these codes. You may also download them from www.traderslibrary.com/tlecorner.

This indicator uses a percent zigzag function on heikin ashi re-calculated OHLC prices. Default, it uses a value of 2.4%, but you can choose a lower and/or a higher value for your stocks depending upon their volatility.

In the simple example of AMD (figure 4.34), the 5 impulse up wave (1) to (5) with an extension in wave (3) can be nicely labeled with the help of this indicator. Counting Elliott waves is very helpful in estimating the direction and also the size of the next move.

Looking at different time periods will give even more information to help you estimate the direction of the next move. As an example, let's look at the evolution of the stock AMD since 2000.

Figure 4.34: AMD 5 impulse up wave (1) to (5) with an extension in wave (3)

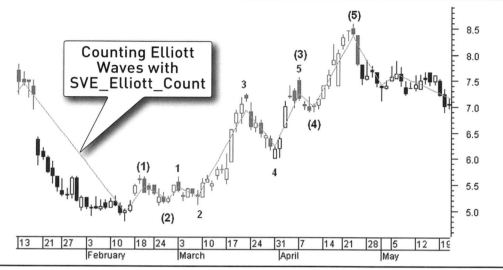

Source - MetaStock® charts courtesy of Equis International.

Figure 4.35: Long-term monthly chart of AMD

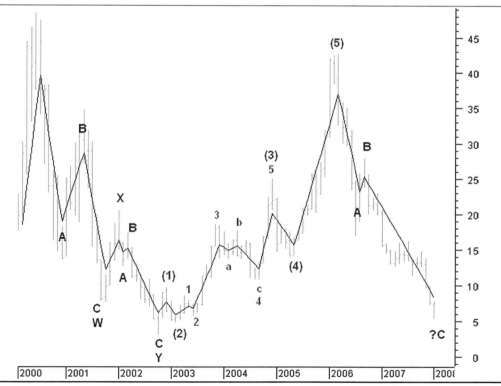

Source - MetaStock® charts courtesy of Equis International.

Figure 4.36: Weekly chart showing a complex wxy correction

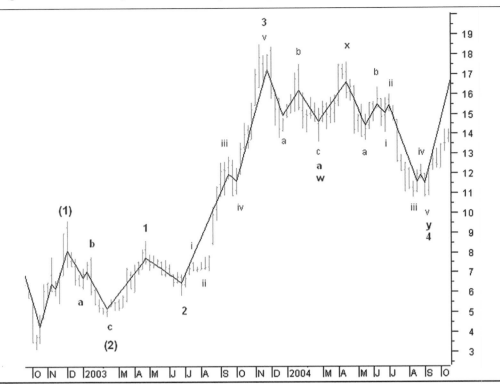

Source - MetaStock® charts courtesy of Equis International.

First, in figure 4.35, we look at the long-term count with a monthly chart. Since we are looking at a long-term chart with big price moves, we will have to adapt the percentage turning point for our "SVE_Elliott_Count" indicator. We bring it up to 3.4% from the standard 2.4%.

Labeling the turning points shows us a long-term downtrend from a price top in 2000 to a price bottom in 2003 with a double zigzag WXY correction. Starting in 2003, we see an impulse move up with a wave (5) top in 2006. Wave (3) has an intermediate wave extension. Since the top in 2006, price has been moving down, and we are now waiting for the end of the correction wave C.

Figure 4.37: Second part of the weekly chart

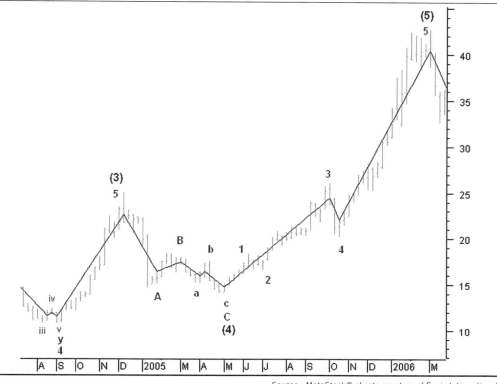

Source - MetaStock® charts courtesy of Equis International.

Switching to a weekly chart and setting "SVE_Elliott_Count" back to 2.4%, we gain even more specific details. Figure 4.36 shows the first part of the weekly chart until intermediate correction wave 4. Wave 4 seems to be a rather complex wxy correction.

The second part of the weekly chart is shown in figure 4.37. The last impulse wave (5) up has an extension. Our "SVE_Elliott_Count" is not showing correction wave 2 here; but, if we go to a daily chart, we would most likely see that count there.

Figure 4.38: Start of the up move in the daily chart

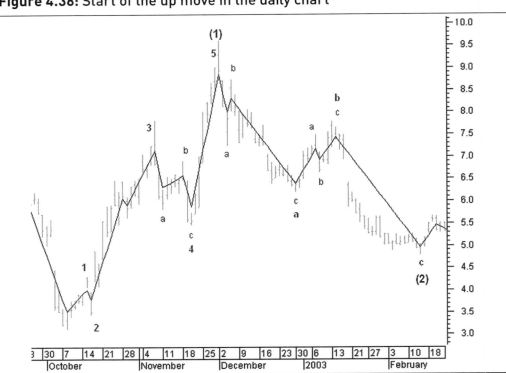

Source - MetaStock® charts courtesy of Equis International.

Finally, let's have a look at the count on a daily chart. To capture even smaller moves on the daily chart, we bring the percentage of the "SVE_Elliott_Count" down from the standard 2.4% to 2.1%.

Figure 4.38 is the start of the up move in the daily chart. Here you can see an extra pivot point near the end of October. You probably would count this as intermediate waves 3 and 4 at that moment in time. So, intermediate top 3 would then become top 5 and top (1), and consequently, intermediate wave 4 would be labeled as correction wave (2). So what do you expect next? Right—a wave (3) up! What do we expect if the count is labeled as on the chart? A move up to make intermediate wave 5 a complete wave (1). So, with both counts you would be correct; price should go up.

When price starts falling in December, you would soon realize that the count (as shown on the chart) is the right one because what you thought was wave (3) could not be. Remember, wave (3) cannot be the smallest wave.

Figure 4.39: The start of wave (3) up with an extension impulse wave and more extensions

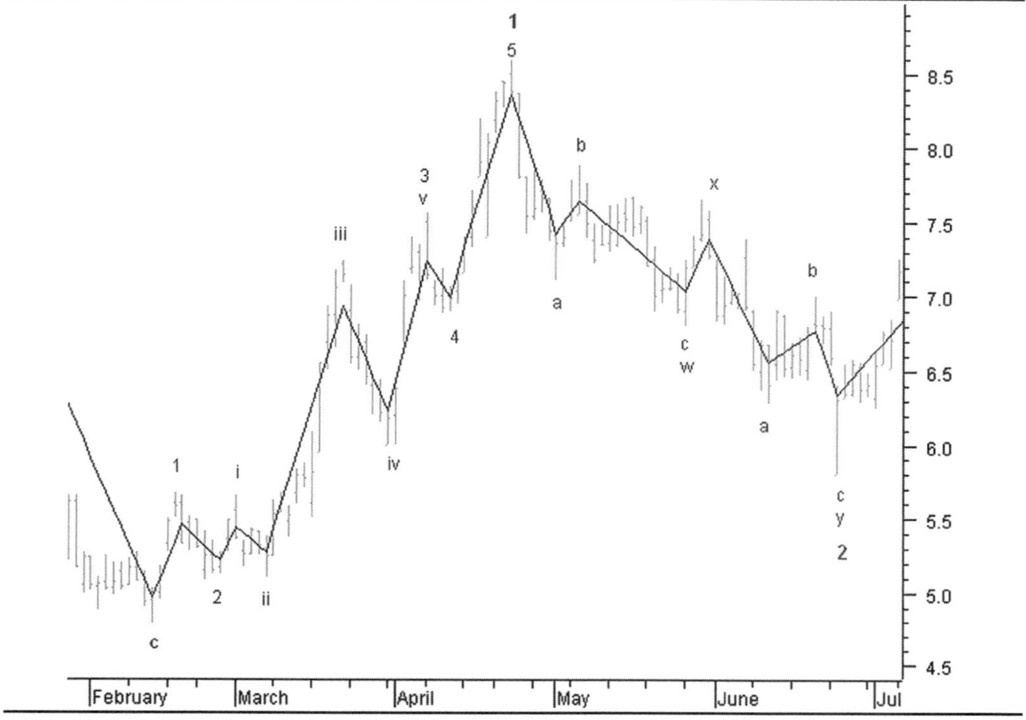

From bottom c and (2) in February (figure 4.39), we have the start of wave (3) up with an extension impulse wave and even more extensions starting in intermediate wave 1. Extension wave 3 also has another lower degree extension. Correction wave 2 is a wxy double zigzag correction.

Figure 4.40: Extension wave 3 has extensions in the lower degree waves 3 and 5

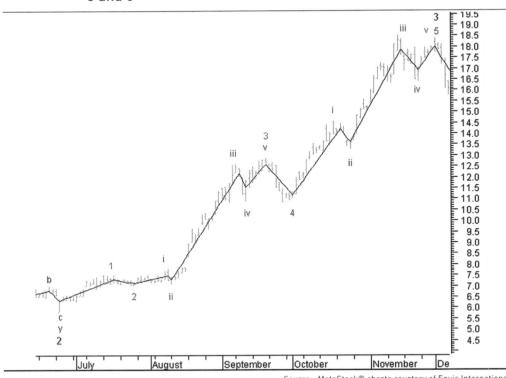

Source - MetaStock® charts courtesy of Equis International.

The extension wave 3 in figure 4.40 has extensions in the lower degree waves 3 and 5, but the "SVE_Elliott_Count" indicator makes a perfect count possible.

In figure 4.41, we see the start of the reaction from extension wave 3 to wave 4. This is a very complex reaction, so you will most likely have to adapt the count a few times.

Let's have a look as price begins moving down in the beginning of December. No problem with wave A and wave B. Next, we have a wave "a" with a bottom still above the bottom of wave A, so we expect an extension for wave C.

We get this extension with waves abc. Now we are at a point where we have to ask the question; is this the end of the correction? Well, the size of the correction might be able to help make that decision. On the other hand, what do we expect next? If this is the end of the correction, we would expect price to move up for a new wave 1. Or if the correction is not finished yet, we would expect a reaction for a wave B, with price also moving up. So in this moment in time, it is not imperative to have an absolutely correct count because whatever the count, we expect the price to move up!

Figure 4.41: Very complex start of the reaction from extension wave 3 to
wave 4

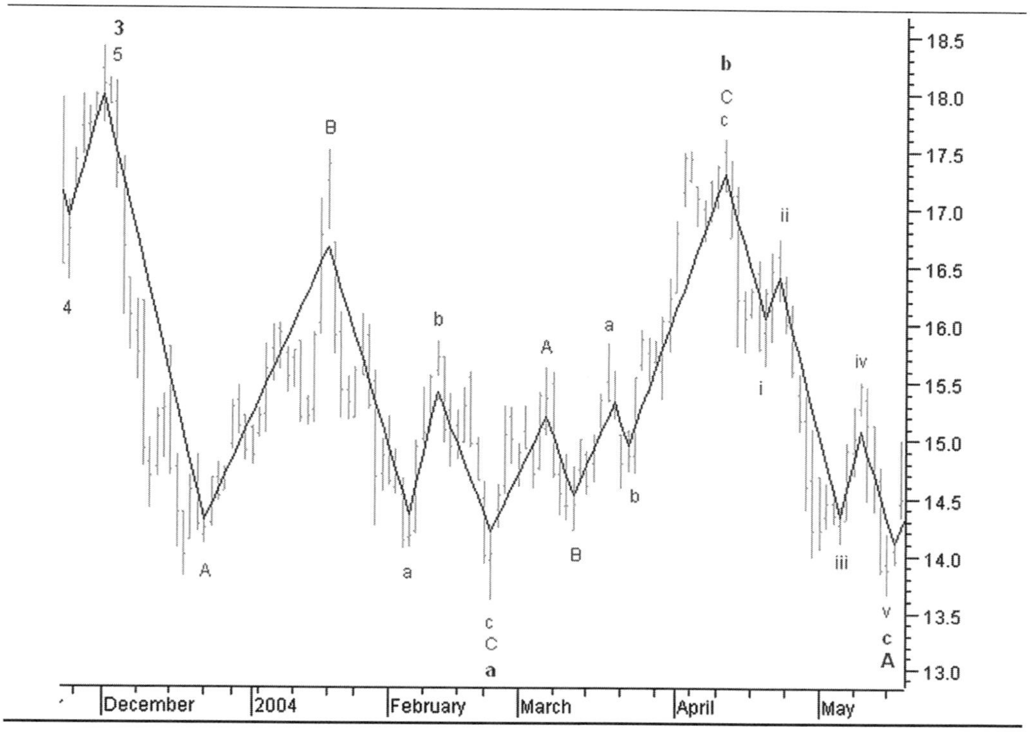

Source - MetaStock® charts courtesy of Equis International.

Beginning at the end of February, we can see this happening. By the end of
April, it is clear that we did not start a new impulse wave up, but a correction wave B. What we expect then is a move farther down below the last low
point. Of course, good Elliott wave practice dictates that once you know that
your count is not correct, you should adapt it so that you stay on the right
track for future price moves.

With the help of the LOCKIT "SVE_Elliott_Count" indicator and
some practice, you will be able to make correct Elliott wave counts.
Used within the LOCKIT system, this will surely help you to make
better estimates as to where price is moving next.

LOCKIT

This concludes PART I where we looked at the technical analysis basics,
indicators, candle chart patterns, and Elliott waves all used in the LOCKIT
application.

**For a closer look at the charts in this chapter,
go to www.traderslibrary.com/TLEcorner.**

TEST YOUR CHAPTER 4 KNOWLEDGE

1. Label this chart with an Elliott wave count.

Source - MetaStock® charts courtesy of Equis International.

_____

_____

_____

_____

_____

_____

_____

_____

2. Label this chart with an Elliott wave count.

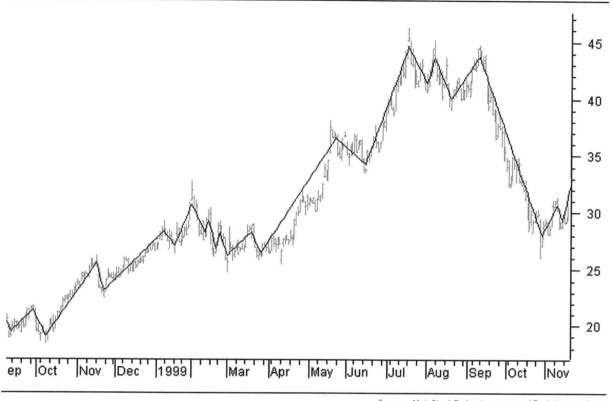

Source - MetaStock® charts courtesy of Equis International.

_____

_____

_____

_____

_____

_____

_____

_____

3. Label this chart with an Elliott wave count.

_____

_____

_____

_____

_____

_____

_____

_____

_____

 For answers, please visit the Traders' Library Education Corner at
www.traderslibrary.com/tlecorner.

PART II

The SVAPO Oscillator and LOCKIT

Chapter 5

SVAPO and ATR Trailing Stop

SVAPO (Short-term Volume And Price Oscillator) is my homemade indicator, which we are going to study in detail here.

> SVAPO is the first indicator below the price chart of the LOCKIT chart template. Within LOCKIT, this is an important oscillator indicating short-term reversal points to enter or exit trades. To trade based on SVAPO, we will also introduce an ATR (Average True Range) trailing stop in this chapter.

LOCKIT

INDICATOR BASICS

Before describing the construction and application of SVAPO, I'll discuss some basics of using an indicator as a buy and sell trigger. In this chapter we will be discussing indicators and oscillators—technically speaking, an oscillator is an indicator that fluctuates above and below a centerline. Not all indicators are oscillators, but all oscillators are indicators!

The indicator must have clear reversal points and be as fast as possible on the entry side. The faster you can get in at a price reversal, the tighter your initial stop-loss can be. This will save you a lot of money on any trades that move the wrong way.

A trailing stop-loss, which is a stop-loss order that follows the prevailing price trend, is best set in relation to your investment horizon. Are you a swing trader trying to catch all the shorter, profitable price moves, or are you a medium- to long-term trader trying to stay in the trade to capture the extended, bigger price moves?

Indicators and Price Relation

There is no ideal indicator, which is why you have to protect your investment with a stop order.

Using a single indicator as the only reference to enter or exit a trade is not a good idea. The indicator should instead be used as an alert. It should alert you to take a closer look at the chart and, only after taking into consideration all possible technical analysis tools, to make a decision. Every now and then, though, the indicator or oscillator you use will be perfect.

Figure 5.1, the daily chart of NCR Corp. (NCR), shows an ideal relation between the oscillator at the top of the chart and the price at the bottom.

- A buy signal is given when the oscillator reaches the lower boundary and turns up.

- A sell signal is given when the oscillator is at the upper boundary and turns down.

The oscillator here is as fast as it can be and marks the exact top and bottom turning points.

Initial Stop

Figure 5.2 illustrates a less-perfect scenario with the daily chart of eBay Inc. (EBAY), but it is saved by the initial stop. A buy signal is generated when the oscillator turns up from below the lower boundary. An appropriate initial stop related to the price volatility and with no previous low available is set at 2% from the buying price.

The price moves farther down, and we are stopped out of the trade five days later with a minimum loss, thanks to the initial stop.

Trailing Stop

Trailing stops are useful for staying in a trade for a longer period of time to keep you in longer price moves. They are also handy when your oscillator is not giving a sell signal. This tends to occur when the price is moving flat or consolidating in a downtrend.

Figure 5.1: NCR daily, an ideal relationship between the oscillator and price

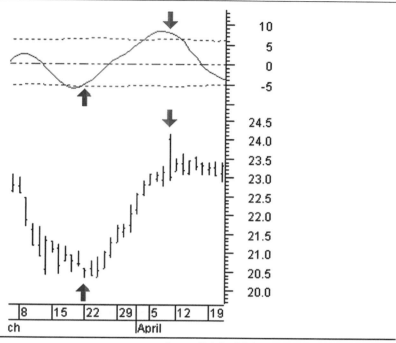

Source - MetaStock® charts courtesy of Equis International.

Figure 5.2: EBAY much less perfect but saved by the initial stop

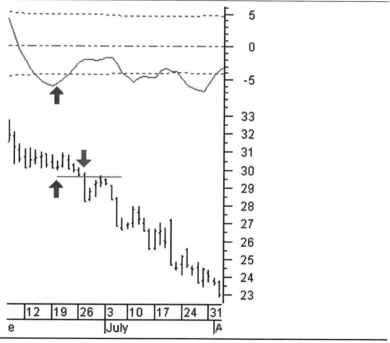

Source - MetaStock® charts courtesy of Equis International.

Figure 5.3: Intel initial stop at 3% and a medium-term 7% trailing stop

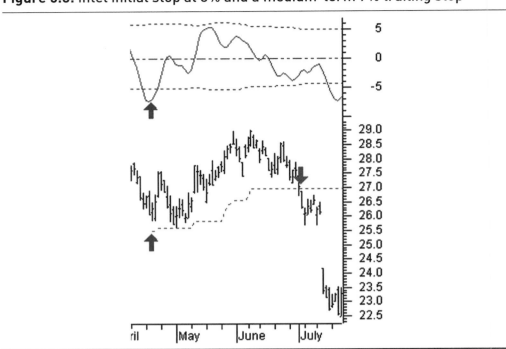

Take a look at figure 5.3 with the chart of Intel Corp. (INTC). The initial stop was set tight at 3%, below the short-term low. A normal medium–term 7% stop is used as a trailing stop.

The oscillator does not pass the upper boundary and, as a result, it does not create a sell signal. Still, the trade could be closed without a loss thanks to the trailing stop, which got you out of the trade just in time.

SVAPO "SHORT-TERM VOLUME AND PRICE OSCILLATOR" CONSTRUCTION

In this section, we're going to take a look at my own indicator, SVAPO (Short-term Volume and Price Oscillator). First, we need to determine our assumptions and what types of objectives we have for this indicator. Then, we can put it into action!

And, by the way, I like the term SVAPO because it starts with my initials!

Basic Assumptions

In order to construct a short-term oscillator based on price and volume, you have to look at the relationship between these two components in up-trending and down-trending markets.

These are their normal relationships:

Up-trending Market	Price	Volume
Uptrend	Up	Up
Correction	Down	Down
Reversal	Down	Up

Down-trending Market	Price	Volume
Downtrend	Down	Up
Correction	Up	Down
Reversal	Up	Up

Combining the relationships based on market direction leaves us with three possible conditions:

Market Direction	Price	Volume	Calculation
Uptrend	Up	Up	+ Volume
Downtrend	Down	Up	- Volume
Corrections	Up/Down	Down	0

In an up-trending market, the price and the volume are moving up. When calculating the oscillator, volume will be added.

In a down-trending market, the price goes down, while the volume is up. When calculating the oscillator, volume will be subtracted. When the volume is moving down and the price is in a consolidation phase moving in either direction, the volume will not be taken into consideration when calculating the oscillator.

Merely combining price and volume will result in a very choppy oscillator. Using conventional smoothing techniques, such as moving averages, will create an unacceptable delay for a short-term oscillator. So, how can we remedy this for price and volume?

Price Smoothing

If you want to determine the short-term market direction, there shouldn't be any delay when you smooth the price trend. You can accomplish this using heikin ashi recalculated prices and a short-term triple exponential moving average (TEMA).

In MetaStock® code, you can do this using the following formula:

haOpen:=(Ref((O+H+L+C)/4,-1) + PREV)/2;

haCl:=((O+H+L+C)/4+haOpen+Max(H,haOpen)+Min(L,haOpen))/4;

haC:=Tema(haCl,5);

Figure 5.4 shows the effect of this price smoothing technique.

Figure 5.4: Effect of TEMA on heikin ashi closing average smoothing technique

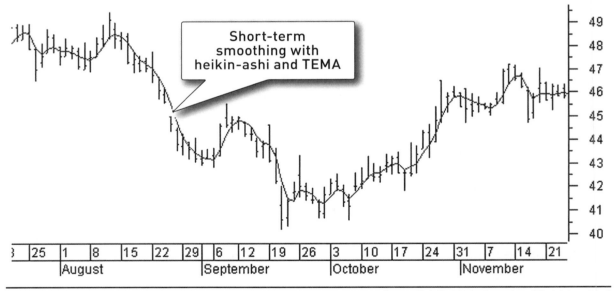

Source - MetaStock® charts courtesy of Equis International.

Figure 5.5: Result of the volume smoothing techniques

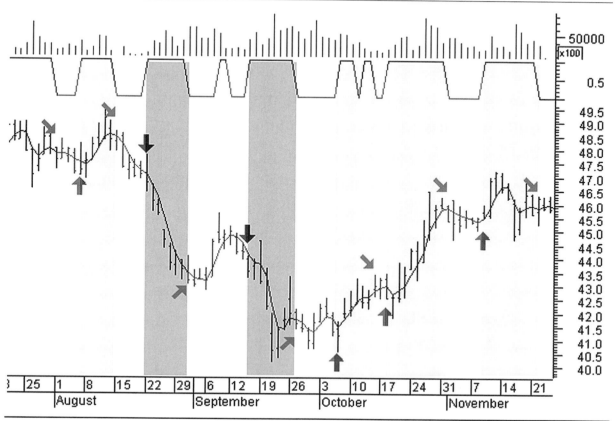

Volume Smoothing

In figure 5.5, taking a look at the volume bars of Dow Chemical at the top of the chart, you can see that determining the short-term volume trend is no simple task. The first action item is to limit single extreme-volume counts. So we compare the volume with a medium-term, simple moving average of the previous volume, and limit an extreme value to no more than twice that moving average.

In MetaStock code, it can be done this way:

```
vave:=Ref(Mov(V,40,S),-1);
vmax:=vave*2;
vc:=If(V<vmax,V,vmax);
```

The second action item is to smooth without creating delays. One of the better methods of tracking the short-term trend of volume is by linear regression. You can smooth the linear regression slope with a short-term TEMA average, but the result will still not be smooth enough. So, in the final step, we maintain the previous calculated result over a period of two bars. The final result of this volume-trend smoothing can be seen as a digital value below the volume bars in figure 5.5.

In MetaStock code, it is done this way:

```
vtr:=Tema(LinRegSlope(vc,8),8);
Alert(vtr >= Ref(vtr,-1),2);
```

The arrows on the price bars in figure 5.5 correspond to the changes in price trend. A vertical up arrow represents volume uptrend with price uptrend, while a vertical down arrow represents volume uptrend with price downtrend. The sideways up arrow represents a downtrend in volume during a correction phase in a price downtrend. The sideways downward arrow represents a volume downtrend during a correction phase in a price uptrend. As you can see, this corresponds quite well with the short-term market direction.

SVAPO IN ACTION

In figure 5.6, you can see the SVAPO oscillator in action on the same chart as on the previous figure. Just using the turning points in the oscillator yields profitable trades.

In addition to calculating and smoothing the heikin ashi closing average and smoothing the volume, we also need to include a minimum required price change before any volume is taken into consideration. Oftentimes, this minimum change will not be reached when the price is creating dojis. This is the price area with uncertainty, which is why it is probably best not to take the volume of these bars into consideration. Because volume often counts in mil-

Figure 5.6: Turning points in SVAPO give profitable trades

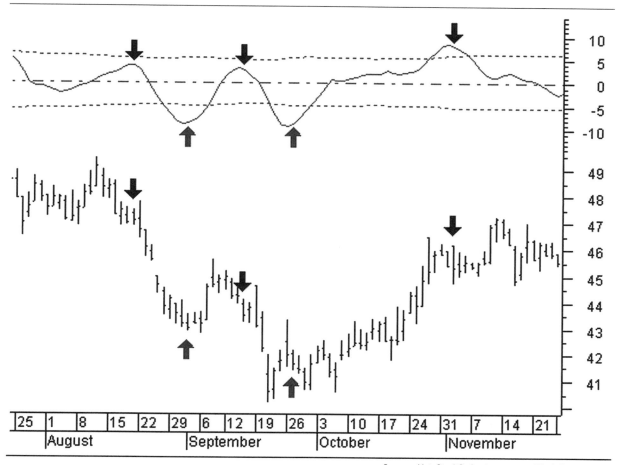

lions, we divide the result by a medium-term average of the volume. This brings the oscillator swing somewhere around a more readable +/-10.

Since tops and bottoms of the SVAPO oscillator are not a fixed value, it is a good idea to have a reference to determine if the oscillator is beyond its normal upper or lower boundary; therefore, I added standard-deviation lines from the mean, with 1.5 at the upper end and 1.3 at the lower end, together with the zero reference.

This is the complete SVAPO MetaStock® formula:

```
{calculate the heikin ashi closing average haCl and get the input
variables}

haOpen:=(Ref((O+H+L+C)/4,-1) + PREV)/2;

haCl:=((O+H+L+C)/4+haOpen+Max(H,haOpen)+Min(L,haOpen))/4;

period:= Input("SVAPO period :", 2, 20, 8);

cutoff:= Input("Minimum %o price change :",0,10,1);

{Inputs for standard deviation bands}

devH:= Input("Standard Deviation High :", 0.1, 5, 1.5);

devL:= Input("Standard Deviation Low :", 0.1, 5, 1.3);

stdevper:= Input("Standard Deviation Period :", 1, 200, 100);

{Smooth HaCl closing price}

haC:=Tema(haCl,period/1.6);

{Medium term MA of Volume to limit extremes and division factor}

vave:=Ref(Mov(V,period*5,S),-1);

vmax:=vave*2;

vc:=If(V<vmax,V,vmax);

{Basic volume trend}

vtr:=Tema(LinRegSlope(V,period),period);

{SVAPO result of price and volume}

SVAPO:=Tema(Sum(If(haC>(Ref(haC,-1)*(1+cutoff/1000)) AND
Alert(vtr>=Ref(vtr,-1),2), vc, If(haC<(Ref(haC,-1)*(1-cutoff/1000))
AND Alert(vtr>Ref(vtr,-1),2),-vc,0)),period)/(vave+1),period);

devH*Stdev(SVAPO,stdevper);

-devL*Stdev(SVAPO,stdevper);

zeroref:=0;

zeroref;

SVAPO
```

 Please utilize the disc in the back of the book for instant access to these codes. You may also download them from www.traderslibrary.com/tlecorner.

Figure 5.7: The SVAPO defaults

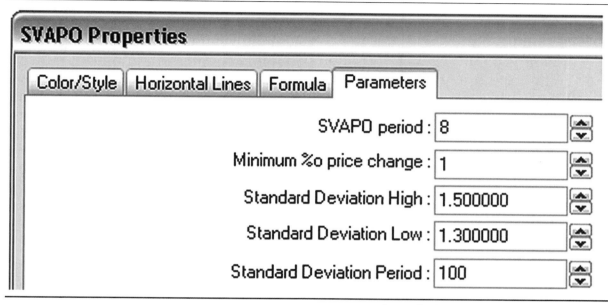

Source - MetaStock® charts courtesy of Equis International.

The defaults used for SVAPO are shown in figure 5.7 with a period of eight bars, a minimum per thousand price change of one, a standard deviation of 1.5 on the upper side and 1.3 on the lower side, with 100 bars as the standard-deviation look-back period.

These defaults work well in all time frames, from minute and hourly charts to daily, weekly, and monthly charts. If you want very short-term signals, you can go as low as a 3-bar SVAPO.

Now that you know how to create SVAPO, I will discuss the SVAPO trading rules, entry/exit signals, and how to determine price targets.

Basic Trading Rules

The trading rules I will discuss here are based on an 8-bar, short-term volume and price oscillator period with a 1/1000 minimum price change and with an upper standard-deviation channel at 1.5 and a lower channel at 1.3 over a 100-day period.

Rule 1

The start of a short-term up-move is signaled when SVAPO turns up from below the lower standard-deviation boundary, as shown in the weekly chart of Hewlett-Packard (HP) in figure 5.8.

Figure 5.8: HP with SVAPO turning up and down from the standard deviation boundaries

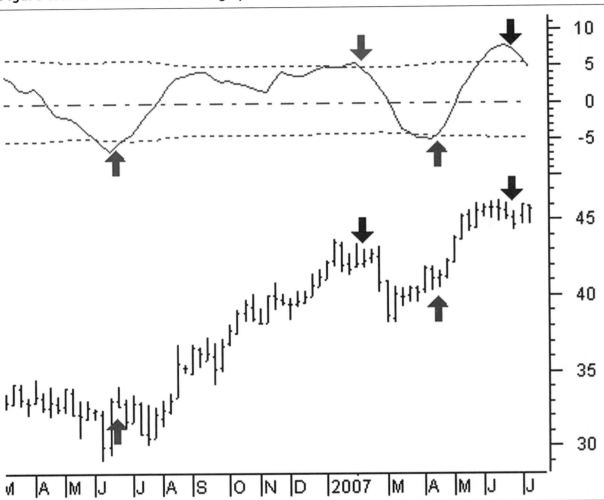

Source - MetaStock® charts courtesy of Equis International.

The same is valid for a short-term down-move when SVAPO turns down from above the upper standard-deviation boundary.

Rule 2

Medium-term turning points in an uptrend or downtrend are usually indicated with a divergence between price and SVAPO, as shown in figure 5.9. See the divergence (1) at the end of April. The SVAPO has higher lows, while the price has lower lows. At the end of the medium-term uptrend at (3), another divergence appears with lower highs in SVAPO and higher highs in price.

Figure 5.9: SVAPO trading rules 1, 2, and 3

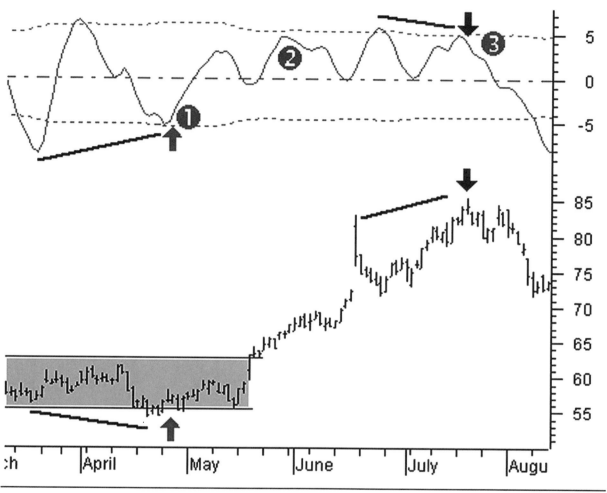

Rule 3

In a medium-term uptrend, SVAPO will generally continue to move above the zero-reference line. Look at reference (2) in figure 5.9. In a medium-term downtrend, SVAPO will generally continue to move below the zero-reference line.

Rule 4

For short-term scalping or for finding additional medium-term entry points, SVAPO can be used with a period of only three bars and no minimum price change.

Figure 5.10: SVAPO rule 4 short-term trading

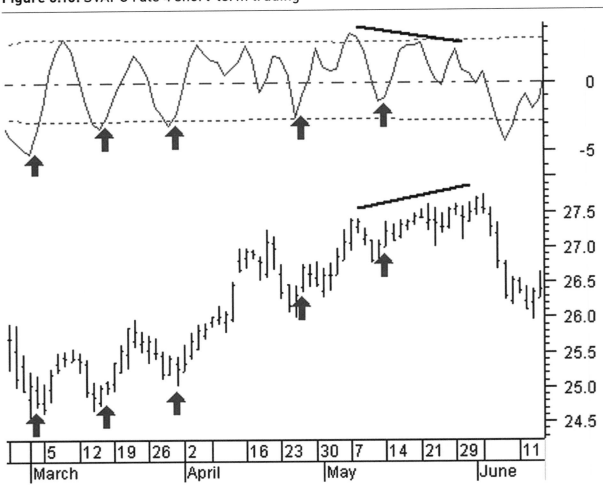

Look at the different entry points in figure 5.10 on the Pfizer chart, indicated by SVAPO at the start of and during the medium-term uptrend. Note how each entry point is a profitable short-term trade on its own. The medium-term turning point is reached when SVAPO passes the upper boundary and diverges by the end of May.

Application Example

The Allis Chalmers Energy Inc. chart (figure 5.11) shows an ideal buying moment when, after a big correction, SVAPO turns up in the beginning of March and creates a divergence with price.

Figure 5.11: Ideal buying moment after a big correction and SVAPO turning up & diverging

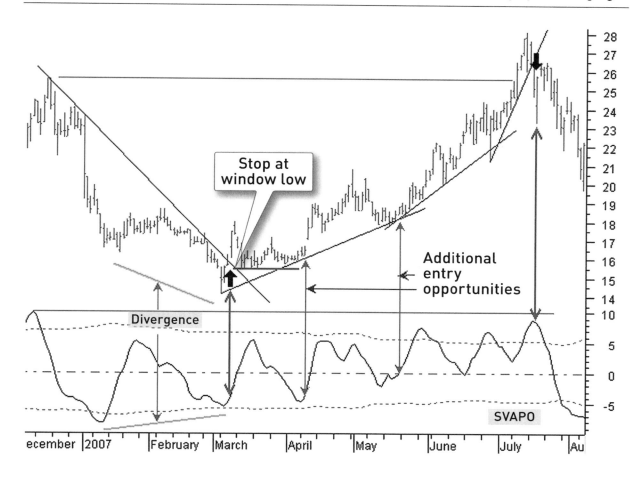

Source - MetaStock® charts courtesy of Equis International.

At the same moment in time, the price moves up, breaking the medium-term downtrend. Interestingly, there is a small window the day before, and the support of this window allows you to maintain a very tight stop.

After a couple of days of reaction, the price remains flat for some time without breaking the initial stop level. At the end of this move, there is a second opportunity to enter the trade when SVAPO turns up once more.

Next, we draw an uptrend line and see that the price touches this trend line again during the second half of May; this is another entry opportunity. With the price now moving up faster, we can draw a sharper uptrend line. Starting from July, the price starts going up even faster. It is clear that this kind of speed will not last very long.

This trend line is broken by the end of July with SVAPO turning down from a higher top; however, looking at the medium-term top from December 2006 and the new top now, we see a divergence between the higher top in price and a lower top in SVAPO.

It's time to take a profit!

"NO VOLUME" SVAPO OSCILLATOR

Some financial data is published without volume. Applying the principles used in SVAPO, but without the volume calculations, I came up with a "SVAPO_No_Volume" oscillator that is quite useful for data series without a volume component.

This is the MetaStock code for "SVAPO_No_Volume":

```
{calculate heikin ashi closing average haCl and get the input vari-
ables}

haOpen:=(Ref((O+H+L+C)/4,-1) + PREV)/2;

haCl:=((O+H+L+C)/4+haOpen+Max(H,haOpen)+Min(L,haOpen))/4;

{input SVAPO period}

period:= Input("SVAPO period :", 2, 20, 8);

{input minimum per thousand price change}

cutoff:= Input("Minimum %o price change :",0.0,10,1);

{Inputs for standard deviation bands}

devH:= Input("Standard Deviation High :", 0.1, 5, 1.5);

devL:= Input("Standard Deviation Low :", 0.1, 5, 1.3);

stdevper:= Input("Standard Deviation Period :", 1, 200, 100);

{Smooth HaCl closing price}

haC:=Tema(haCl,period/1.6);

{MA of closing price to limit extremes}
```

```
vave:=Ref(Mov(C,period*5,S),-1);

vmax:=vave*2;

vc:=If(C<vmax,C,vmax);

{Basic price trend}

vtr:=Tema(LinRegSlope(C,period),period);

{SVAPO result of price, extremes and basic trend}

SVAPONoVol:=Tema(Sum(If(haC>(Ref(haC,-1)*(1+cutoff/1000)) AND
Alert(vtr>=Ref(vtr,-1),2), vc, If(haC<(Ref(haC,-1)*(1-cutoff/1000))
AND Alert(vtr>Ref(vtr,-1),2),-vc,0)),period)/(vave+1),period);

devH*Stdev(SVAPO,stdevper);

-devL*Stdev(SVAPO,stdevper);

zeroref:=0;

zeroref;

SVAPONoVol
```

 Please utilize the disc in the back of the book for instant access to these codes. You may also download them from www.traderslibrary.com/tlecorner.

Example Chart with "SVAPO_No_Volume" Oscillator

The Dutch AEX index is one of those indices that does not publish volume. Figure 5.12 shows this index with the "SVAPO_No_Volume" oscillator below. The same basic trading rules used with SVAPO apply also for the "SVAPO_No_Volume" oscillator. Most interesting are the divergences between price and the oscillator.

In the chart of figure 5.12 on the next page, the index makes a higher top by the end of April, while the oscillator makes a lower top. This is a selling condition. The index turns down until half of June when there is a new divergence visible with lower bottoms in the index and higher bottoms in the oscillator. This is a buying condition.

The next divergence to show up is a hidden divergence with higher bottoms in the index and lower bottoms in the oscillator. This pushes the index higher and confirms a further up trend until the beginning of September when there

Figure 5.12: The same basic trading rules are used for the "SVAPO_No_Volume" oscillator

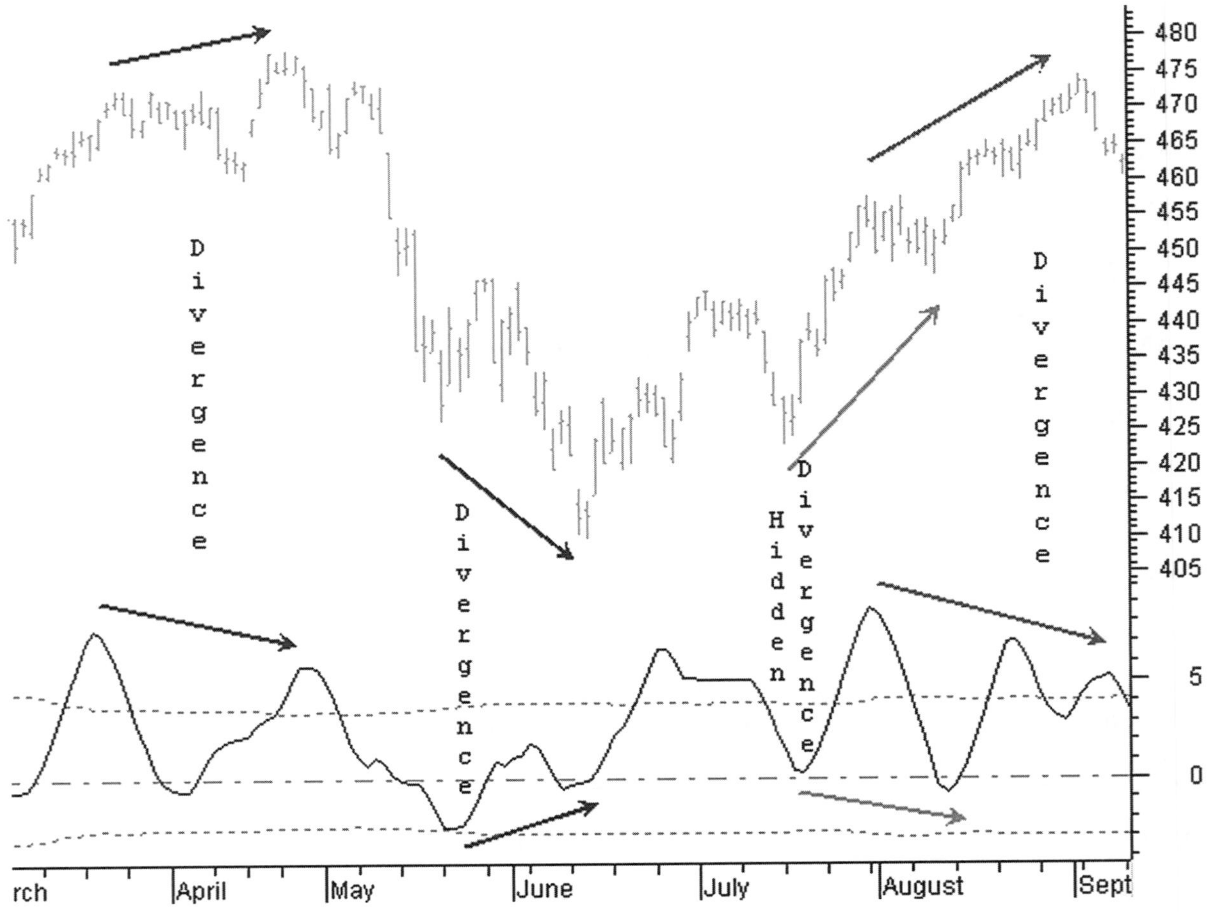

Source - MetaStock® charts courtesy of Equis International.

are again divergences with higher tops in the index and lower tops in the oscillator. This is a selling condition.

TRADING WITH SVAPO

By simply looking at price and SVAPO, it is possible to find early entries for buying or selling a stock.

In figure 5.13, a chart of AMD, there was a big down move over six months. Notice how lower tops in price during July and August made a hidden di-

Figure 5.13: AMD lower tops in price made a hidden divergence with higher tops in SVAPO

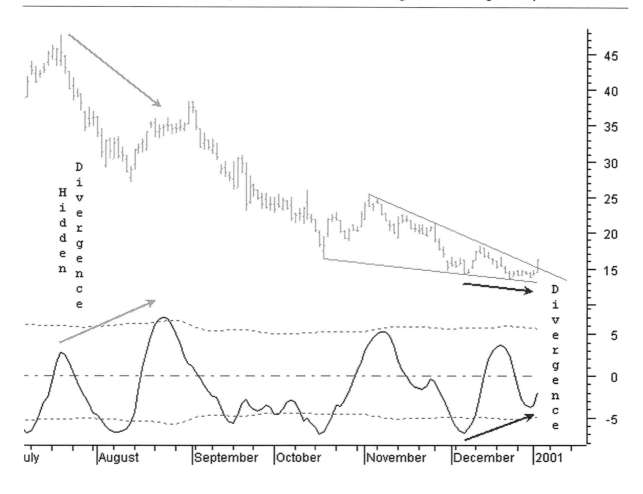

Source - MetaStock® charts courtesy of Equis International.

vergence with higher tops in SVAPO; a nice indication that the downtrend would continue.

Until the end of December, price went farther down in a convergent move. But beginning 2001, price made a divergent move with lower bottoms in price and higher bottoms in SVAPO. This was a buying signal that was further confirmed by price breaking the last downtrend line and by price breaking out of a falling wedge reversal pattern.

In figure 5.14, we can see the evolution of the uptrend. Price moved up until the beginning of February when a correction started. This correction brought

Figure 5.14: AMD uptrend evolution

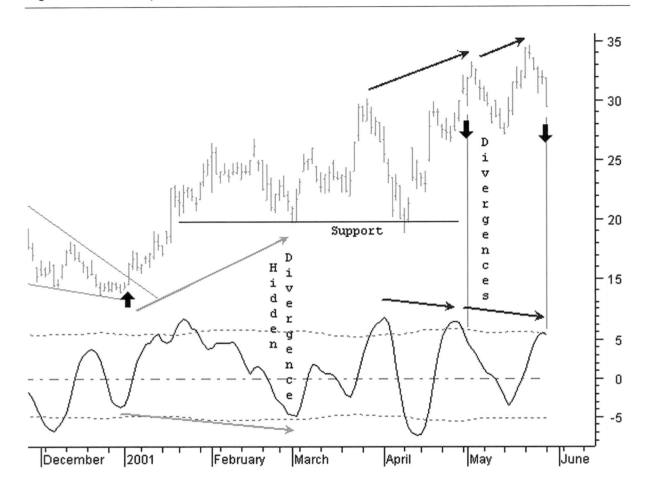

Source - MetaStock® charts courtesy of Equis International.

price back to a support level and by the beginning of March, a hidden divergence was visible with higher bottoms in price and lower bottoms in SVAPO, pointing to a continuation of the up trend. Price moved up in a convergent way, with another correction to the support level until the beginning of May. There, we have a small divergence between price and SVAPO with higher tops in price and lower tops in SVAPO. This might have been a selling moment; however, if you missed it, there was a second, more explicit divergence at the end of May. This signaled that it was time to close the position.

> Looking at price and SVAPO alone is, however, not a good idea. As you know from LOCKIT, you must always also use an initial and a trailing stop to get you out of a trade with a minimum loss in case SVAPO does not give a sell signal.

LOCKIT

Next, I have included another more dynamic trailing stop method that you can use both here and within LOCKIT.

ATR (AVERAGE TRUE RANGE) TRAILING STOP

Once a buying order is executed, you must always limit the risk by keeping an initial stop. The initial stop itself is variable from trade to trade because it will be based on different technical analysis techniques. On the other hand, you must use a trailing stop as the ultimate selling signal to avoid losing too much of your profit.

Average True Range (ATR) was developed by J. Welles Wilder and introduced in his book, *New Concepts in Technical Trading Systems* (Wilder, 1978). The ATR indicator measures a security's volatility.

Wilder started the true range concept, defined as the greatest value of:

- The current high less the current low.

- The absolute value of the current high less the previous close.

- The absolute value of the current low less the previous close.

He then calculated an average of this value, thus creating the ATR.

Like most technical analysis programs, MetaStock® has a predefined ATR indicator (ATR(period)). If you need to calculate it yourself, it can be created as follows:

```
{Get the required ATR period;}
period:=Input("ATR Period :",1,100,5);
{Calculate the biggest difference based on the true range concept;}
diff1:=Max(H-L,Abs(H-Ref(C,-1)));
diff2:=Max(diff1,Abs(L-Ref(C,-1)));
{Use Wilders' moving average method to calculate the Average
True Range;}
Mov(diff2,period*2-1,E)
```

 Please utilize the disc in the back of the book for instant access to these codes. You may also download them from www.traderslibrary.com/tlecorner.

With this formula you can create an ATR value based on something other than the closing price, say an average price for example.

To create a trailing stop based on the ATR value, we calculate the maximum allowed loss based on the ATR value multiplied by a factor. Since the number of input parameters in MetaStock® is limited to six, we have to create separate formulas for a long or a short position.

The following MetaStock® formula "SVE_StopLong_Trail_ATR_Date" creates an initial and long position ATR trailing stop on the price chart from an entry date:

```
{SVE_StopLong_Trail_ATR_Date- ATR trailing stop long from date}
InpMonth:=Input("Month",1,12,1);
InpDay:=Input("Day",1,31,2);
InpYear:=Input("Year",1800,2050,2009);
InitStop:=Input("Initial Stop Price",0.1,10000,10);
atrper:=Input("ATR period :",1,100,5);
atrfact:=Input("ATR multiplication :",1,10,3.5);
loss:=atrfact*ATR(atrper);
EntryLong:= InpYear=Year() AND InpMonth=Month() AND
```

InpDay=DayOfMonth();

EntryLock:=If(Ref(EntryLong,-1)=0 AND EntryLong=1,1,PREV);

support:=C-loss;

TrailStopLong:= If(EntryLock=0 OR EntryLong=1,InitStop,

If(support>Ref(Support,-1),Max(support,PREV),PREV));

TrailStopLong

 Please utilize the disc in the back of the book for instant access to these codes. You may also download them from www.traderslibrary.com/tlecorner.

The following MetaStock® formula "SVE_StopShort_Trail_ATR_Date" creates an initial and short position ATR trailing stop on the price chart from an entry date:

{SVE_StopShort_Trail_ATR_Date- ATR trailing stop Short from date}

InpMonth:=Input("Month",1,12,1);

InpDay:=Input("Day",1,31,2);

InpYear:=Input("Year",1800,2050,2009);

InitStop:=Input("Initial Stop Price",0.1,10000,10);

atrper:=Input("ATR period :",1,100,5);

atrfact:=Input("ATR multiplication :",1,10,3.5);

loss:=atrfact*ATR(atrper);

EntryLong:= InpYear=Year() AND InpMonth=Month() AND InpDay=DayOfMonth();

EntryLock:=If(Ref(EntryLong,-1)=0 AND EntryLong=1,1,PREV);

support:=C+loss;

TrailStopShort:= If(EntryLock=0 OR EntryLong=1,InitStop,

If(support>Ref(Support,-1),Min(support,PREV),PREV));

TrailStopShort

 Please utilize the disc in the back of the book for instant access to these codes. You may also download them from www.traderslibrary.com/tlecorner.

Formula Construction

First, we ask for the starting date:

InpMonth:=Input("Month",1,12,1);

InpDay:=Input("Day",1,31,2);

InpYear:=Input("Year",1800,2050,2009);

For the initial stop, we simply ask for the stop price because it will be set based on technical analysis. This way you can use the exact initial stop price:

InitStop:=Input("Initial Stop Price",0.1,10000,10);

Then, we ask for the ATR average period. As the default, we will use a 5-day average because we have found this to be the most commonly profitable value when using more volatile stocks.

atrper:=Input("ATR period :",1,100,5);

Next, we ask for the ATR average multiplication factor. As the default we will use a value of 3.5 because this seems to be the most common profitable value when using more volatile stocks.

atrfact:=Input("ATR multiplication :",1,10,3.5);

After that, we calculate the loss value based on the ATR value and the multiplication factor.

loss:=atrfact*ATR(atrper);

We reach the entry point in the daily price data series when the required starting date corresponds with a date displayed in the chart. Please make sure the requested date exists in the chart, otherwise nothing will be displayed.

EntryLong:= InpYear=Year() AND InpMonth=Month() AND InpDay=DayOfMonth();

Next we lock the starting date.

EntryLock:=If(Ref(EntryLong,-1)=0 AND EntryLong=1,1,PREV);

Figure 5.15: Trailing stop nicely captures a five wave Elliott up move

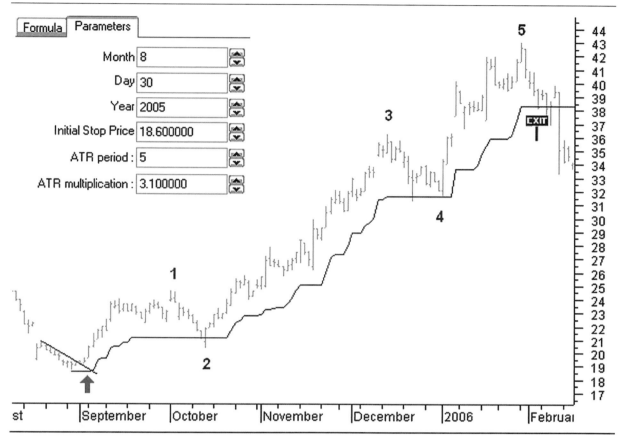

Source - MetaStock® charts courtesy of Equis International.

Figure 5.15 is a chart of Salesforce Com Inc. You can see how the trailing stop nicely captures a five wave Elliott up move. The formula input settings are displayed in the chart. The trailing stop is broken when the closing price falls below the trailing stop line.

Figure 5.16: AMD example start with SVAPO and trailing stop

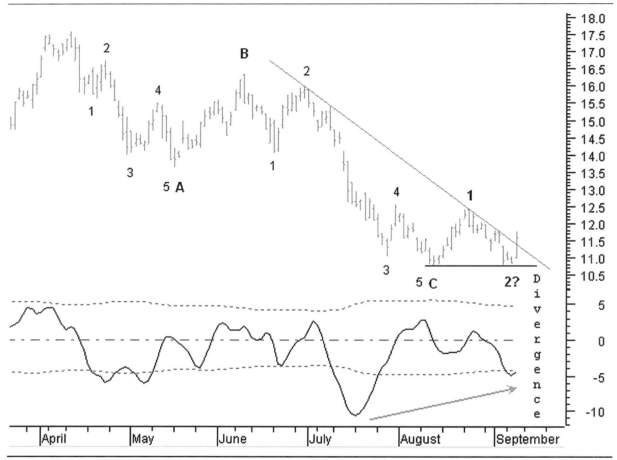

SVAPO AND ATR TRAILING STOP APPLICATION

Let me show you a few examples of trading with SVAPO and the use of the ATR-based trailing stop.

In figure 5.16, we have a chart of AMD up to September 9, 2004.

There are a number of reasons why we should open a long trade:

1. Looking at SVAPO, we have a nice positive divergence with a higher bottom in SVAPO and lower to equal bottoms in price.

2. The last medium-term trend line in the previous descent is broken by the closing price.

Figure 5.17: AMD up move, with ATR trailing stop settings

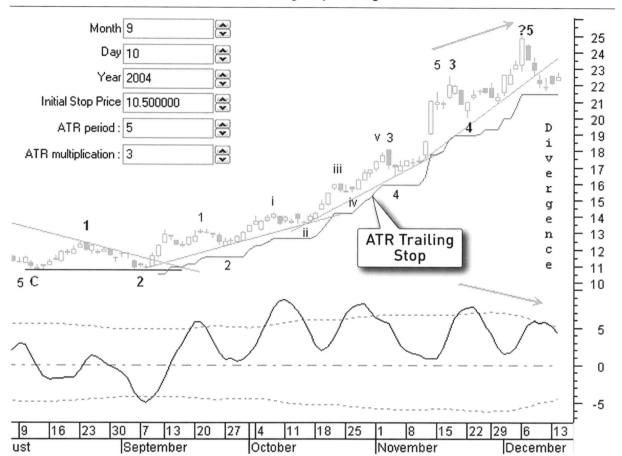

Source - MetaStock® charts courtesy of Equis International.

3. AMD has completed an ABC correction wave down and is now most likely starting an impulse wave 3 up.

4. The previous low of August support is confirmed by a new upward turning point.

To open a long trade here, we have to set an initial stop, and we must use a trailing stop. The initial stop can be set a fraction below the support line at $10.50. For the trailing stop, we can use the ATR trailing stop method, using a 5-day ATR and a multiplication factor of 3, considering the moderate volatile price move in the recent past.

Figure 5.17 shows the price up move that followed. The settings of the ATR trailing stop are also visible in the chart. The whole way up this trailing stop is never broken. Note how SVAPO remains above the zero-level during the entire

Figure 5.18: Neither the initial nor the trailing stop is broken up to now

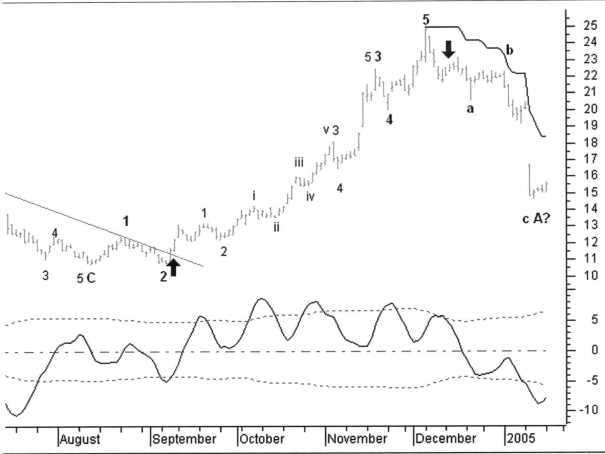

uptrend. Also, notice how price accelerates in three steps confirmed by steeper trend lines. We also seem to have a complete Elliott impulse wave count.

Moving along the chart, we now see a bigger divergence between higher tops in price and lower tops in SVAPO. The two top candles make up a bearish harami reversal pattern confirmed with a lower closing price in the next candle. On these technical grounds, I would now close the long position and take the almost 100% profit. In any case, the trade must be closed if the trailing stop is broken.

If a correction is coming next, it could be reasonably big after the 100% price move up. Opening a short position now, therefore, has a nice profit target. With an initial stop at $25.00, the top of the bearish harami pattern, the risk-reward-ratio is acceptable. We would also continue to keep a trailing stop with the same values as before.

Figure 5.19: The smaller ATR trailing stop is broken and SVAPO is turning down

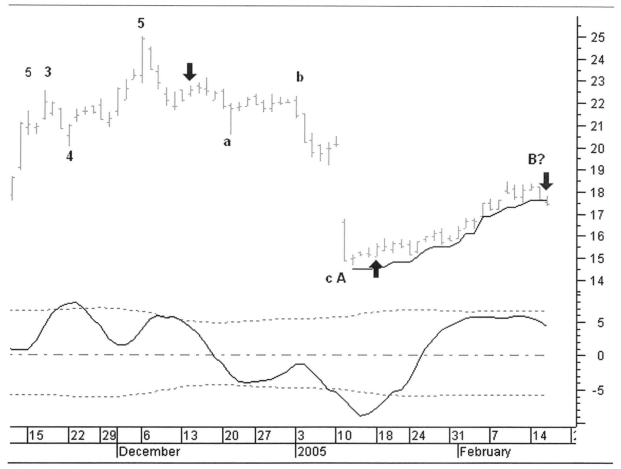

Source - MetaStock® charts courtesy of Equis International.

In figure 5.18, you can see that neither the initial nor the trailing stop has been broken up to now. There was a one day down move of more than 25%. In general, you should always profit from this kind of move and take profit. Most of the time, however, there will be a consolidation period. With SVAPO making a low and turning up, price may continue its correction up. Looking at the wave count, we are most likely making a wave 2 correction of a higher order. The abc correction up to now is probably the start of a longer-term ABC correction. I would expect a correction wave B up and, after that, a correction wave C down a fraction lower than where the chart is currently.

It is important to see that we do not have much to lose. Closing the short position now gives us a very nice profit. Opening a new long position with an initial stop just below the last low point limits a possible loss to a small percentage. On the other hand, since we expect just a limited up move, we will

Figure 5.20: Price moves down and breaks the ATR trailing stop

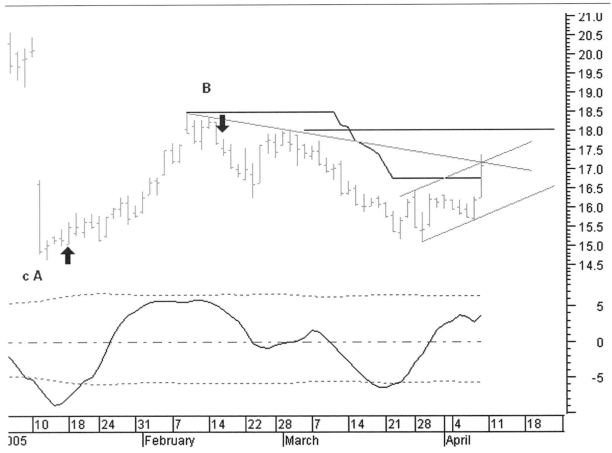

Source - MetaStock® charts courtesy of Equis International.

use a small ATR trailing stop of 5 days and a multiplication factor of 1 to get us out of the trade fast.

In figure 5.19 on the previous page, the small ATR trailing stop has been broken, while SVAPO has turned down from the upper side. Is this the top of correction wave B? Again, we do not have much to lose. Closing our long position gives us a profit and opening a new short position requires only a small initial stop. We will hope for a move below the previous low point, and again, we will use our normal ATR trailing stop of 5 days with a 3 times multiplication factor.

Price does move down (figure 5.20) but it now breaks the ATR trailing stop. If we close the position, we make a very small profit. There is resistance from the downtrend line and resistance from the upper side of the new up channel.

Figure 5.21: Price finally makes a longer-term WXY double zigzag correction

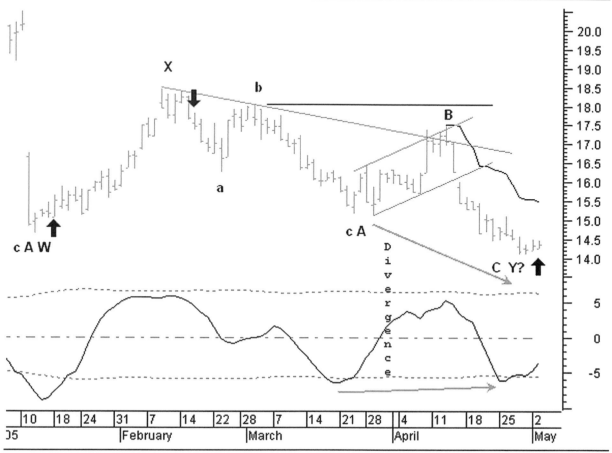

More important, resistance is found at about $18. If we do not sell yet and keep this resistance as a selling point, we will have to close the trade with a small loss. Looking at the last price move, it is not impossible that we had a low correction point already at "A" and that we have started a new impulse wave up with waves 1 and 2 and the beginning of wave 3; however, I have my doubts that we will make a new low for correction wave C. If price started a new longer-term wave 3, then why isn't there a divergence between price and SVAPO? Ok, I think this is reason enough to hold on to the short trade for the moment and keep a stop at $18.00, for only a very small risk.

In figure 5.21, we can see how price finally made a longer-term WXY double zigzag correction with a lower low. Price and SVAPO are turning up now and showing divergence. This is more likely the start of a new longer-term

Figure 5.22: The result, a very profitable trade

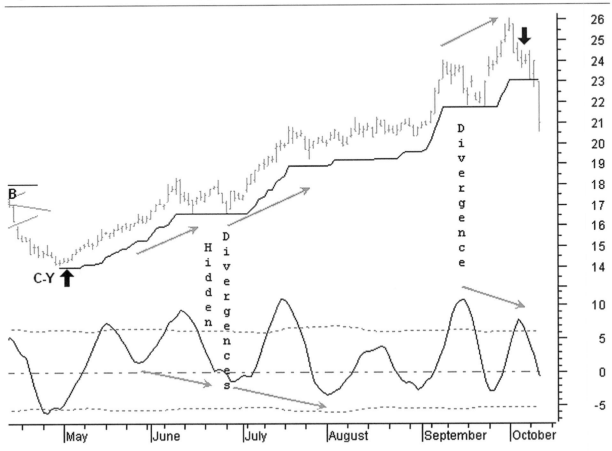

Source - MetaStock® charts courtesy of Equis International.

uptrend move. Again, we have the advantage that we can start with a small initial stop, limiting our possible loss to a small amount of money. We close the short trade with a nice profit and open a new long trade. We will keep a trailing stop with a 5-day ATR and a multiplication factor of 3.

Figure 5.22 shows the result: Another very profitable trade! The trailing ATR stop has now been broken, but basically we would have closed the long position when SVAPO made a larger divergence with price a few days earlier. On the way up, notice the hidden divergences between SVAPO and price, which pushed price farther up and continued the previous trend.

LOCKIT

It is clear that using SVAPO as a reference oscillator and using an ATR trailing stop is a winning team. Use it to your advantage as part of the LOCKIT system.

**For a closer look at the charts in this chapter,
go to www.traderslibrary.com/TLEcorner.**

TEST YOUR CHAPTER 5 KNOWLEDGE

1. After a previous downtrend, this stock is now in an uptrend. Below the price chart is the SVAPO oscillator. Would you now buy or sell this stock.

What are your arguments?

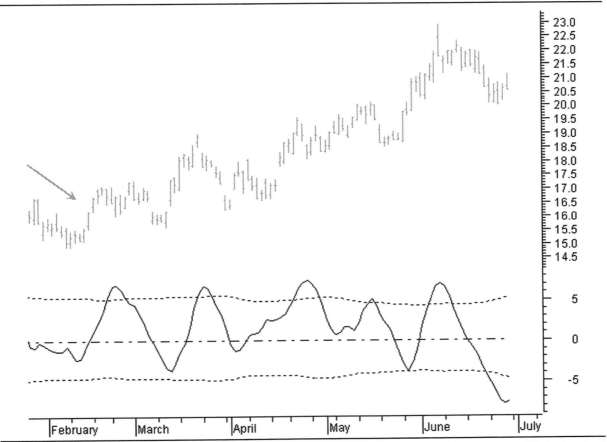

Source - MetaStock® charts courtesy of Equis International.

2. SVAPO is diverging with a lower top compared to a higher top in price. Would you sell here?

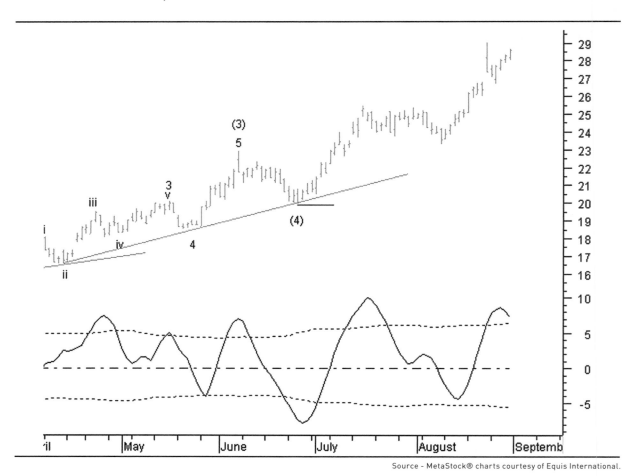

Source - MetaStock® charts courtesy of Equis International.

3. Price went up and again SVAPO is diverging with a lower top compared to a higher top in price. Would you sell here?

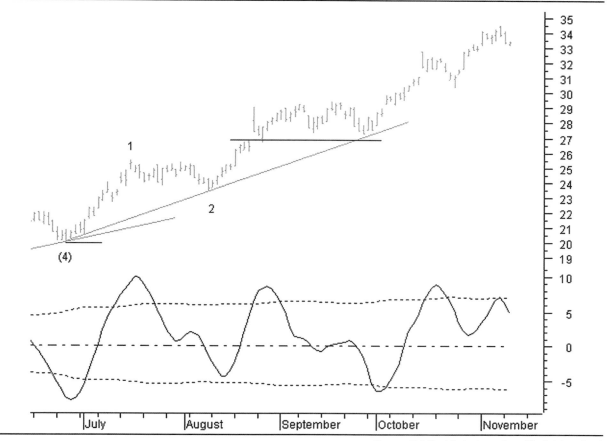

_____

_____

_____

_____

_____

_____

_____

Q&A **For answers, please visit the Traders' Library Education Corner at www.traderslibrary.com/tlecorner.**

PART III
LOCKIT PRICE PROJECTIONS

Chapter 6

Price Projection Techniques

Making price projections with LOCKIT is important in determining the risk/reward ratio. You simply cannot calculate the risk/reward ratio if you have no idea what price levels could be reached. On the other hand, knowing different techniques for estimating future price levels also will be a great help when deciding where to close a trade.

BASIC PRICE PROJECTIONS

Basic support and resistance will be found at price turning points and windows. More support levels will be found at the level of trend lines and trend channels, as well as at reaction lines.

In figure 6.1 we see a buying signal after the closing price moved above a last downtrend line during the first half of August. Assuming that price would not continue moving up, there is only one important line to consider, and that is the support line. This is also usually the initial stop level.

The first target price level is "Resistance_1," a previous price reversal point. Next, we expect some resistance from the 50-day simple moving average. Then follows "Resistance_2," representing support levels and a window in the previous downtrend; thereby, previous support becomes resistance. At around the same time, there is resistance from the medium-term downtrend line. Not far away from this level, we find resistance from the 200-day simple moving average.

Figure 6.1: Basic support and resistance levels

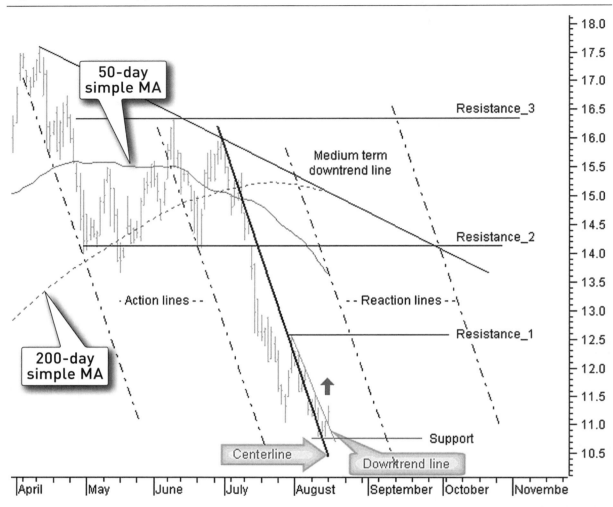

Source - MetaStock® charts courtesy of Equis International.

Finally, we have "Resistance_3," an important turning point in the previous downtrend. Close to this level, multiple turning points in the previous downtrend will show resistance.

Drawing a centerline through the last big downtrend move, we can create some action lines (action-reaction lines will be discussed in the last part of this chapter) through past turning points, where these previous downtrends show equal inclinations as the centerline. Projecting parallel lines into the future at the same distance as the action lines creates corresponding reaction lines. These reaction lines will also represent price resistance levels.

Figure 6.2: Future price move and the basic resistance levels

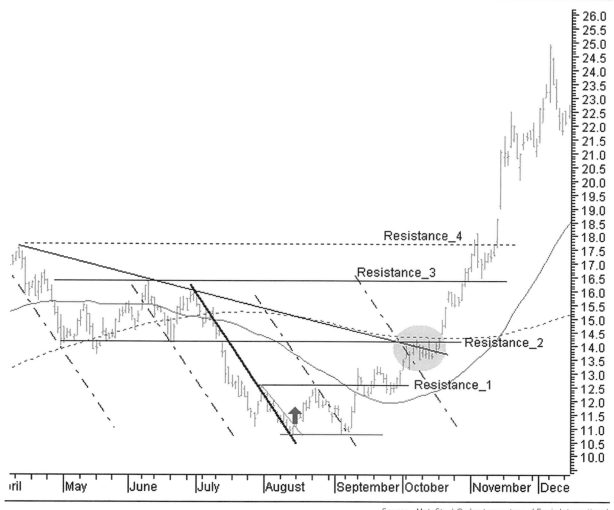

In figure 6.2 you can see how the future price made a big up move. As expected, there was a first level of resistance at "Resistance_1" that, together with the first reaction line, pushed price back down to the start of the up move. The next attack took some time to break through resistance for a move up to the next level of resistance. Note that there was support from the 50-day simple moving average.

At the level of "Resistance_2" there were more forces posing resistance. There was of course "Resistance_2," a previous support level in the downtrend now acting as resistance, and the downtrend line. There was also resistance from the 200-day simple moving average and some resistance from the second reaction line.

On the rest of the move up, there was only slight resistance from the levels "Resistance_3" and "Resistance_4." Resistance_3" was a previous resistance level in the downtrend, which turned to a support level for the further uptrend.

LOCKIT

> In LOCKIT we use the basic support and resistance found at price turning points and windows, the support or resistance levels of trend lines and trend channels, and the use of reaction lines in order to project future price levels.

We will, however, make use of additional price projection techniques discussed next.

FIBONACCI STUDIES

Leonardo Pisano (Fibonacci) was an Italian mathematician born in 1170. He was considered by some to be the most talented mathematician of the Middle Ages.

In *Liber Abaci* (c. 1202), Fibonacci introduced the so-called *modus Indorum* (method of the Indians), which today is known as Hindu-Arabic numerals.

Liber Abaci also presented, and solved, a problem involving the growth of a hypothetical population of rabbits, which was based on idealized assumptions. The solution was a sequence of numbers that, over several generations, became known as Fibonacci numbers.

The number sequence was known to Indian mathematicians as early as the 6th century, but it was Fibonacci's *Liber Abaci* that introduced it to the West.

Fibonacci numbers have the following sequence: 1, 1, 2, 3, 5, 8, 13, 21, 34, 55, 89, 144, 233, and so on. Each number is the sum of the two previous numbers. The higher up in the sequence, the closer two consecutive numbers of the sequence divided by each other will approach the golden ratio (approximately 1: 1.618, or 0.618: 1).

Fibonacci numbers, or patterns, are found in seashells, flower petals, sunflower seed heads, pine cones, palm fronds, pineapple rinds, and 90% of plant leaf and petal arrangements.

Fibonacci Levels

Charting Fibonacci levels is done by first drawing a fictive vertical line between two turning points that you wish to examine for Fibonacci levels.

Figure 6.3: Fibonacci levels giving support and resistance to future price movement

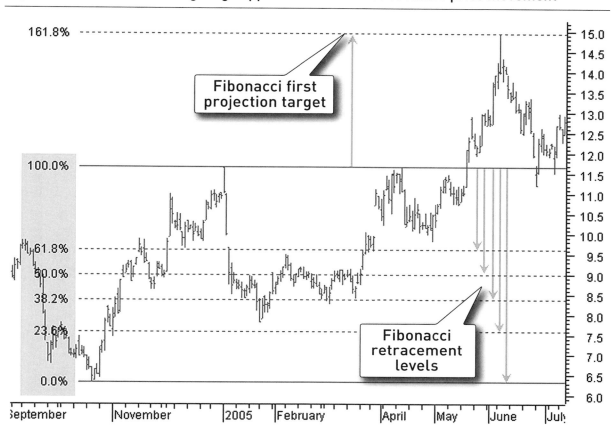

Source - MetaStock® charts courtesy of Equis International.

Next, you draw horizontals through retracement levels at 100%, 61.8% (100★0.618), 50%, 38.2% (61.8★0.618), 23.6% (38.2★0.618), and 0%; then, draw horizontals at three or more Fibonacci target levels at 161.8% (100★1.618), 261.8% (161.8★1.618), and 423.6% (261.8★1.618).

After the price moves up or down, there often will be a partial retracement, which will find support and resistance on Fibonacci levels.

Fibonacci Levels in an Uptrend

We use the chart of AMR Corp. to show Fibonacci levels in an uptrend.

In figure 6.3, the Fibonacci levels from a 0% rise until a 100% price up-move between the end of September and December 2004 show a number of horizontal lines of support and resistance to future price movement.

Figure 6.4: New Fibonacci projection targets on a weekly chart

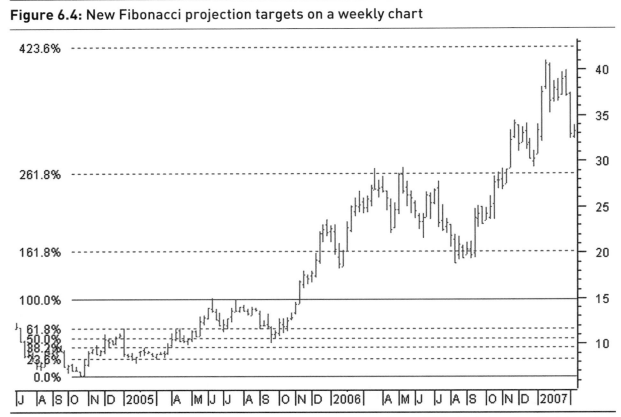

Source - MetaStock® charts courtesy of Equis International.

By the end of May, previous top levels around $11.70 were broken (Figure 6.3). The price then continued to move right up to the next Fibonacci level at 161.8%, or $15.

In figure 6.4, the same chart with weekly bars and a new Fibonacci projection between the start of the up-move in September 2004 until the first reached target at $15 in June 2005 gave us new future price targets. Where do you think price moved to? Believe it or not, right up to Fibonacci levels 161.8%, 261.8%, and very close to 423.6%.

Figure 6.5: Fibonacci retracements and projection levels in a downtrend

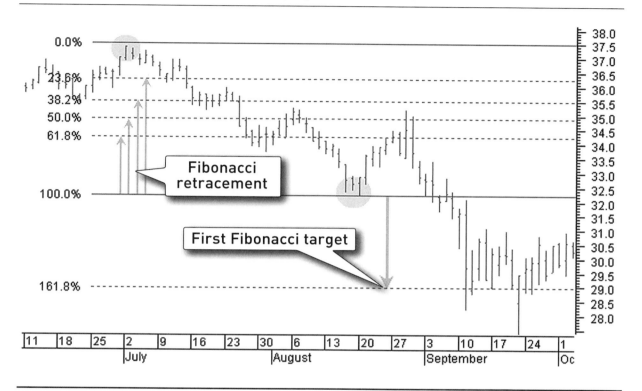

Fibonacci Levels in a Downtrend

We use a chart of AHOLD, a Dutch stock, to look at Fibonacci levels in a downtrend.

Creating the Fibonacci levels in figure 6.5 from a 0% price drop until a 100% price down between the beginning of July and mid-August shows a number of horizontal Fibonacci retracement levels, which give support and resistance to future price movement. At the beginning of September, a previous bottom at €32.2 was broken. The price then continued to move down until the next Fibonacci level at 161.8%, or €29.0.

Figure 6.6: Fibonacci projection levels reached

Source - MetaStock® charts courtesy of Equis International.

Next, have a look on the weekly chart of figure 6.6 to see what other levels have been reached. Do you find this hard to believe?

Historical Fibonacci Projections

When price changes from, for example, a downtrend to an uptrend, it is only possible to draw Fibonacci retracement levels for the past downtrend move, using these retracement levels as price targets for the new up move.

It is clear that at the start of a price turning point, there is no second reference point available for a Fibonacci projection. Since support and resistance levels from the past are also continued in the future, it is not unusual that previous support or resistance can be used as the second reference point for a Fibonacci projection into the future.

Figure 6.7: Fibonacci historical projection principle

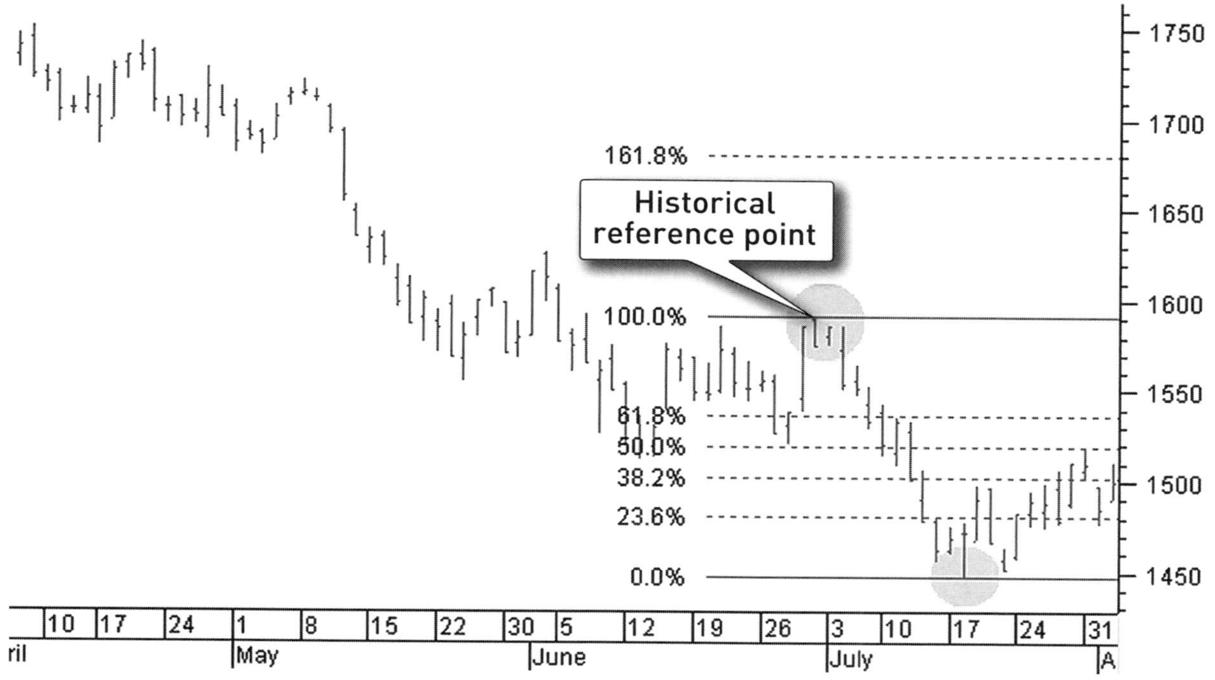

Source - MetaStock® charts courtesy of Equis International.

The NASDAQ index in figure 6.7 went down from 1750 to 1450. After the turning point in July, we expected an up-move. For a future price estimation, we created a Fibonacci projection with the reference low point in mid-July and the last previous top, which gave us a first target at a level of 1680.

Figure 6.8: Fibonacci historical projection confirmed

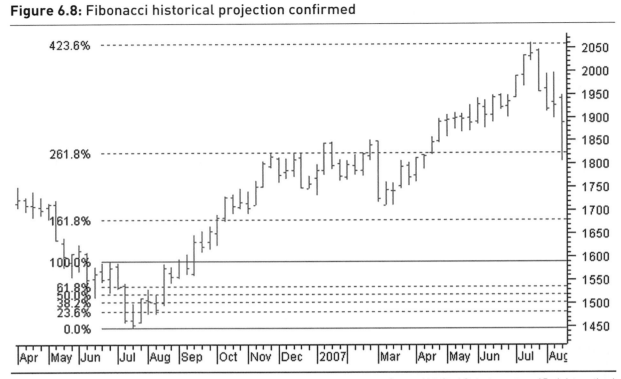

Source - MetaStock® charts courtesy of Equis International.

Figure 6.8 shows that we not only reached the target at 1680, but we also reached the Fibonacci projections at 261.8% and 423.6% from the same historical reference point.

> **LOCKIT**
>
> Fibonacci retracements and projections are a very important tool used within LOCKIT for making future price projections. Reaching a Fibonacci target level is an important part of the signals used to close a position.

Next, we are going to introduce the Andrews pitchfork and discuss action/reaction lines more closely.

ANDREWS PITCHFORK

Alan Hall Andrews is known in technical analysis for creating a method called the "Andrews pitchfork."

Andrews describes his application as the median line method. The application of the median line method came from the ideas of Sir Isaac Newton and Roger Babson, including, among other things Newton's third law of motion: "For each action, there is an equal and opposite reaction."

Figure 6.9: Construction of the median line

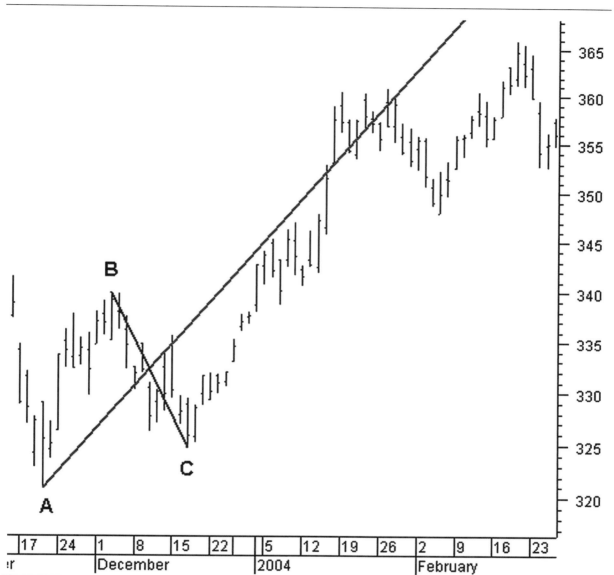

Source - MetaStock® charts courtesy of Equis International.

The Median Line

Construction

1. Calculate the mid-point of the reaction B-C (the line B-C is normally not drawn).

2. From a previous reference, high or low point, draw a line through this mid-point. This is the median line.

Figure 6.10: Price returning to the median line 80% of the time

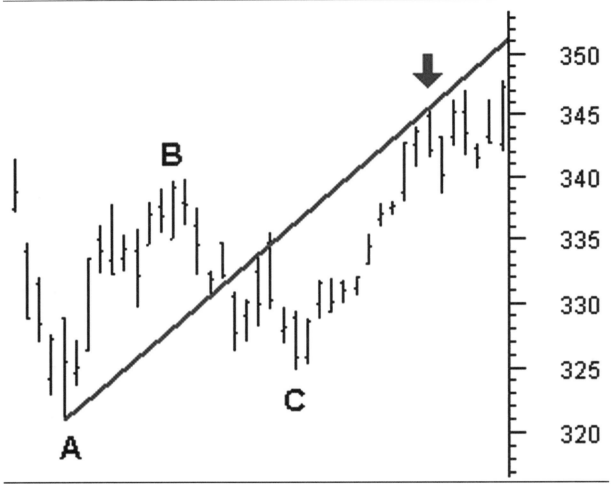

Trading Based on the Median Line

1. The price will return to the median line about 80% of the time (figure 6.10).

Figure 6.11: Median line showing support and resistance

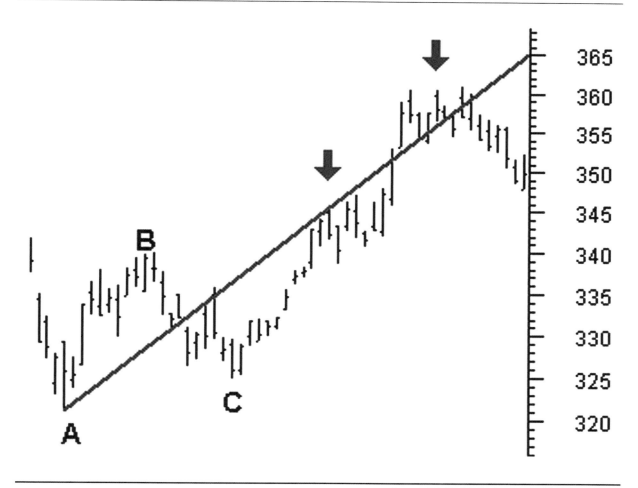

Source - MetaStock® charts courtesy of Equis International.

2. The median line is a resistance and support line. The price will react around the median line (figure 6.11).

3. The price returning to the median line often will move for some time around that median line before a new direction is chosen (figure 6.11).

Figure 6.12: Price not touching the median line will push price in opposite direction

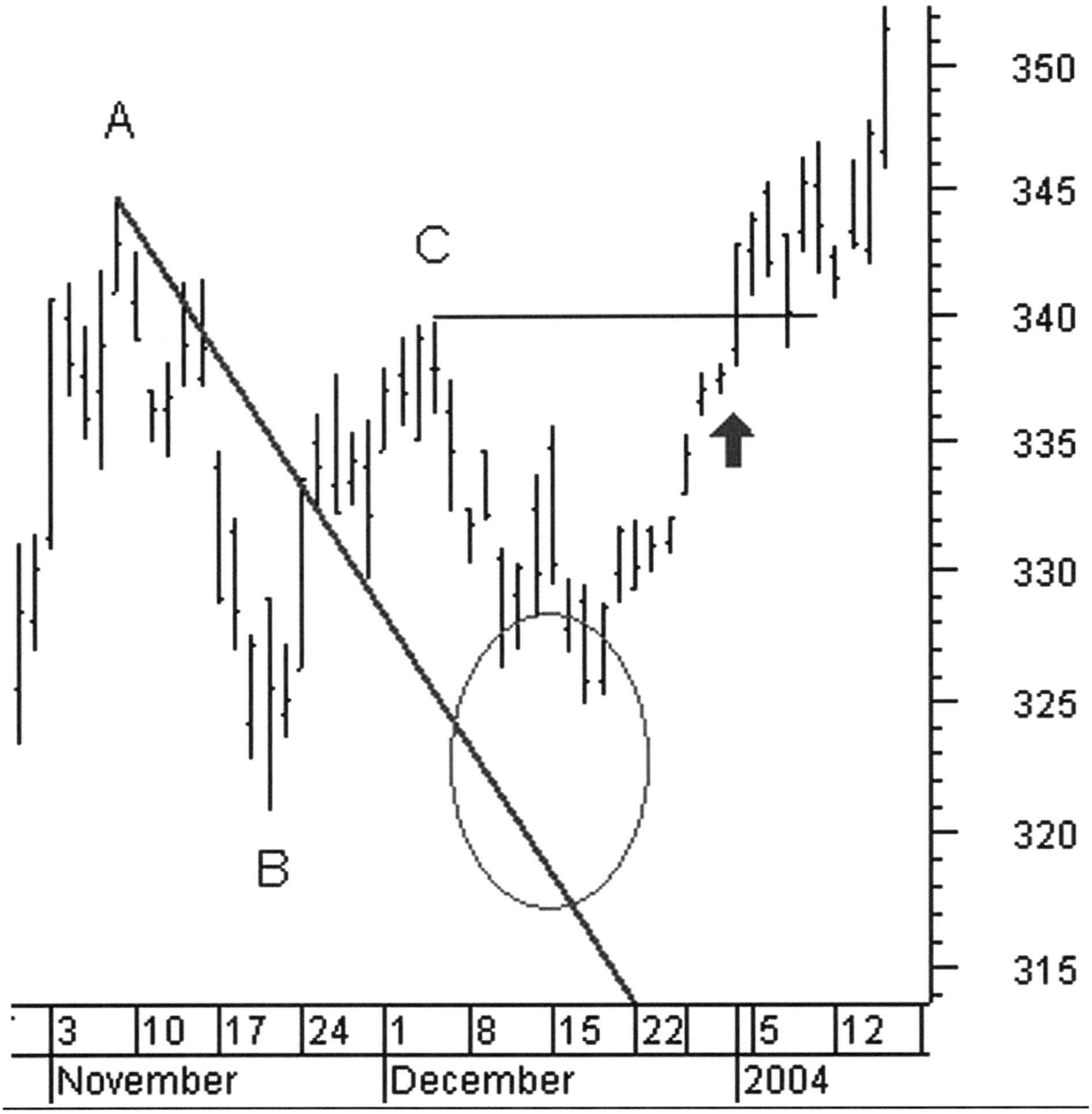

Source - MetaStock® charts courtesy of Equis International.

4. If the price does not complete touching the median line, it will move in the opposite direction, past the price turning point used for the construction of the median line (figure 6.12).

Figure 6.13: Andrews pitchfork channel

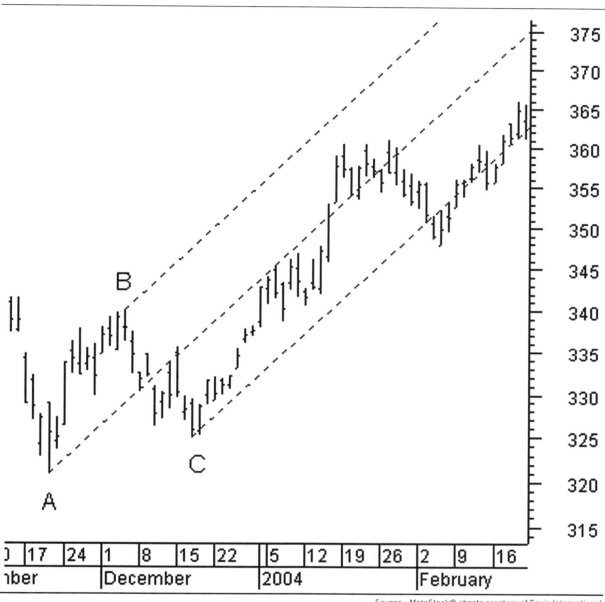

The Pitchfork

After calculating and drawing the median line, Andrews added two additional lines parallel to the median line, from the points B and C. This created parallel lines above and below the median line.

Figure 6.14: Pitchfork warning lines

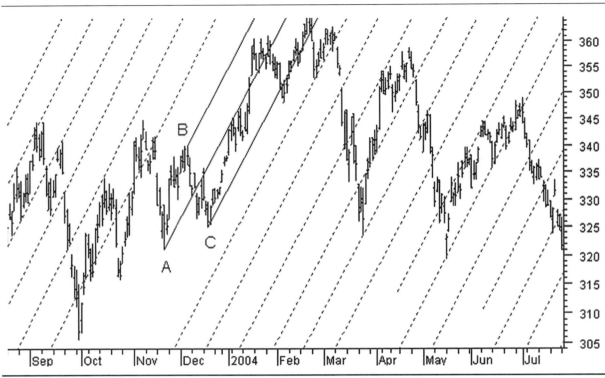

These three lines are called the Andrews pitchfork (figure 6.13 on previous page). Prices tend to move for some time within this pitchfork channel, similar to a trend channel.

Like in a trend channel, prices find support and resistance at the lower and upper side of the pitchfork channel.

Warning Lines

Andrews then added parallel lines in the past and the future at the same distance as the parallel lines from the median line; he called these warning lines.

In figure 6.14, you will notice that the price will move regularly to and within the boundaries of these warning lines.

> In LOCKIT we use the Andrews pitchfork mainly as a price target tool to see if price reaches the median line (80% of the time). If price does not reach the median line, we know to what level it will move next as a minimum. Additionally, the outer lines of the pitchfork are quite effective as a trend channel, which gives us upper and lower boundaries for future price moves.

LOCKIT

ACTION AND REACTION LINES

Action-Reaction Method 1

The action-reaction method 1 uses three lines: the reference line, the action line, and the reaction line.

Look at figure 6.15 for an application using the action-reaction method 1. The reference line can be a median line, a trend line, a centerline, or a multi-reversal line.

Figure 6.15: Action-Reaction method 1

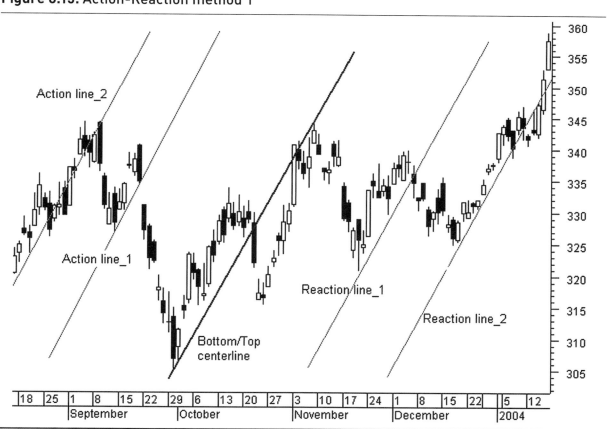

Source - MetaStock® charts courtesy of Equis International.

The action is the left side of the chart, or the past; the right side of the chart is the reaction into the future. Action lines are drawn under the same angle as the reference line, through a past pivot point. Reaction lines are drawn under the same angle as the reference line and at the same distance as the corresponding action lines.

Action-Reaction Method 2

The action-reaction method 2 uses the same three lines as the action-reaction method 1: the reference line, the action line, and the reaction line.

Figure 6.16: Action-Reaction method 2

Source - MetaStock® charts courtesy of Equis International.

Look at figure 6.16 for an application of the action-reaction method 2. The reference line can be a median line, a trend line, a centerline, or a multi-reversal line.

Only one action line, a parallel line with the reference line, is drawn through a pivot point in the past.

Reaction lines are drawn parallel to the reference line and at equal distances from each other using the distance between the action line and the reference line as the basic measure.

> **In LOCKIT we mainly use the action-reaction methods to find crossings with other price projection techniques to get an indication on the time axis when a target could be reached.**

LOCKIT

This concludes PART III where we looked at basic LOCKIT price projections, Fibonacci studies, the Andrews pitchfork, and action-reaction lines to complete the different price projection methods used in LOCKIT.

 For a closer look at the charts in this chapter, go to www.traderslibrary.com/TLEcorner.

TEST YOUR CHAPTER 6 KNOWLEDGE

1. We are probably starting wave 3 of a new up trend. Can you make some projections for what price levels could be reached?

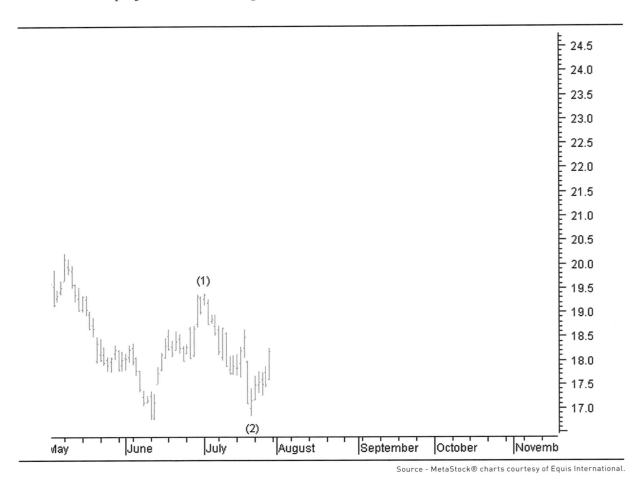

Source - MetaStock® charts courtesy of Equis International.

_____

_____

_____

_____

_____

_____

_____

_____

2. We have most likely made correction wave (A) and correction wave (B). Can you make a projection for wave (C) down?

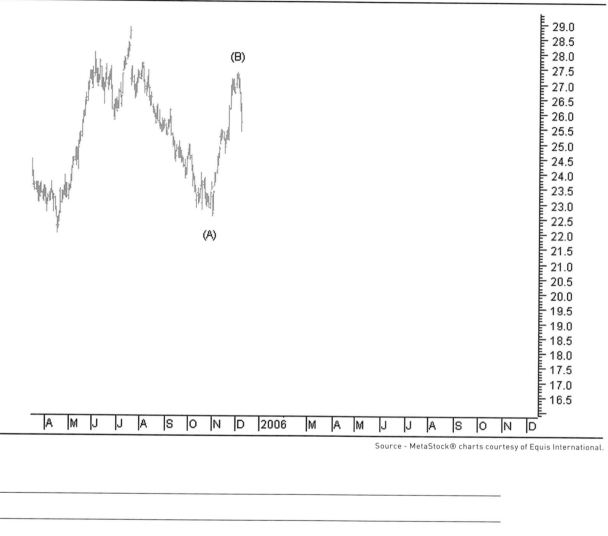

Source - MetaStock® charts courtesy of Equis International.

 For answers, please visit the Traders' Library Education Corner at www.traderslibrary.com/tlecorner.

PART IV
LOCKIT STRATEGY AND RESULTS

Chapter 7

LOCKIT Application and Rules

LOCKIT is a stock-trading method based on applying technical analysis and money and risk management techniques. Please note that special indicators used within LOCKIT are available in MetaStock® code. I have included a disc in the back of this book that has all of these codes ready for upload. If, however, you don't use Metastock, the Appendix gives you a list of other programs that have all or most of the used code available for their application.

Also, please keep in mind that this chapter will give you an overview of the entire LOCKIT system in a step-by-step process. Now that you have a working knowledge of the basic technical analysis tools we use within LOCKIT, I think you will be impressed with how well the methodology works. If you need a refresher on the basics as you move through this next part, you have to no further to look than the previous chapters.

LOCKIT is an acronym that stands for:

L "Long term" What is the Long-term trend?

O "Open" The rules for Opening a position.

C "Close" The rules for Closing a position.

K "K-ratio" Keep risk under control and manage your money.

I "Initial stop" Set an Initial stop loss.

T "Trailing stop" Set a Trailing stop loss.

STEP 1: LONG-TERM TREND

First, we look at the long-term trend. We prefer to trade only in the direction of the long-term trend. Even with the use of technical analysis, you will have to leave enough price reaction potential for the intermediate-term in order to keep a stock in your portfolio for the longer-term.

Figure 7.1: Bankrate Inc. with a 17% trailing stop

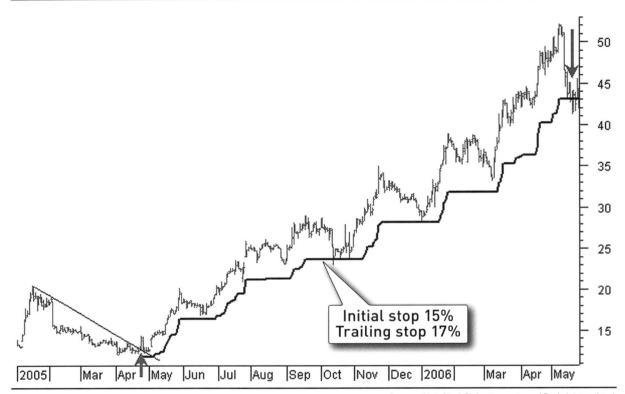

Initial stop 15%
Trailing stop 17%

Source - MetaStock® charts courtesy of Equis International.

Look at figure 7.1, Bankrate Inc. We have to keep a 17% trailing stop to keep us in the trade for the long term. Many times, this means we will have to use an initial stop in the same order; however, it is clear that we cannot permit many losing trades that cost us 15% or more. It is, therefore, important to understand what the long-term trend is doing.

Estimating the Long-term Trend

To estimate the long-term trend for the whole of the stock market, we use a stock index. During a long-term uptrend, we only trade on the long side.

Figure 7.2: S&P 500 Index monthly chart

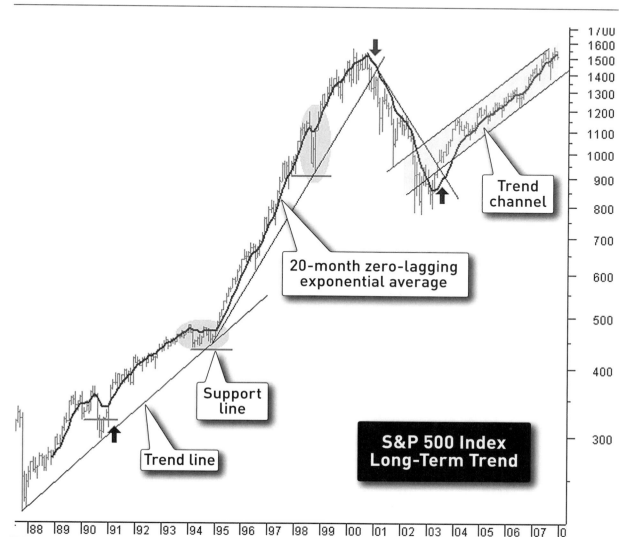

Source - MetaStock® charts courtesy of Equis International.

On the other hand, we will only trade from the short side in a long-term falling market.

We use a monthly chart (Figure 7.2) to look at the long-term trend. Remember that it is easier to make money in a rising market than in a falling market, simply because a stock can go up from $1 to $100, or 10,000%, but it can only fall from $1 to $0, or 100%.

Detailed information about technical analysis used within LOCKIT can be found in PART I chapters 1 to 4.

We can say that a chart with higher price bottoms and higher price tops is in an uptrend. Lower price tops and lower bottoms means price is in a downtrend. The first indication of a possible trend reversal in an uptrend is a lower top compared to the last one. You get a confirmation when the next bottom is lower than the last bottom. In a downtrend, a first indication of a reversal is a higher bottom than the last one. You get a confirmation with a higher top than the last one.

The use of a moving average on monthly prices is the first tool that we will use in LOCKIT to look for the long-term trend; however, to avoid the lagging of the average used as much as possible, we will use a short 20-month exponential moving average with a zero-lagging compensation.

The long-term trend is considered up as long as this moving average is going up. When this average starts moving flat or slightly downward, you can use recent price support or resistance and trend lines to find confirmation for an eventual long-term trend change.

In MetaStock® you can create a zero-lagging exponential moving average as follows:

```
Period:= Input("Exponential Average period?",1,250,20);
EMA1:= Mov(CLOSE,Period,E);
EMA2:= Mov(EMA1,Period,E);
Difference:= EMA1 - EMA2;
ZeroLagEMA:= EMA1 + Difference;
ZeroLagEMA
```

 Please utilize the disc in the back of the book for instant access to these codes. You may also download them from www.traderslibrary.com/tlecorner.

Additionally, it is best to use trend lines and trend channels for confirmation. Because we are looking at big price moves, we will use a logarithmic scale on the vertical axis. In most cases, trend lines tend to accelerate on the way to a longer-term target. A trend line broken by the closing price is basically a reversal signal.

Looking at figure 7.2, there was doubt in the S&P 500 long-term up-move during the second half of the year 1990, with the average moving down and breaking a shorter-term uptrend line (not shown). We had a more flat correction in 1994, but here the price remained above the uptrend line and above the

Figure 7.3: S&P 500 Index in the period 2003 till 2007 with a 7% trailing stop

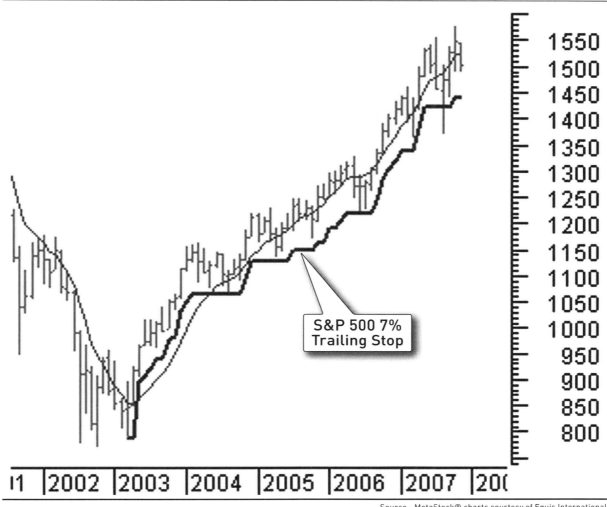

S&P 500 7%
Trailing Stop

Source - MetaStock® charts courtesy of Equis International.

last support level. Finally, there was a bigger correction at the end of 1998. But even here, the price remained above the trend line and the last support line.

Of course, we can also use or combine the previous techniques with a trailing stop. If the closing price breaks the trailing stop, then we can assume a trend reversal.

As a reference, look at figure 7.3, which shows the period 2003 until 2007 on the S&P 500 Index. The closing price trailing stop used was 7%.

> This is the first step in the LOCKIT system: Find out the long-term trend and take trades only in the direction of that trend.

LOCKIT

STEP 2: OPENING A POSITION

After examining the long-term trend in **LOCKIT** step 1, let's investigate the medium-term using a weekly chart. Keep in mind that you are looking for the bigger medium-term trades. Are you, conversely, a short-term trader? If so, you would only look at the weekly chart to find out whether the price is or is not coming to a medium-term reversal point.

CA Inc. Weekly Chart
The Day of 08/13/2004

Let's look at figure 7.4, the weekly chart of CA Inc.

Because of the big price shift in this longer period, we use a semi-logarithmic scale for this weekly chart. First, we look for a probable Elliott wave count. If our count is correct, we may be near the end of a longer-term correction wave (4). Correction wave (2) was a sharp correction; most of the time, wave (4) would then follow with a flat correction, which seems the case here. Drawing a trend line through the tops (1) and (3) and a parallel line through the bottom of wave (2) show that we have reached a target price for wave (4) at the bottom of this channel. At the same time, we reach support at the 200-day simple moving average (dashed line), and we are finding support at a previous low point (wave (4) bottom) at a price level of $22.

We use three indicators: 1) SVAPO with the standard settings, 2) the standard 14 (weeks) SVE_RSI_StDev, and 3) the standard 18 (weeks) SVE_BB%b_ HA. It is important to examine whether these indicators are making convergent or divergent moves.

These indicators are now moving in the lower part of their normal space, making a convergent move. Remember, there are usually no divergences in a wave 4 because the up move is still intact; therefore, we are not really looking at a price reversal. If there is a divergence, it will probably be a hidden one. We can now see that there is room for an up-move to create the next impulse wave (5), which must bring price above the top of wave (3), or above $29.60.

Looking at figure 7.5 (on page 208) and assuming that we reached a not-yet-confirmed bottom of wave (4), we could try to make a future price projection for wave (5). A Fibonacci projection with a first target at $22.50 already has given support three times for different wave (4) corrections.

Figure 7.4: Investigating the medium-term trend on the weekly chart of CA Inc.

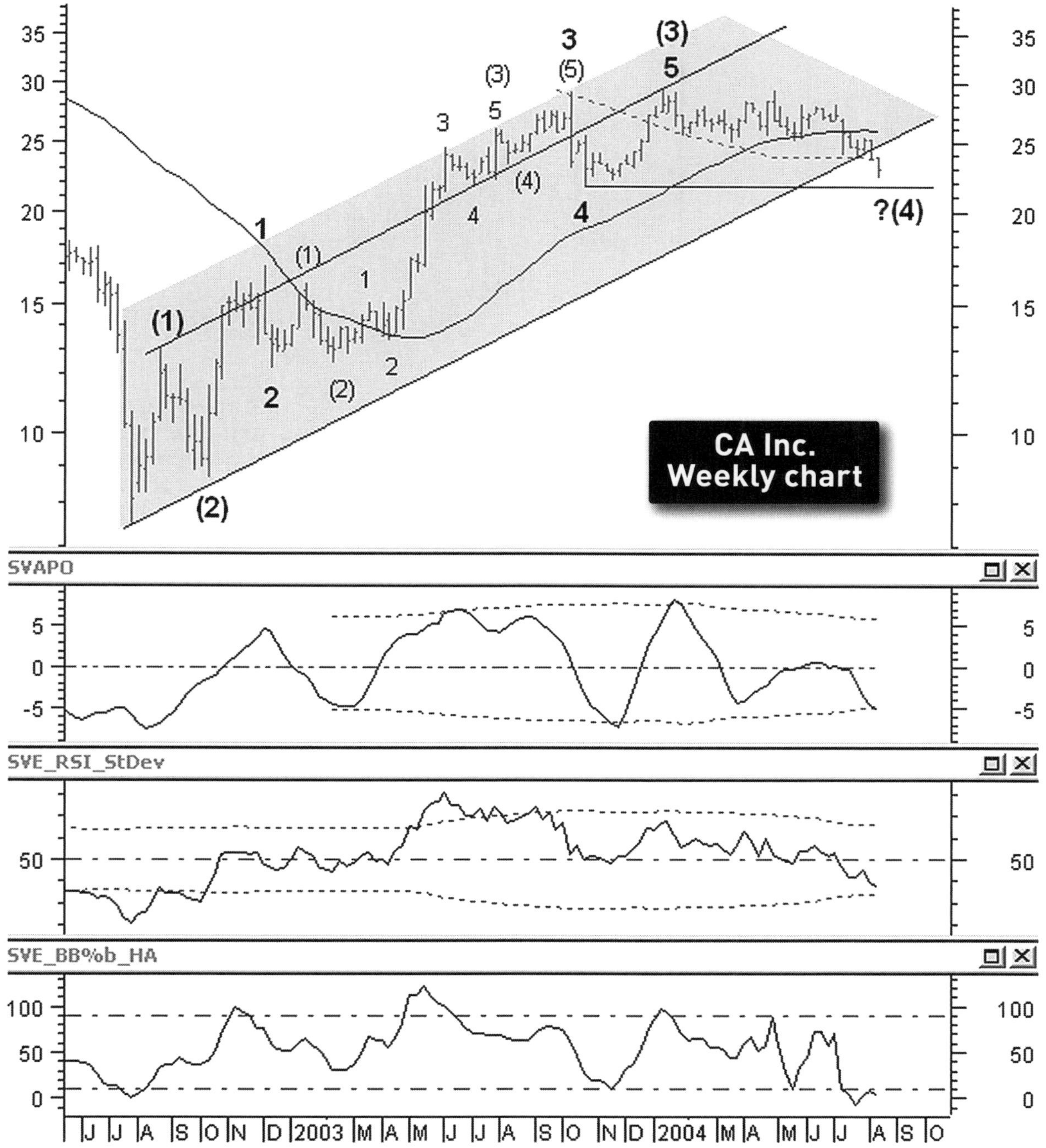

Source - MetaStock® charts courtesy of Equis International.

Figure 7.5: Projecting the long-term price target on the weekly chart of CA Inc.

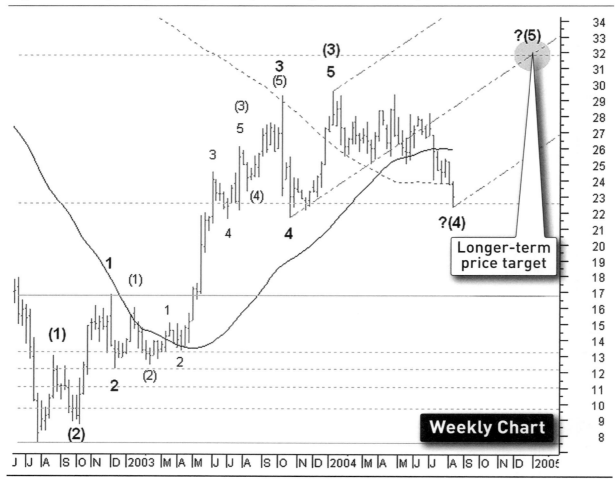

A rising pitchfork, in line with the rising prices and the average, would cross the second Fibonacci target at $32. This is the closest target for the medium term to be reached in about 20 weeks.

But, be careful! This projection is only valid if we really have reached the turning point that starts impulse wave (5). Considering the solid support here, there is a good chance we are at the turning point. Do we have a confirmation on the daily chart?

Figure 7.6: Analyzing the daily candlestick chart of CA Inc.

Source - MetaStock® charts courtesy of Equis International.

CA Inc. Daily Chart

Finally, let's look at the daily candlestick chart for the last few months.

In figure 7.6, correction wave (4) consists of an ABC correction. The C correction itself has a lower order wave with another (A)(B)(C) correction, of which the (C) correction finally is an impulse wave.

We can see a number of signs indicating a possible end of this correction.

The price is reaching a second Fibonacci target at $22.40, drawn from the top of the B-wave and the first correction in the down-move. Also, the first Fibonacci target at $25 was touched exactly by intermediate wave (A).

A falling pitchfork between B and (A) and 2 gives a medium-term, down-moving channel. The price reaches the median line of this pitchfork again in the neighborhood of the second Fibonacci projection target.

The price now also touches the median line of a short-term, down-moving pitchfork drawn between the wave points 2, 3, and 4, and this happens exactly on the second Fibonacci target.

The price is moving far away from its 50- and 200-day simple moving averages. A move toward these averages is expected.

The last two candles make up a bullish harami pattern: a candlestick bottom reversal pattern.

Let's also have a look at the indicators on the daily chart of figure 7.7.

Figure 7.7: Interpreting the indicators on the daily chart of CA Inc.

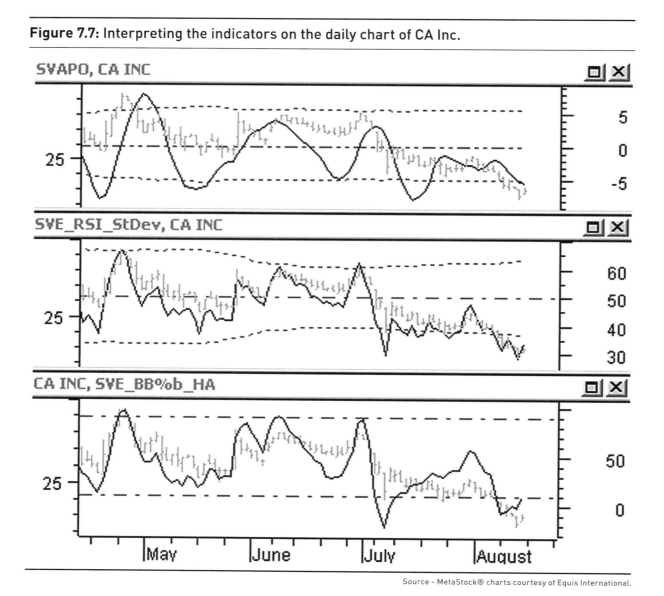

Source - MetaStock® charts courtesy of Equis International.

If this is going to be the turning point, we will see a divergence in the SVA-PO indicator next.

The RSI indicator is below the lower standard deviation line in the oversold territory.

And the BB%b indicator already has a divergence with the price and is moving up from below the 10-reference line.

Clearly, a turning point cannot be far away!

> This is the second step in LOCKIT: Make use of the complete arsenal of LOCKIT technical analysis tools to decide if opening a position is the right thing to do.

LOCKIT

STEP 3: CLOSING A POSITION

Step 3, closing a position, will be discussed after steps 4, 5, and 6.

STEP 4: MONEY AND RISK MANAGEMENT

Money Management

To comply with LOCKIT money management, we will invest in a fixed number of stocks. Each stock will get starting capital that is equal to the total capital divided by the fixed number of stocks. There is no profit or loss sharing between the stocks. My testing showed this to be the most effective system with the best results in the long run. We will go over this in more detail in chapter 10.

With a starting capital of $25,000 and a selection of 20 stocks, each stock will get $1,250 from the start. Losing 10% in one stock and one trade will be limited to $125, or just 1% of the total portfolio value. Furthermore, the total loss of one stock can never be more than $1,250, or 5% of the total portfolio value. This kind of money management makes the trading system crash resistant.

In PART V, you will find all the details about money and risk management as applied by LOCKIT.

Risk Management

Risk management means looking for an initial stop and a price target that gives you a good risk-to-reward ratio. The initial risk should be as low as possible, but it must have solid technical grounds.

Figure 7.8: Price targets and risk/reward ratio on the daily chart of CA Inc.

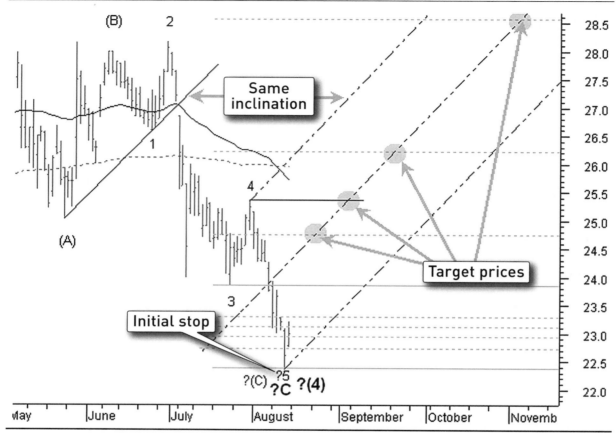

Source - MetaStock® charts courtesy of Equis International.

Remember the reversal candlestick pattern in figure 7.6? We will take the low side of this pattern as the initial stop level. A closing price below this level is a selling signal. In this case, it means buying at $23 with a stop at $22.35, or a very low risk of only 3%.

In figure 7.8 you can see how, for the moment, we can only create a Fibonacci price target using a historical Fibonacci projection. If we calculate from the actual low point to the previous low point, the bottom of wave 3, it will give us three possible targets.

An important target is the first price resistance at the top of wave 4 at $25.35. At this level, we also expect resistance from the 50- and 200-day moving averages. Our initial stop and this target give us a good risk-to-reward ratio and justify opening a long position now.

To have an idea of when this target could be reached, we need this target crossing with some other line. There is, however, nothing we could use as a reference for the moment. We could try to create a fictitious pitchfork. To find an acceptable inclination for this pitchfork, we could use the previous uptrend line between (A) and 1 as a reference.

Buying at $23 we comply with good money and risk management. On 08/13/2004, we buy $1,250/$23 = 54 shares of CA Inc. The possible loss is $0.65 per share, and the first price target is $2.35 higher. This gives us a minimum risk-to-reward ratio in our favor better than 3. This is exactly the type of trade we like to find in LOCKIT.

STEP 5: INITIAL STOP

We always set an initial stop right from the start.

The most important and most difficult decision is closing the position if the initial stop gets broken by the closing price. Here, it means the closing price should not fall below $22.35. Making the decision to sell on the break of the initial stop is not dependent on whether you are involved with long- or short-term investing. There must be no doubt, no discussion, no "yes but," or any other excuses. If the closing price breaks your initial stop, you MUST sell!

STEP 6: TRAILING STOP

Equally important (in relation to holding on to as much profit as possible) is closing the position when the price falls through the trailing stop. Technical analysis has given you selling signals before; but, if you misinterpret them, you will need a trailing stop to take care of closing the position before you lose all of the profit. So, if price falls through the trailing stop, you MUST close the position. The trailing stop used is not only dependent on the investment period (short, medium, or long term), but is also related to the volatility of the stock.

To get an idea of the fixed stop percentage to apply for a certain stock in a certain period, you can use the following trailing stop MetaStock® formula:

```
{SVE_Stop_Trail%}
perc:=Input("Trailing Loss % :",0,100,14);
loss:=C*perc/100;
trail:=
If(C>PREV AND Ref(C,-1)>PREV,
Max(PREV,C-loss),
```

If(C<PREV AND Ref(C,-1)<PREV,

Min(PREV,C+loss),

If(C>PREV,C-loss,C+loss)));

Trail

 Please utilize the disc in the back of the book for instant access to these codes. You may also download them from www.traderslibrary.com/tlecorner.

Figure 7.9: More short-term reversals with a small 3% trailing stop on Intel Corp.

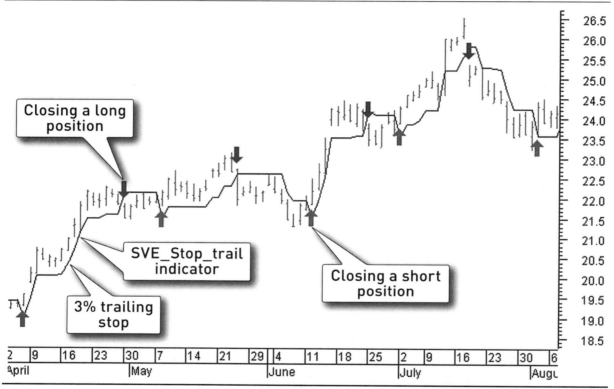

Source - MetaStock® charts courtesy of Equis International.

Short-term Trailing Stop

If you do not use extremely volatile stocks and you invest over the short term, then the trailing stop will be in the order of 3% to 5%, using daily charts. It is best to apply a trailing stop on a previous period to get a visual idea of what could be the best trailing stop for your particular stock. For that you can use the previous formula, SVE_Stop_Trail%.

Figure 7.10: Less short-term reversals with a 5% trailing stop on Intel Corp.

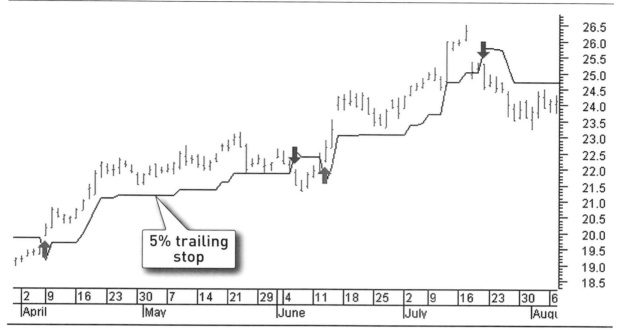

Source - MetaStock® charts courtesy of Equis International.

With a 3% trailing stop, you have (in figure 7.9) four selling points for Intel Corp. looking at long positions.

During the same period, you can see in figure 7.10 only two selling points using a 5% trailing stop.

Medium-term Trailing Stop

A 7% to 11% trailing stop will be adequate for the medium term, using daily charts. The best thing is to apply a trailing stop on a previous period to get a visual idea for what could be the best trailing stop for this stock in this particular moment in time. For this, again, you can use the formula SVE_Stop_Trail%.

With an 8% trailing stop, you can see in figure 7.11 just one selling point for a long position in Intel Corp., looking at the same period as before.

Long-term Trailing Stop

A long-term trailing stop will have to be in the order of 11% to 15%. It is best to switch to a weekly chart when looking at the longer term.

Figure 7.11: An 8% medium-term trailing stop on Intel Corp.

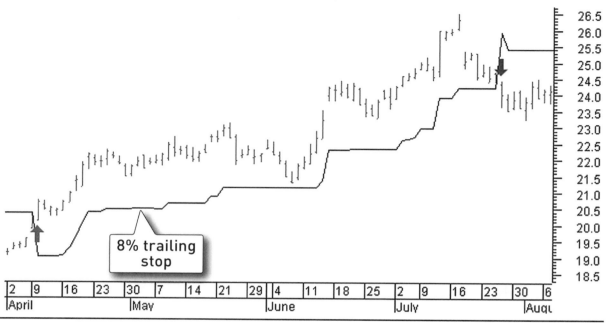

8% trailing stop

Source - MetaStock® charts courtesy of Equis International.

Figure 7.12: A long-term 12% trailing stop on the weekly chart of Intel Corp.

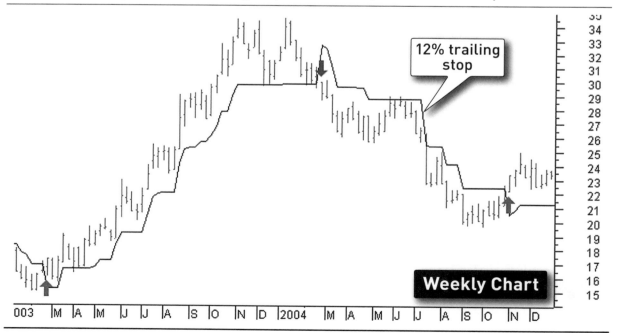

12% trailing stop

Weekly Chart

Source - MetaStock® charts courtesy of Equis International.

Figure 7.13: Buying point and short-term follow-up of CA Inc. with a 5% trailing stop

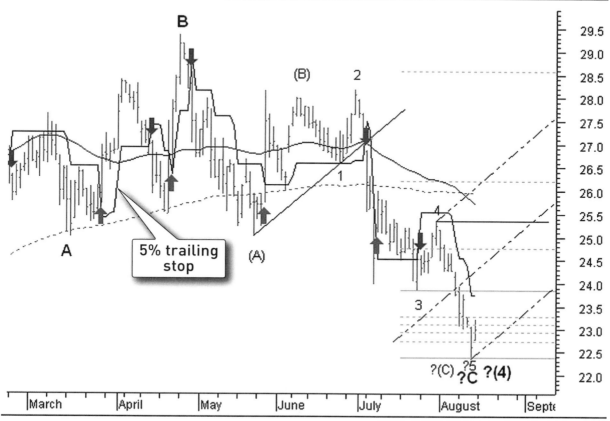

Source - MetaStock® charts courtesy of Equis International.

In figure 7.12, note that with a 12% trailing stop in Intel Corp., there were two closing buys for short positions and one closing sell for a long position in the period 2003–2004.

STEP 3: CLOSING THE TRADE

Long Position CA Inc. Short-term Follow-up

Looking for short-term trading with CA Inc., you can see in figure 7.13 that a 5% trailing stop seems to follow the short-term price movement best.

We buy CA Inc. on 08/13/2004 for $23. The initial stop is set at $22.35. We keep a short-term trailing stop at 5%.

The important short-term price targets to keep in mind: $25.40, which was a previous top, and resistance from the 50- and 200-day simple moving averages. The next target is at $28.50, the third Fibonacci projection in the neighborhood of a total of four previous tops with previous wave tops (B) and 2.

Figure 7.14: A lot of resistance in the daily chart, time to close CA Inc.

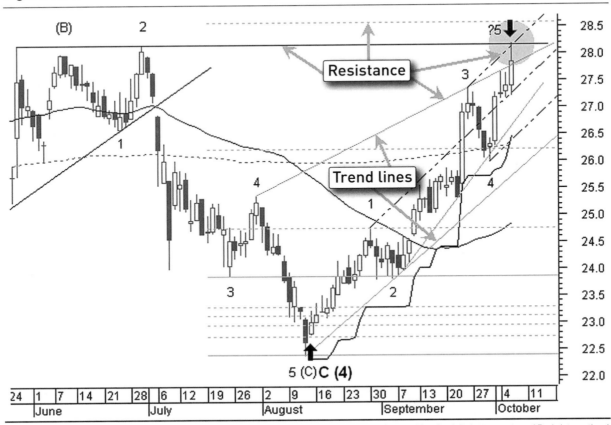

Source - MetaStock® charts courtesy of Equis International.

On 10/06/2004, are we ready to sell now? After opening the position, the price moves straight up to the first Fibonacci target at $24.75.

In figure 7.14 we see a short-term correction at the end of August. If we do a Fibonacci projection from this new pivot point, we get exactly the same targets as before, proving that historical Fibonacci projections do work.

After this short-term correction, the price continued its move up to the second Fibonacci target. During this time, the 50- and 200-day moving averages were broken. The original uptrend line from the start of wave 1 and the bottom of wave 2 can, from now on, be drawn more sharply.

Next, there was a short correction back to the Fibonacci level, which is now support. At the sharper uptrend line, there was enough support to turn price back up again.

On 10/6/2004 – What Happens?

Price reaches a new high value at a level where a lot of resistance is found:

- We are exactly at the resistance of the line through (B) and 2;

- We are close to the third Fibonacci price target;

- We reach the upper side of a short-term, sharp up-moving pitchfork;

- We reach the resistance of an inverse trend line; and

- We essentially are completing an Elliott impulse wave count. Most likely, we are looking at the end of wave 5.

If there were good arguments to close our position on the way up, this seems to be the right moment. During the way up, there was no problem with the initial stop or the trailing stop.

We will always try to close the position based on good technical arguments and not wait for the trailing stop to be broken. If, however, the trailing stop is broken and we have not yet closed the position, the position MUST be closed!

Of course, before closing, we also have a look at our indicators in figure 7.15.

We can see a divergence with a second lower top in SVAPO, the RSI indicator is topping and is likely to diverge, and there is divergence with lower tops in SVE_BB%b_HA.

Conclusion: The indicators are in agreement that a top will be reached.

We sell our 54 shares of CA Inc. at a closing price of $27.85, for a total amount of $1,503.9, minus the buying cost of $1,242, which yields a profit of $261.9 or 21%.

The new available capital for buying this stock the next time is $1,250 + $261.9=$1,511.9. Remember; there is no profit or loss sharing with other stocks in portfolio.

Figure 7.15: CA Inc. diverging indicators give a selling agreement

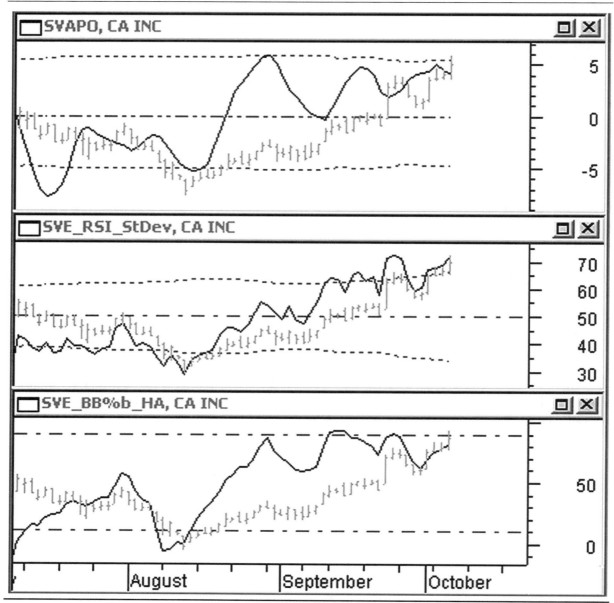

10/18/2004: Opening a New Long Position?

Have a look at figure 7.16 to see if we should consider buying again. What are the arguments for opening a new long position?

Figure 7.16: A new entry point in CA Inc. after a short-term correction

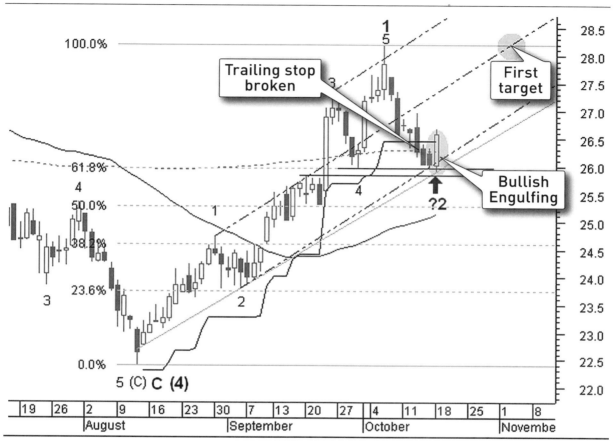

- The price has retraced back to the 61.8% Fibonacci retracement level, probably ending correction wave 2 of a medium-term uptrend impulse wave.

- There is support from the previous turning point of wave 4.

- A fraction lower, there is support of a previous doji candle top.

- Price reaches the lower side of the up-moving pitchfork channel.

- Price has fallen back between the 200- and 50-day moving averages, which are very close together.

- Price has exactly fallen back to the upward trend line.

- The last two candles in the chart are a bullish engulfing reversal pattern.

Figure 7.17: Indicators confirm continuation of previous uptrend

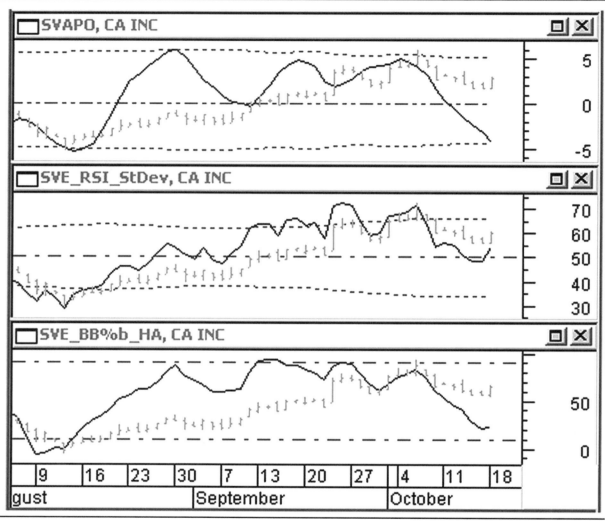

These are a lot of good technical reasons to buy this stock now!

OK, but what about the risk-to-reward ratio?

The short-term price target is the previous top at $28.20. With the long-term projection we did on 08/13/2004, we had a long-term target of $32. We can put an initial stop at the bullish engulfing pattern or just below at the trend line support at $25.80, and buy now at a closing price of $26.58. The possible loss will be limited to $0.78, and the first price target is $2.40 away. This is a good risk-to-reward ratio to open the position.

Looking at the indicators in figure 7.17, we notice that SVAPO is very close to the lower standard deviation line, RSI is turning above the 50 level, and SVE_BB%b_HA is moving close to the lower side.

If we just had a temporary reaction in the uptrend, a reversal in the indicators is possible; it is normal that there are no divergences. If there were divergences, they would most likely be hidden, indicating a previous trend continuation.

This looks like a buy with a high chance for a profitable trade. You could profit from this and increase the buying power with 50% for this specific trade. The effect of increasing the buying power will be visible on the longer-term only. We will keep our normal buying power in our example.

Based on these positive arguments, we are buying 56 CA Inc. shares at a closing price of $26.58, for a total amount of $1,488.50. We keep an initial stop at $25.80 and continue to use a trailing stop at 5%.

12/07/2004: Time to Close the Position?

The price is moving up with almost no reactions within the up-moving pitchfork channel.

Look at figure 7.18 on the following page. On 12/07/2004, there seems to be a good chance for a price reaction.

- The price has reached a Fibonacci target level;

- The price has reached the estimated long-term target at $32;

- The price is moving up against the upper side of the pitchfork channel;

- The wave 3 up-move has been made with three consecutive sharper uptrend lines. The last sharpest trend line is now broken; and

- The last three candlesticks come close to what could be an evening doji star reversal pattern.

These provide more than enough reasons to believe that a reaction is coming and that it is best to take a profit now.

Figure 7.18: Price reaction expected after up move, time to close CA Inc. position

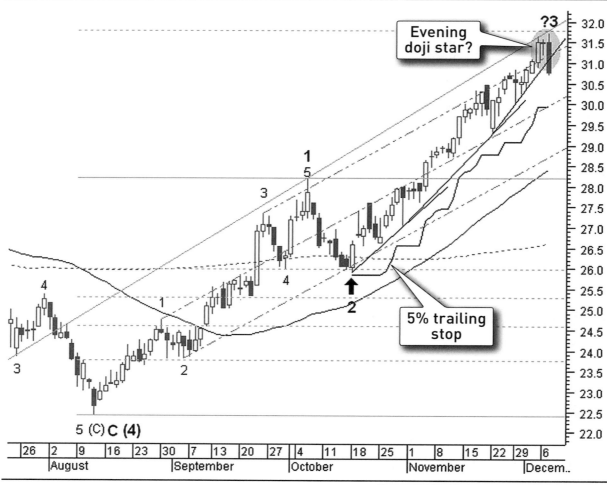

Source - MetaStock® charts courtesy of Equis International.

Looking once more at the indicators in figure 7.19, we see that SVAPO recently turned down from above the standard deviation level, but is moving up again. If, however, it turns down again, it will create a divergence. The RSI has turned already and is showing a divergence and SVE_BB%b_HA has a number of divergences too.

Chances are big that we have reached a top!

We sell the 56 shares of CA Inc. at a closing price of $30.75. The profit is $30.75-$26.58=$4.17, or a total of $4.17*56=$233.52—more than 15%.

Figure 7.19: Topping indicators with divergences confirm possible top in price

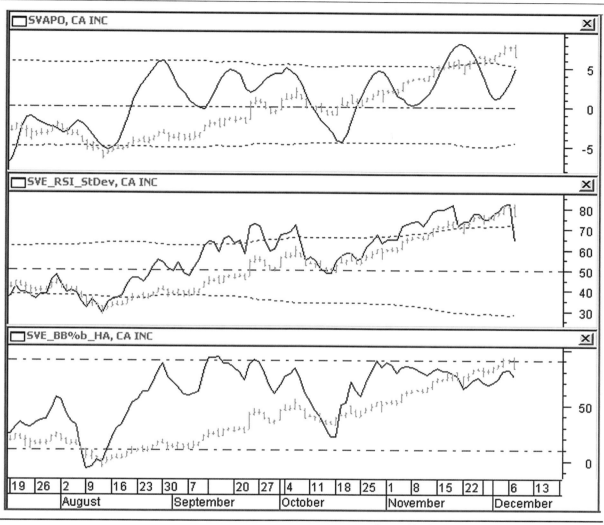

Source - MetaStock® charts courtesy of Equis International.

The total available capital for the following trade in this stock is now $1,511.9 + $233.52= $1,745, for a profit of $495 on the starting capital of $1,250 in less than four months.

> Using the LOCKIT system for trading, based on a thorough knowledge of the basic technical analysis techniques, gives you a good chance for making more profit in the stock market.

LOCKIT

LOCKIT RULES FOR OPENING AND CLOSING POSITIONS

I've compiled an overview of the LOCKIT rules for opening and closing long or short positions. Please read through these carefully and continue to use these examples as a reference.

LOCKIT Trend Reversal Rules for Opening a Long Position

A trend reversal will be more certain when more rules are giving a signal. We will use the following reference letters to indicate which rules are complied with where on the example charts.

General Rules – Opening a Long Position

F. Price reverses with a higher bottom in a downtrend.

G. Price reaches support. This support is given by the 100- or 200-day simple moving average, a support line, or the lower side of a trend channel or pitchfork.

H. Price breaks through the last steepest downtrend line.

I. There is a rising breakout or continuation window.

J. Price reaches a Fibonacci target level or retracement level.

K. Price moves in a trend and is far below the 50-day simple moving average.

L. A clear complete Elliott wave count is visible.

M. The zero-lagging TEMA average on closing prices (ZLTMACL) crosses above the zero-lagging TEMA average on re-calculated OHLC heikin ashi prices (ZLTMAHA).

N. The indicators (SVAPO, RSI, and SVE_BB%b) are in the oversold area, preferably having divergences with price. If you are keeping hourly, daily, and weekly charts, you can find the ideal entry time when buying signals are becoming apparent in all time frames.

O. A price-reversal pattern is visible in the price chart.

P. A candlestick pattern confirms the reversal. The next candle confirms the new uptrend direction with at least a closing price in that direction.

Q. AVOID trading while in a trend move and when the indicators keep moving close around their median value.

An Example

As an example, let's look at figure 7.20, the medium-term chart of AMR Corp.

G. The price reaches a solid support level at the bottom of a sub-wave 4 (January 2006) of the previous uptrend; a window before that (December 2005) is still not closed.

J. The price reaches a 50% retracement level over the complete move up from September 2005 until May 2006. The level of 50% is a common retracement, providing good support.

K. The price is far below the simple moving averages. An upward move to the 50-day average is expected.

Figure 7.20: LOCKIT trend reversal rules for opening a long position

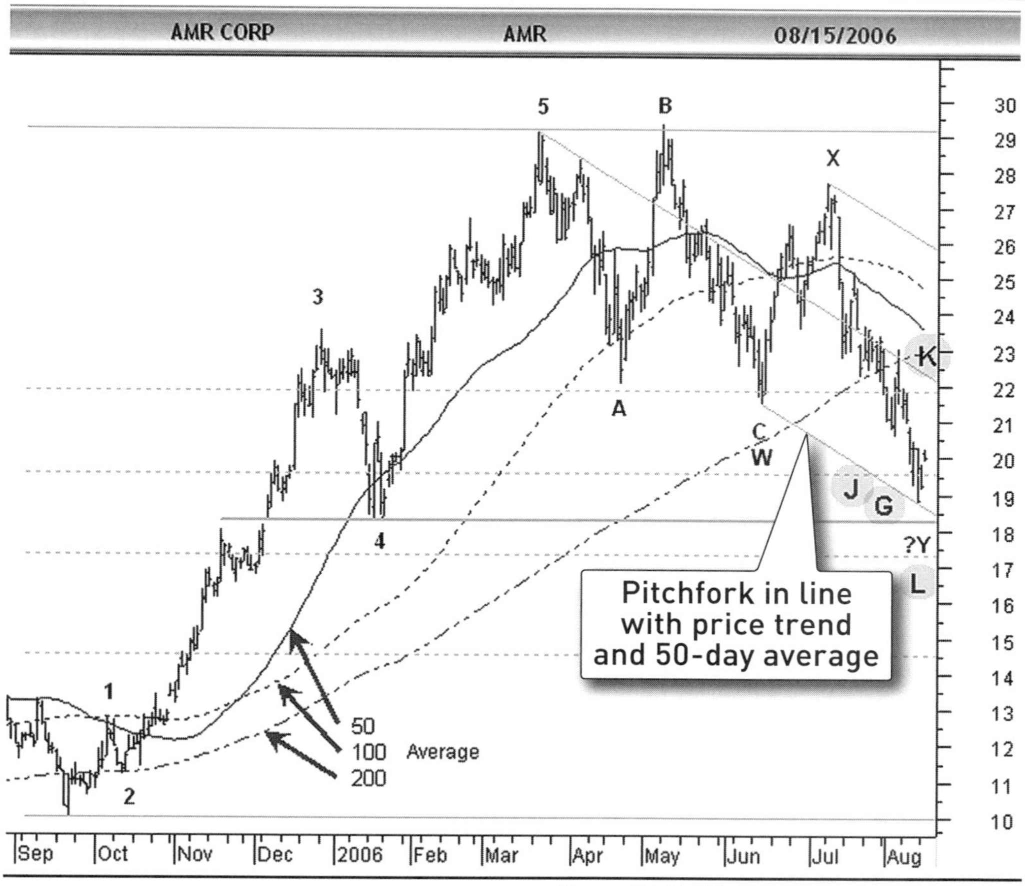

Source - MetaStock® charts courtesy of Equis International.

L. After the impulse move up from September 2005 until March 2006, we are likely to finish the correction wave with a double zigzag. If this is the turning point, we have now completed wave Y.

Next with figure 7.21, let's look at the shorter term with a candle chart and our indicators.

G. The price turns at the lower side of the pitchfork. This pitchfork is nicely in line with the slope of the 50-day moving average.

H. The price breaks the third downtrend line with the sharpest inclination.

I. There is a window between the last and the previous candle; this could be a breakaway window.

Figure 7.21: More LOCKIT trend reversal rules on a short-term candlestick chart

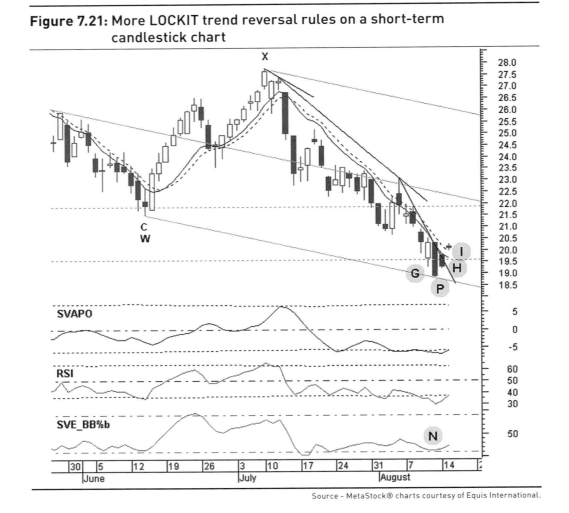

Source - MetaStock® charts courtesy of Equis International.

Figure 7.22: LOCKIT trend reversal rules applied for buying AMR Corp.

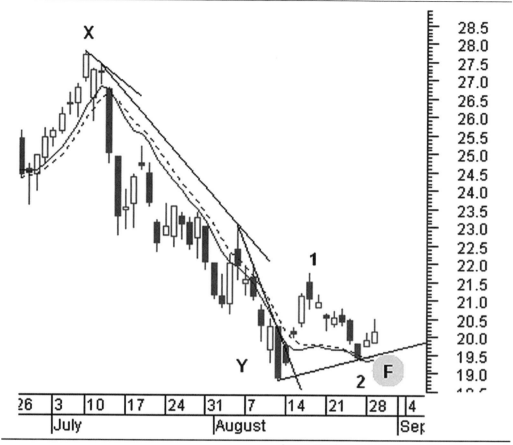

Source - MetaStock® charts courtesy of Equis International.

N. All indicators are in the oversold territory; however, two out of the three indicators are not showing divergence with price, which could be an indication that this is still not the ideal moment to open a trade.

P. There is a bullish harami reversal pattern, followed by a candle with a window and a higher closing price.

These are more than enough reasons to open a long position. This is especially true because we have a good risk-to-reward ratio if we buy at $20.04 and keep an initial stop at the low of the bullish harami pattern, at $18.78.

This gives us an initial stop with a possible loss limited to 6%.

F: In figure 7.22, notice the possible start of an Elliott impulse wave 3 a couple of weeks later. We now have a higher bottom in price, which is an important trend reversal signal for the medium-term trend.

Figure 7.23: AMR Corp. price targets

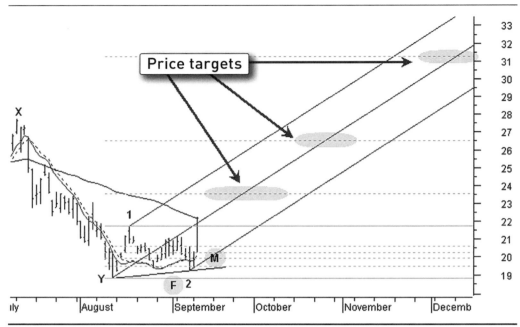

Source - MetaStock® charts courtesy of Equis International.

Next, the correction wave 2 in figure 7.23 makes a flat zigzag ABC correction, bringing the price still a fraction lower. We can now draw a pitchfork between the turning points of waves 1 and 2 and the start (Y) of wave 1, giving direction to the future price movement.

A Fibonacci projection over wave 1 gives us some future price targets. The crossings of these targets with the median and outer lines of the pitchfork give us some idea of when these targets could be reached.

> **M:** The zero-lagging TEMA average based on the closing price (ZLT-MACL) crosses the zero-lagging TEMA average based on re-calculated OHLC heikin ashi prices (ZLTMAHA). This is another confirmation that the uptrend has started.

LOCKIT Long Position Trend Reversal Closing Rules

The more rules that are followed, the more trustworthy the selling signal will be. We will continue to use the AMR Corp. example charts and the reference letters of the rules to indicate where each one falls on the chart.

General Rules – Closing a Long Position

F. After opening a position, the price keeps moving flat while indicators move in the expected direction. There is serious doubt about the expected price up-move, and it's possible that the price will turn down after the flat move.

G. Price breaks the initial stop.

H. The price breaks through the last steeper uptrend line, or a support line, while the price is moving flat.

I. The price reaches a Fibonacci target level.

J. A clear complete Elliott wave count is visible.

K. A candlestick pattern confirms the top reversal. The next candle is preferably a candle confirming the new downtrend direction with at least a closing price in that direction.

L. The price reaches the upper side of a pitchfork or trend channel.

M. The indicators (SVAPO, RSI, and SVE_BB%b) are in the overbought area, preferably having divergences with price. If you are keeping hourly, daily, and weekly charts, you can find the ideal selling time when selling signals become apparent in all time zones.

N. The price moves in a trend and is more than average above the 50-day simple moving average.

O. The zero-lagging TEMA average on closing prices (ZLTMACL) crosses below the zero-lagging TEMA average on re-calculated OHLC heikin ashi prices (ZLTMAHA).

P. The chart shows a price reversal pattern.

Q. The price breaks the trailing stop.

If you get a selling signal and it's obvious that it is a temporary reaction coming to an end, you could close half of the open position. If it turns out to be a temporary reaction, you will still make a profit with the other half.

Figure 7.24: LOCKIT trend reversal closing rules selling AMR Corp.

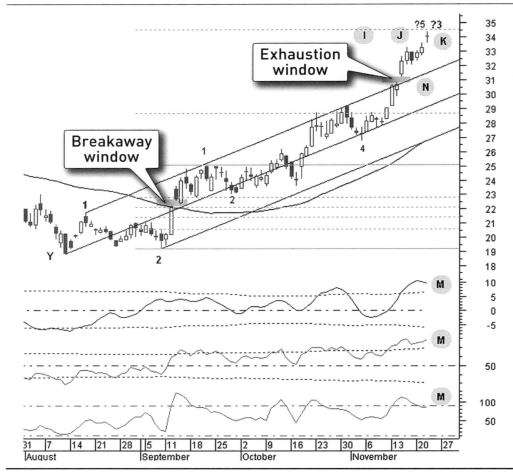

Source - MetaStock® charts courtesy of Equis International.

If, on the other hand, it's really a turning point, then there is more room for closing the trade because losses are only half of what they would have been with the original quantity.

Note how in figure 7.24 the prices stay nicely within the up pitchfork: Halfway through November, price breaks above the pitchfork channel. A Fibonacci projection that started from intermediate wave 1 of extension wave 3 is reached.

I: The price reaches a Fibonacci target level.

J: There is a good chance that we have reached the top of wave 3; there is an intermediate impulse wave 1 to 5.

K: The doji in the candle chart is probably the first indication for a reversal. There is a chance that we will get an evening doji star as a reversal pattern.

M: All indicators are turning down from the overbought level; there is no divergence visible. This is an indication that the price will continue the move up after correction wave 4.

N: The price is moving far away from the 50-day simple moving average.

At the start of wave 3 we saw a breakaway window. Then, we got an exhaustion window, which is a good indication that, at least, this moment in time, we are at a top level.

The most sensible action is to take profit. If the next wave is really a wave 4, we will try to enter a new position at the start of wave 5.

Next, we will list the LOCKIT rules for opening and closing a short position after a trend reversal.

LOCKIT Trend Reversal Rules for Opening a Short Position

F.   The price reverses with a lower top in an uptrend.

G.   The price reaches resistance. This resistance is given by the 100- or 200-day simple moving average, a resistance line, or the upper side of a trend channel or pitchfork.

H.   The price falls through the last steeper uptrend line.

I.   There is a falling breakout or continuation window.

J.   The price reaches a Fibonacci target level or retracement level.

K.   The price moves in a trend and is far away from the 50-day simple moving average.

L.   A clear, complete Elliott wave count is visible.

M.   The zero-lagging TEMA average on closing prices (ZLTMACL) is downward crossing the zero-lagging TEMA average on re-calculated OHLC heikin ashi prices (ZLTMAHA).

N.   The indicators (SVAPO, RSI, and SVE_BB%b) are in the overbought area, preferably diverging with price. If you are keeping hourly, daily, and weekly charts, you can find the ideal entry point when sell signals become apparent in all time zones.

O. There is a chart pattern reversal in the price chart.

P. A candlestick pattern confirms the reversal. The next candle is preferably a candle confirming the new downtrend direction with at least a closing price in that direction.

Q. **AVOID** trading when, while in a trend move, the indicators keep moving close around their median value.

LOCKIT Short Position Trend Reversal Closing Rules

F. After opening a position, the price keeps moving flat, while indicators move in the expected direction. There is serious doubt about the expected price down-move, and it's possible that the price will turn the other way around after this flat move.

G. Price breaks the initial stop.

H. The price breaks through the last steeper falling trend line, or a resistance line, while the price is moving flat.

I. The price reaches a Fibonacci target level or retracement level.

J. A clear complete Elliott wave count is visible.

K. A candlestick pattern confirms the reversal. The next candle is preferably a candle confirming the new uptrend with at least a closing price in that direction.

L. The price is reaching the lower side of a pitchfork or trend channel.

M. The indicators (SVAPO, RSI, and SVE_BB%b) are in the oversold area, preferably diverging with price. If you are keeping hourly, daily, and weekly charts, you can find the ideal buy-back time when closing buy signals become apparent in all time zones.

N. The price moves in a trend and is far below the 50-day simple moving average.

O. The zero-lagging TEMA average on closing prices (ZLTMACL) crosses above the zero-lagging TEMA average on re-calculated OHLC heikin ashi prices (ZLTMAHA).

P. The chart shows a price reversal pattern.

Q. Price breaks the trailing stop.

LOCKIT Trend Correction Rules for Opening a Long Position

The buying signal will be more trustworthy if more rules are applied. We will continue to use the AMR Corp. charts for indicating the rules (with the use of reference letters) that are followed on the charts.

General Rules

F. The price reaches support. This support is the 50-, 100-, or 200-day simple moving average, a support line, or the lower side of a trend channel or pitchfork.

G. The price reaches the end of an Elliott impulse wave 2 or 4, or wave A of a correction wave.

H. The price breaks through the last steeper downtrend line.

I. There is a breakout with a rising (continuation) window.

J. The price reaches a Fibonacci retracement level.

K. There is a continuation chart pattern in the price chart.

L. The indicators (SVAPO, RSI, and SVE_BB%b) are close to the over-sold range, but are still around median levels. If you are keeping hourly, daily, and weekly charts, you can find the ideal entry time when buying signals become apparent in the smaller time zones.

M. Trade in the direction of the medium to longer-term trend.

N. A candlestick pattern confirms the reversal. The next candle is preferably a candle confirming the new uptrend direction with at least a closing price in that direction.

O. The zero-lagging TEMA average on closing prices (ZLTMACL) crosses above the zero-lagging TEMA average on re-calculated OHLC heikin ashi prices (ZLTMAHA).

Figure 7.25: LOCKIT trend correction rules applied for buying AMR Corp.

Source - MetaStock® charts courtesy of Equis International.

As you can see in figure 7.25, the correction in AMR Corp. is an Elliott ABC zigzag pattern.

We now arrive at the point where everything seems to indicate a continuation of the previous uptrend.

F: The price finds support at the 50-day simple moving average, and the price turns up from the lower side of the pitchfork channel.

G: An ABC zigzag correction is complete; it is likely that we reached the end of wave 4.

H: The last descending trend line is broken to the upper side.

J: We closely reach a 61.8% Fibonacci retracement level, which is sufficient for a wave 4 move.

L: There is enough room for an up-move by the indicators.

N: In the candle chart, we have a bullish engulfing reversal pattern, followed by a hammer with a higher closing price.

With a stop at the low side of the bullish engulfing pattern, we have a good risk-to-reward ratio.

There is no doubt that we must open a new long position here.

LOCKIT Long Position Trend Correction Closing Rules

The selling signal is more reliable when more rules are applicable. As before, we are using the AMR Corp. charts to illustrate where the rules (reference letters) are followed.

General Rules

F. After opening a position, the price keeps moving flat, while indicators move in the expected direction. There is serious doubt about the expected price up-move, and it's possible that the price will turn the other way around after the flat move.

G. Price breaks the initial stop.

H. The price breaks through the last steeper trend line or a support line while price starts moving flat.

I. The price reaches a Fibonacci target level.

J. A clear complete Elliott impulse wave count is visible.

K. A candlestick pattern confirms the top reversal. The next candle is preferably a candle confirming the new downtrend direction with at least a closing price in that direction.

L. The price reaches the upper side of the last pitchfork or trend channel.

M. The indicators (SVAPO, RSI, and SVE_BB%b) are in the overbought area, preferably diverging with price. If you are keeping hourly, daily, and weekly charts, you can find the ideal selling time when selling signals become apparent in all time zones.

N. The price moves in a trend and is far above the 50-day simple moving average.

Figure 7.26: LOCKIT trend correction closing rules selling AMR Corp.

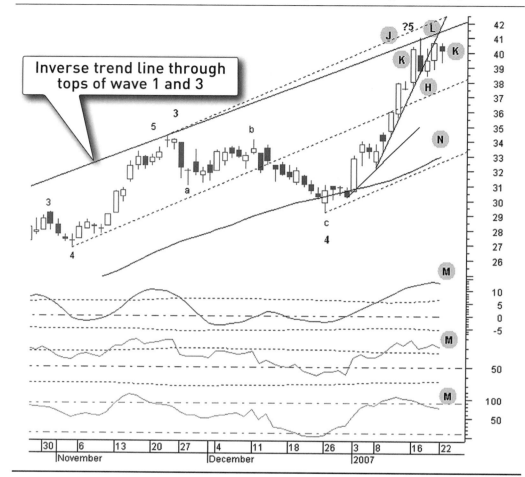

Source - MetaStock® charts courtesy of Equis International.

O. The zero-lagging TEMA average on closing prices (ZLTMACL) crosses below the zero-lagging TEMA average on re-calculated OHLC heikin ashi prices (ZLTMAHA).

P. The chart shows a price reversal pattern.

Q. Price breaks the trailing stop.

Closing the Position

Look at figure 7.26 to see how the price moves up in a short period of time with high acceleration. Looking for selling signals? There are clearly a number of them. Is it time to close this position? Let's investigate.

H: The last ascending trend line is broken to the lower side.

J: We reached a top for Elliott impulse wave 5.

K: We have two consecutive bearish harami patterns in the candlestick chart.

L: The price reaches the upper side of the last pitchfork. The price also reaches an inverse trend line drawn over the tops of waves 1 and 3, possibly the upper side of a longer-term up-channel.

M: Indicators are turning down in the overbought area. There are divergences visible with the RSI and SVE_BB%b indicators.

N: The price has moved far away from the 50-day simple moving average.

These are enough good reasons to take profit and to close the position now!

Looking at figure 7.27, you must agree it was a good decision!

Finally, we list the rules for opening and closing a short position after a trend correction.

Figure 7.27: Further price evolution confirms LOCKIT decision

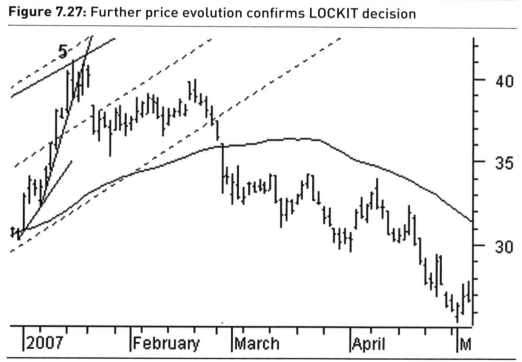

LOCKIT Trend Correction Rules for Opening a Short Position

F. The price reaches resistance. This resistance is the 50-, 100-, or 200-day simple moving average, a resistance line, or the upper side of a trend channel or pitchfork.

G. The price breaks through the last steeper uptrend line.

H. The price reaches a Fibonacci target or retracement level.

I. There is a falling (continuation) window.

J. A clear complete Elliott wave count is visible.

K. The zero-lagging TEMA average on closing prices (ZLTMACL) is downward crossing the zero-lagging TEMA average on re-calculated OHLC heikin ashi prices (ZLTMAHA).

L. The indicators (SVAPO, RSI, and SVE_BB%b) are in the overbought area, preferably diverging with price. If you are keeping hourly, daily, and weekly charts, you can find the ideal entry point when sell signals become apparent in all time zones.

M. There is a chart reversal pattern in the price chart

N. A candlestick pattern confirms the reversal. The next candle is preferably a candle confirming the new downtrend direction with at least a closing price in that direction.

LOCKIT Short Position Trend Correction Closing Rules

F. After opening a position, the price keeps moving flat, while indicators move in the expected direction. There is serious doubt about the expected price down-move, and it's possible that the price will turn the other way around after this flat move.

G. Breaking the initial stop.

H. The price breaks through the last steeper falling trend line, or a resistance line, if the price is moving flat.

I. The price reaches a Fibonacci target level or retracement level.

J. A clear, complete Elliott wave count is visible.

K. A candlestick pattern confirms the reversal. The next candle is preferably a candle confirming the new uptrend but at least a closing price in that direction

L. The price reaches the lower side of the last pitchfork or trend channel.

M. The indicators (SVAPO, RSI, and SVE_BB%b) are in the oversold area, preferably diverging with price. If you are keeping hourly, daily, and weekly charts, you can find the ideal buy-back time when closing signals become apparent in all time zones.

N. The price moves in a trend and is far below the 50-day simple moving average.

O. The zero-lagging TEMA average on closing prices (ZLTMACL) crosses above the zero-lagging TEMA average on re-calculated OHLC heikin ashi prices (ZLTMAHA).

P. The chart shows a price-reversal pattern.

Q. The price breaks the trailing stop.

 For a closer look at the charts in this chapter, go to www.traderslibrary.com/TLEcorner.

TEST YOUR CHAPTER 7 KNOWLEDGE

1. LOCKIT is a short name that stands for?

L _____

_____

_____

O _____

_____

_____

C _____

_____

_____

K _____

_____

_____

I _____

_____

_____

T _____

_____

_____

2. Why are we looking at the long-term market trend?

_____

_____

_____

3. To open a trade we use?

_____

_____

_____

4. To close a trade we use?

_____

_____

_____

5. How do we apply good money management with LOCKIT?

_____

_____

_____

6. How do we limit risk with LOCKIT?

_____

_____

_____

7. The initial stop setting is based on?

_____

_____

_____

8. Why do we use a trailing stop with LOCKIT?

_____

_____

_____

Q&A — **For answers, please visit the Traders' Library Education Corner at www.traderslibrary.com/tlecorner.**

Chapter
8

LOCKIT Application Results

I n this chapter, we will examine an example of how the LOCKIT rules from the previous chapter work with real charts. We will review a couple of different scenarios, applying the LOCKIT rules and discovering how they impact our trading. In this chapter, we're going to move fast so that you can see the overall effectiveness of LOCKIT; however, this means we won't be stopping to discuss every technique. If you are confused at any point, please refer back to the previous chapters. There you will have explanations of all the technical tools used.

LOCKIT APPLICATION EXAMPLE: CMS ENERGY CORP.

Opening a Long Position

On, 03/31/2006 we are looking at buying CMS Energy Corp. stock. We already know from the S&P 500 Index that the long-term trend is up; therefore, we want to buy CMS Energy Corp.

Figure 8.1: Monthly chart CMS Energy Corp in a long-term uptrend

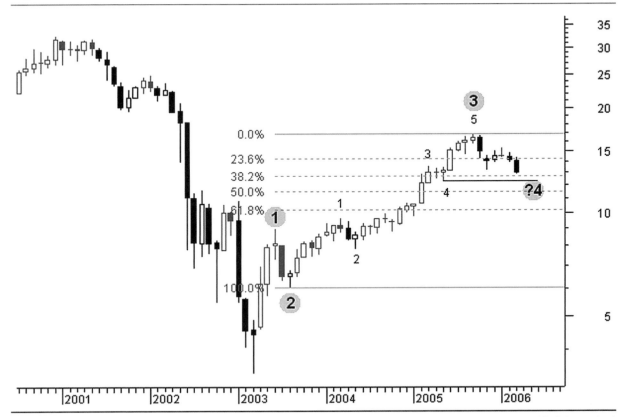

Source - MetaStock® charts courtesy of Equis International.

A monthly chart of CMS (figure 8.1) shows a long-term uptrend since 2003, but there is a reaction phase. Introducing an Elliott wave count shows a consolidation phase for wave 4. We have an impulse wave up with waves 1, 2, and 3. Wave 3 has an extension with intermediate waves 1 to 5.

Looking at theoretical values, we know that wave 4 usually retraces 23.6% up to 38.2% of wave 3; this often is the level of intermediate wave 4.

This would mean that we are close to a price reversal; however, don't forget that we are looking at a monthly chart, so it still may take some time!

Figure 8.2: CMS weekly chart confirms possible end of reaction phase

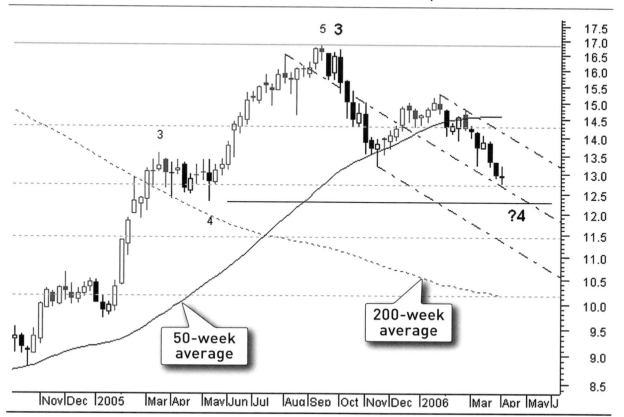

Source - MetaStock® charts courtesy of Equis International.

Weekly Chart

The weekly chart in figure 8.2 confirms that we must be close to the end of correction wave 4. The price is moving below the 50-week simple average but above the 200-week simple moving average, which is still moving down, although less steep.

A pitchfork (dashed line) touching the price at different levels offers a good idea of the price's directional move; however, the price has not yet touched the median line. We expect a move farther down to penetrate the median line.

Figure 8.3: CMS 1 week later, price now touching the pitchfork median line

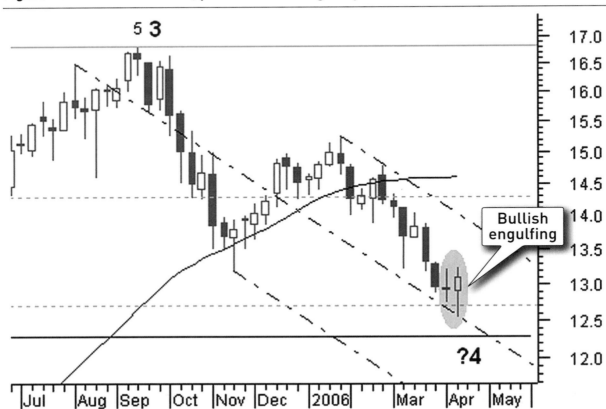

Source - MetaStock® charts courtesy of Equis International.

04/13/2006: One Week Later

In figure 8.3, the low price is now touching the median line of the pitchfork. We have a bullish engulfing signal in the candlestick chart, and we are at a greater distance from the 50-week average. A retrace to this average is probably the first step in creating an Elliott impulse wave 5.

Figure 8.4: CMS, SVAPO oscillator standard settings

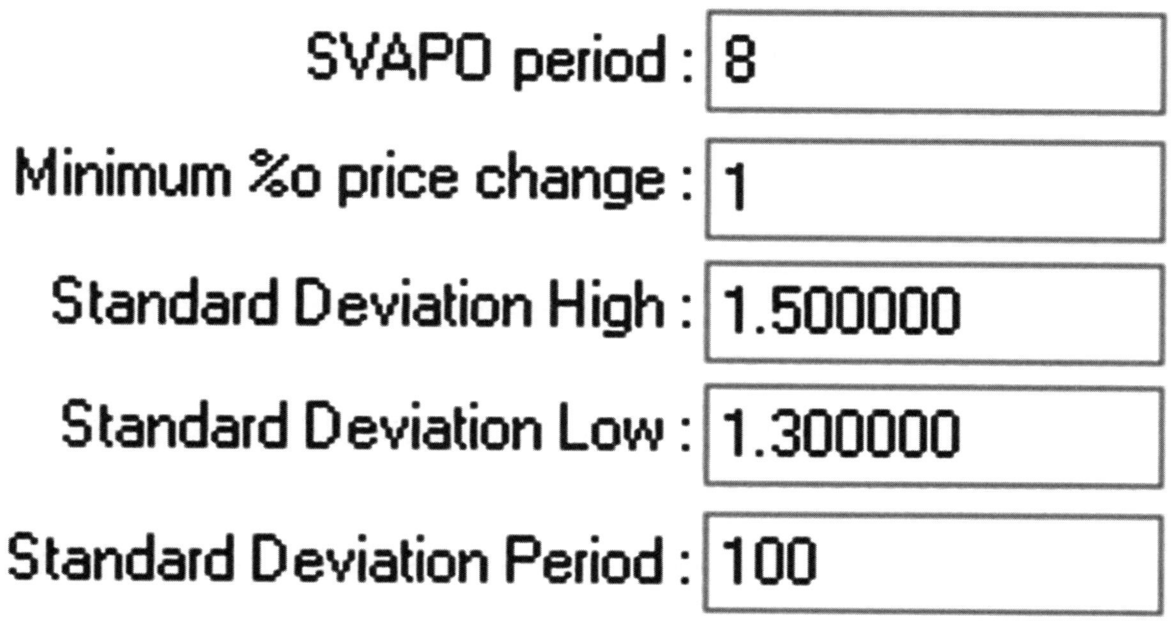

$$SVAPO\ period: \boxed{8}$$

$$Minimum\ \%o\ price\ change: \boxed{1}$$

$$Standard\ Deviation\ High: \boxed{1.500000}$$

$$Standard\ Deviation\ Low: \boxed{1.300000}$$

$$Standard\ Deviation\ Period: \boxed{100}$$

Source - MetaStock® charts courtesy of Equis International.

The Indicators on the Weekly Chart

Let's see if our indicators confirm the end of wave 4 on the weekly chart. To get this confirmation, we use three indicators.

- The SVAPO oscillator with standard settings, as shown in figure 8.4

- The RSI indicator with a 14-week SVE_RSI_StDev and deviations at 1.5 over a 100-day period.

- The Bollinger %b oscillator SVE_BB%b_HA over an 18-week period with reference levels at 10 and 90.

Figure 8.5: CMS weekly indicators

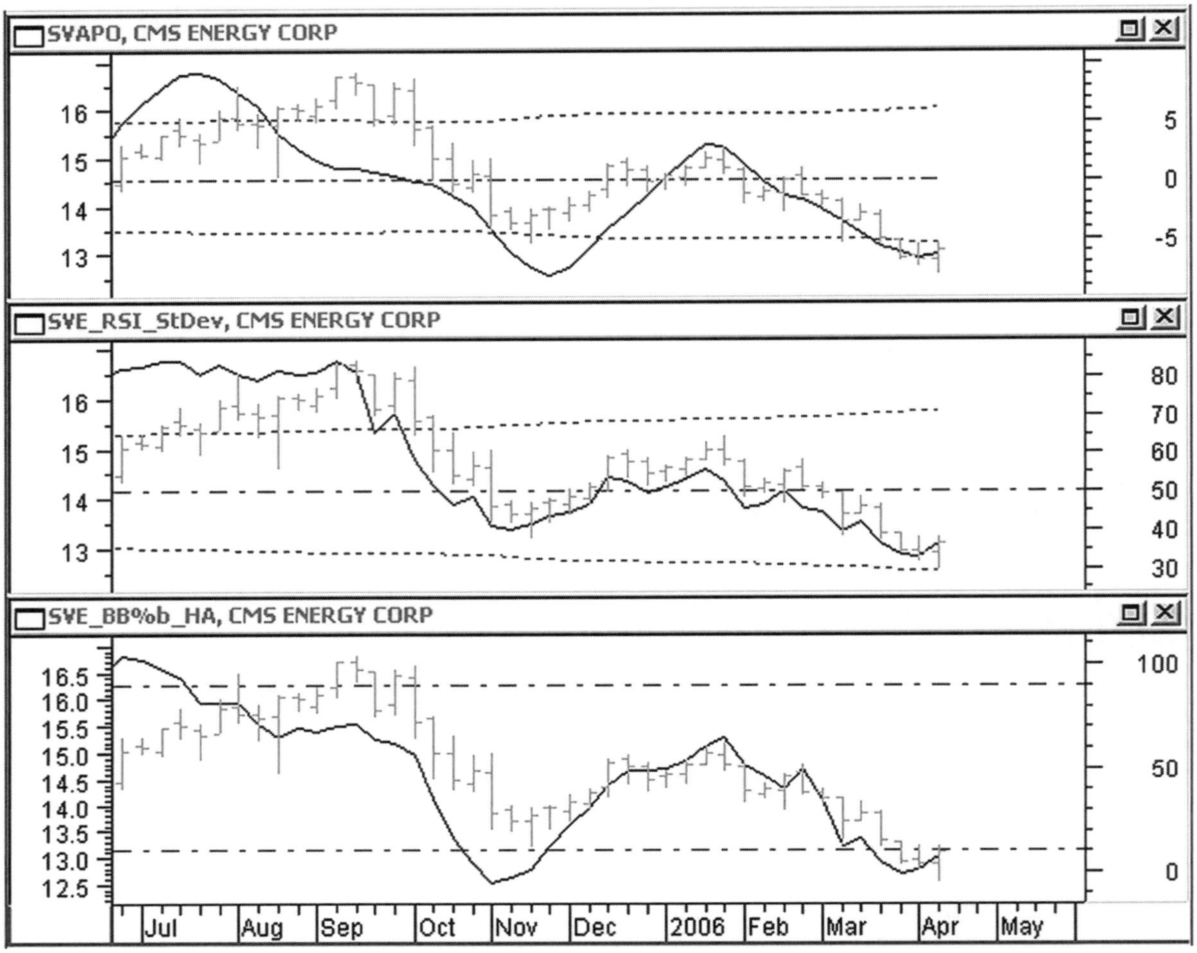

Note in figure 8.5 that SVAPO is turning from below the lower standard deviation, the oversold area, and is making a divergence with the price, showing lower bottoms in price with higher bottoms in SVAPO.

The RSI is turning up from below, close to the 30-level.

The Bollinger %b oscillator is turning up from below the 10-level, and diverging with the price.

So it seems that the indicators also are showing the start of a medium-term up-move.

Figure 8.6: CMS daily chart, detail of wave 4

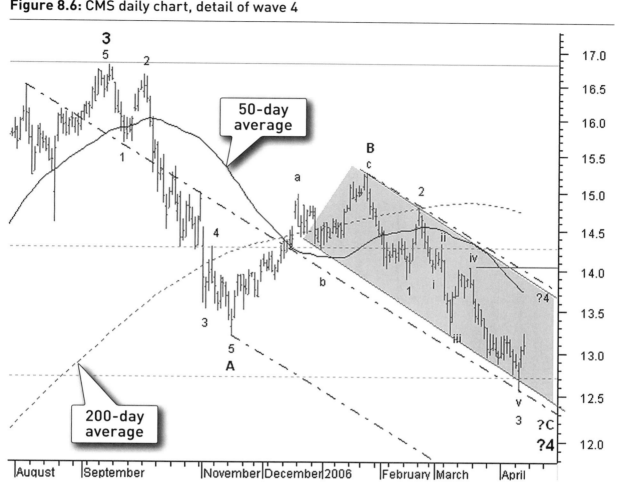

Source - MetaStock® charts courtesy of Equis International.

Daily Chart

In the daily chart, we can analyze in more detail the development of the wave 4. In a large correction wave, waves A and C are basically impulse waves, and wave B is a correction wave.

An impulse wave of the same order generally moves within the same trend channel; figure 8.6 shows that this is clearly the case. Looking at the wave count, it seems that now we have a sub-wave 4 within wave C. In other words, we are still expecting impulse wave 5 to move down, which should bring the price below $12.55.

Wave C is not only moving within the same channel, but it also is moving within the upper side of a downward pitchfork with the exact same slope. We

Figure 8.7: CMS daily, down wave 5 complete, opening the trade

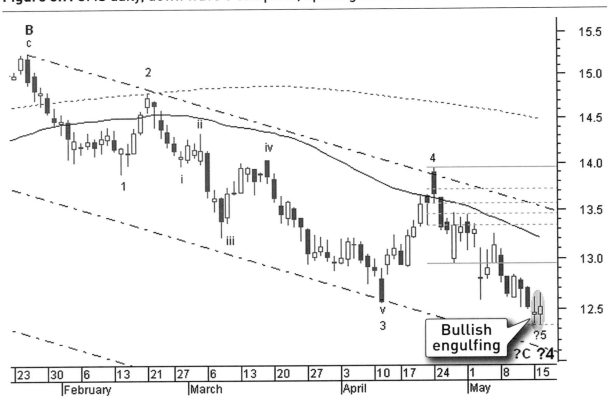

Source - MetaStock® charts courtesy of Equis International.

expect the up-move of wave 4 to find resistance at the upper side of this pitch-fork, against the 50-day simple moving average and close to a resistance at $14. This seems to be a good scenario to end wave 4 and to start wave 5 down.

The weekly chart shows a possible start of a medium-term up-move. But buying now would not give a good risk-to-reward ratio. If, however, we are wrong about not buying now, we can still buy when the price breaks the resistance just mentioned. We will follow up on the daily chart's price evolution. We expect a short-term up-move, followed by a continuation of the down-trend to make a new low.

Open Buy

In figure 8.7, we see that wave 4 completed by touching the upper side of the trend channel and the upper side of the pitchfork. Wave 5 started down and made a lower bottom than wave 3; wave 5 has become a fact.

On 05/15/2006, the price reaches a short-term Fibonacci target, and the candlestick chart has a bullish engulfing reversal pattern. Is this the end of waves 5, C, and longer-term wave 4? If so, we are looking at a bright future. We now are starting the up-move for wave 5, which must bring us, at minimum, above wave 3, or above $16.80.

After the "*L*" and "*O*" of *LO*CKIT, and still before we decide to buy, we must take into account the "*K*" of LOC*K*IT and have a look at the risk-to-reward ratio. We also must, of course, take into account good money management, and divide our investment capital among 20 fixed stocks.

> **Remember our acronym: LOCKIT's L stands for long-term trend; O means opening a position; and K is the K-ratio—let's make sure our trade is a high-probability one!**

LOCKIT

With the low of the bullish engulfing pattern, together with the longer-term support of the line through sub-wave 4 of impulse wave 3, we have a solid and close initial stop. If we are wrong, the loss will be limited, which gives us a very good risk-to-reward ratio.

Buying at $12.52 with support at $12.33, we can put in a very small initial stop: the "*I*" of LOCK*I*T. This initial closing price stop is only 1.6%. Taking into account a rather low volatility of this stock in the recent past, we also can keep a relatively low trailing stop of 5% (the "*T*" of LOCKI*T*).

With a starting capital of $25,000 divided among 20 stocks, we have the starting capital for one stock equal to $1,250. We buy [1250/12.52] or 99 shares of CMS Energy Corp.

Possible Targets

On 07/03/2006, as shown in figure 8.8 on the next page, closing prices remain above the initial and trailing stop. The price now breaks the resistance of the top of wave 1. We have an Elliott impulse wave 1 and the correction wave 2. Wave 3 seems to be started with extension waves 1 and 2, and with extension wave 3 on the way.

A pitchfork between points 1 and 2 and the bottom of the big wave 4 gives an up-move that is too sharp. If, however, we use a previous bottom a few days before, we get a much more acceptable slope that is more in line with the present price trend.

Drawing a trend line from bottom C through the bottom of wave 2, we expect the impulse wave to move within a channel. To create this channel, we draw a parallel line through a previous intermediate bottom (3). The slope

Figure 8.8: CMS daily, up wave 3 started; projection for medium-term targets

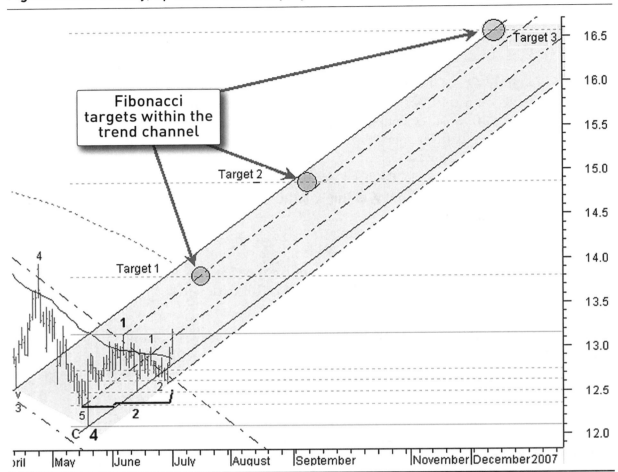

Source - MetaStock® charts courtesy of Equis International.

and the width of this channel is acceptable and, apparently, completely in line with the pitchfork.

Possible price targets are given by a Fibonacci price projection from bottom C and top 1.

Target_1 at $13.80 looks quite logical, with the crossing of the first Fibonacci target and with the upper side of the pitchfork and the 200-day simple moving average giving resistance at that same level. This would be a sharp move up, but is somewhat expected after the longer period of the flat consolidation.

Target_2 at $14.85 gives a moderate price acceleration and will probably reach the upper side of the trend channel. This is possibly the end of wave 3, so there is enough room for wave 4 to fall back to the lower side of the channel.

Target_3 at $16.60 could be anywhere in the channel at that level. We rather expect the price to move a bit higher to finish the longer-term wave 5 above the previous top of the long-term wave 3, meaning above $16.80.

Up to 10/31/2006, price levels and time periods follow our estimates quite well.

Following the Wave Count

Looking at figure 8.9, we are now at a critical point in our Elliott wave count. We cannot exclude the fact that wave 5 is complete and that a bigger reaction will follow. But we have not yet reached the longer-term wave 5 top, which means that there is still a big chance for a continuation of the up-move.

Additionally, there also is the possibility that the current wave 5 has an extension and that we now are seeing correction wave 2 of this extension. In that

---

Figure 8.9: CMS daily, a critical point

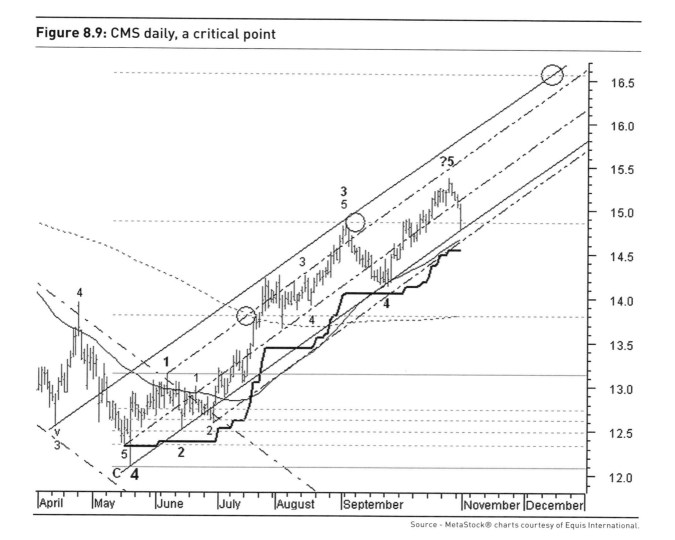

Figure 8.10: CMS daily, we have a wave 5 extension and now the trailing stop is broken

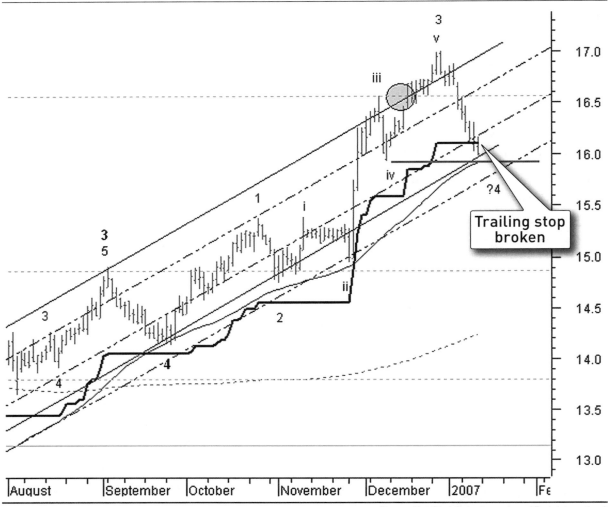

Source - MetaStock® charts courtesy of Equis International.

case, the correction probably will be limited to the lower side of the trend channel. There is additional support from the lower side of the pitchfork and from the 50-day simple moving average. And, all of this support is close to the 5% trailing stop.

Because we are close to the stop level, it will certainly be worthwhile to believe in an extension of wave 5. If we keep to the rules, we will sell if the closing price breaks the trailing stop level.

On 01/12/2007, we have, without a doubt, a wave 5 extension.

In figure 8.10, correction wave 2 remained above our trailing stop level. The price went through the third Fibonacci target and made a higher top than the previous long-term wave 3 top. We now may be at the long-term wave 5 top. If this is the case, our intermediate Elliott count does not fit because our count here is at a wave 4 correction. So we expect wave 5 above the top of intermediate wave 3, or above $17.

But wave 4 is now breaking the trailing stop. Shall we close or wait one more day?

Well, there is solid support from the 50-day simple moving average, from the lower side of the trend channel, and the pitchfork, and from a support line of a previous low.

Furthermore, figure 8.11 shows that all indicators are in the oversold area. SVAPO and SVE_Bb%b_HA are already reversing, providing good reasons to put things on hold; however, we will keep a stop at $15.80, just below the previous price support line or just a fraction below our trailing stop.

Figure 8.11: CMS daily, all indicators are in oversold territory

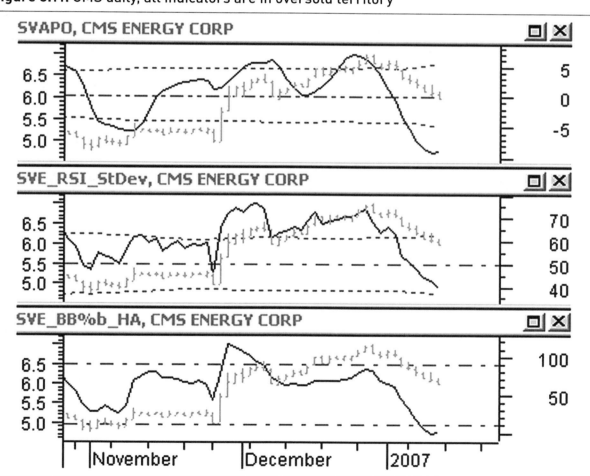

Source - MetaStock® charts courtesy of Equis International.

Figure 8.12: CMS daily, looking for the selling point

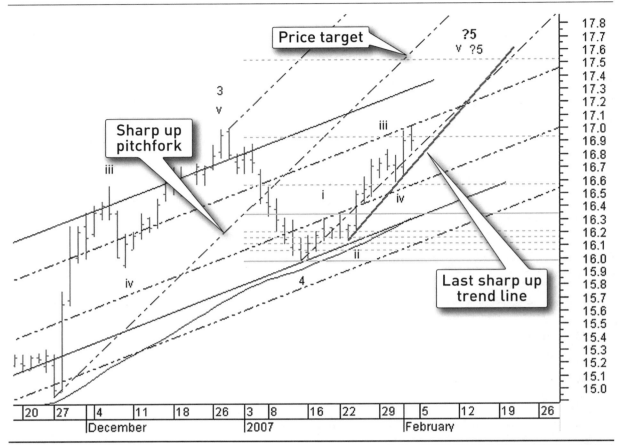

Source - MetaStock® charts courtesy of Equis International.

On 02/02/2007, our temporary stop at $15.80 was obsolete because price reversed immediately, as you can see in figure 8.12.

If the price moves farther up past the previous tops, then all 5 waves will come to an end. It is best to estimate a price target and to close the position at this target, even considering that the last wave "v" could have another extension. Taking profit is a better idea; another extension is an uncertain move.

We have a few choices for closing the position.

- A first choice is reaching the first Fibonacci target at $17.50 from the projection over wave "i."

- A second choice is to close the trade based on reaching the median line of the new sharp up pitchfork, which clearly gives direction to the latest price move.

- A third choice is not really aimed at a price target, but instead gives away as little as possible of the profit from a top turning point. This would mean selling when the last sharp uptrend line is broken.

To avoid having to make a choice, we will trade on the first possibility presented!

Closing our Long Position

Uh oh, look at 02/06/2007. That was really fast!

Look how price reaches the third Fibonacci target and the median line of the pitchfork in figure 8.13.

Figure 8.13: CMS daily, closing the long position

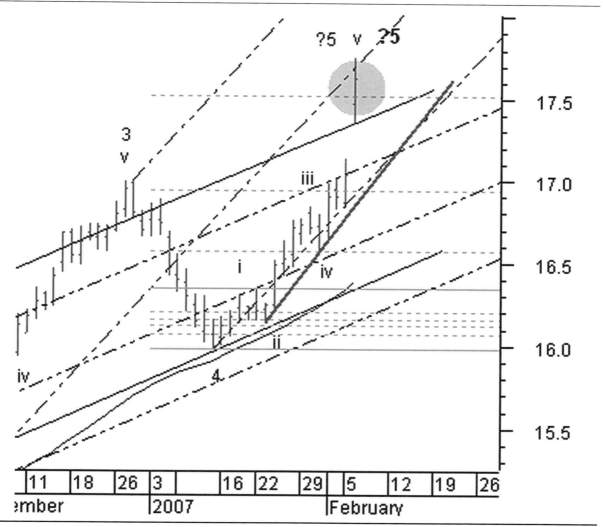

Source - MetaStock® charts courtesy of Equis International.

We sell at a closing price of $17.63, minus the buying price of $12.52, which yields a profit of $5.11 times 99 shares, for a total profit of $505.89.

Now we have a total capital of $1,755.89 for the next trade in this stock.

We made a 40% profit!

Opening a Short Position

The day after closing our position (02/26/2007) there was a big, volatile one-day move.

Figure 8.14: CMS daily, hanging man top reversal, opening new short position

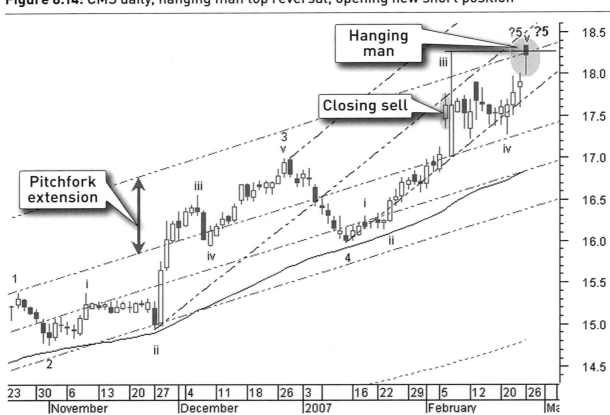

Source - MetaStock® charts courtesy of Equis International.

Next, there was consolidation (figure 8.14), and we now have a hanging man top reversal pattern in the candlestick chart with a new top. We have to adapt our last Elliott wave count.

Is this the long-term impulse wave 5 top?

Figure 8.15: CMS daily, overview indicators starting the new short position

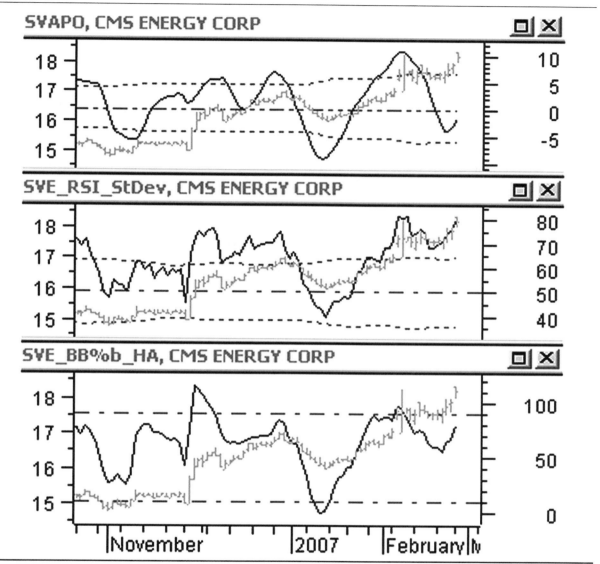

Source - MetaStock® charts courtesy of Equis International.

The indicators in figure 8.15 are not showing divergence, which could indicate that we have not reached a longer-term turning point. If that is the case, we will have to review our entire Elliott wave count.

RSI and BB%b are topping and may make a short-term divergence.

SVAPO appears to be in an uptrend, but it can turn around at the 0–reference level.

Still, a short position now can be profitable, with a reaction back to the older and not that sharp pitchfork channel and back to the 50-day simple moving average (figure 8.14).

Because we can set a very close initial stop at the top of the hanging man candlestick pattern, we can achieve an ideal risk-to-reward ratio. The possible loss is so small that we can, without hesitation, open a short position.

We sell now (opening a short position) at a closing price of $18.21. We do not want to take any more risk in a short position compared to opening a long position. So we will only trade for the same amount as we would for a long position and not use any margin conditions to open a larger short trade. We sell $1,755/$18.21 or 96 shares.

We place an initial stop at $18.40. Losing this trade will cost fewer than $20.

Closing the Short Position and Opening a New Long Position

The day after opening the short position (03/05/2007), the price makes a large, volatile one-day move.

In figure 8.16, you can see how the price fell back to an intermediate uptrend line, the lower side of a down-moving pitchfork, the 50-day simple moving

Figure 8.16: CMS daily, price fallen back to a number of support levels

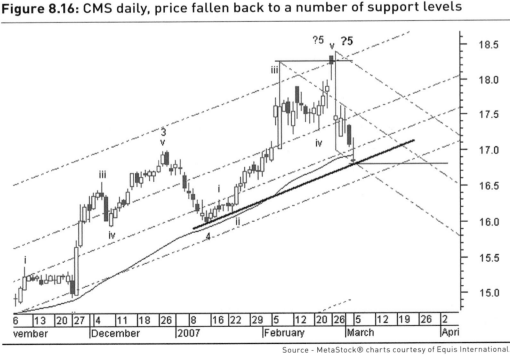

Figure 8.17: CMS daily, indicators have room to turn around, opening a new long position

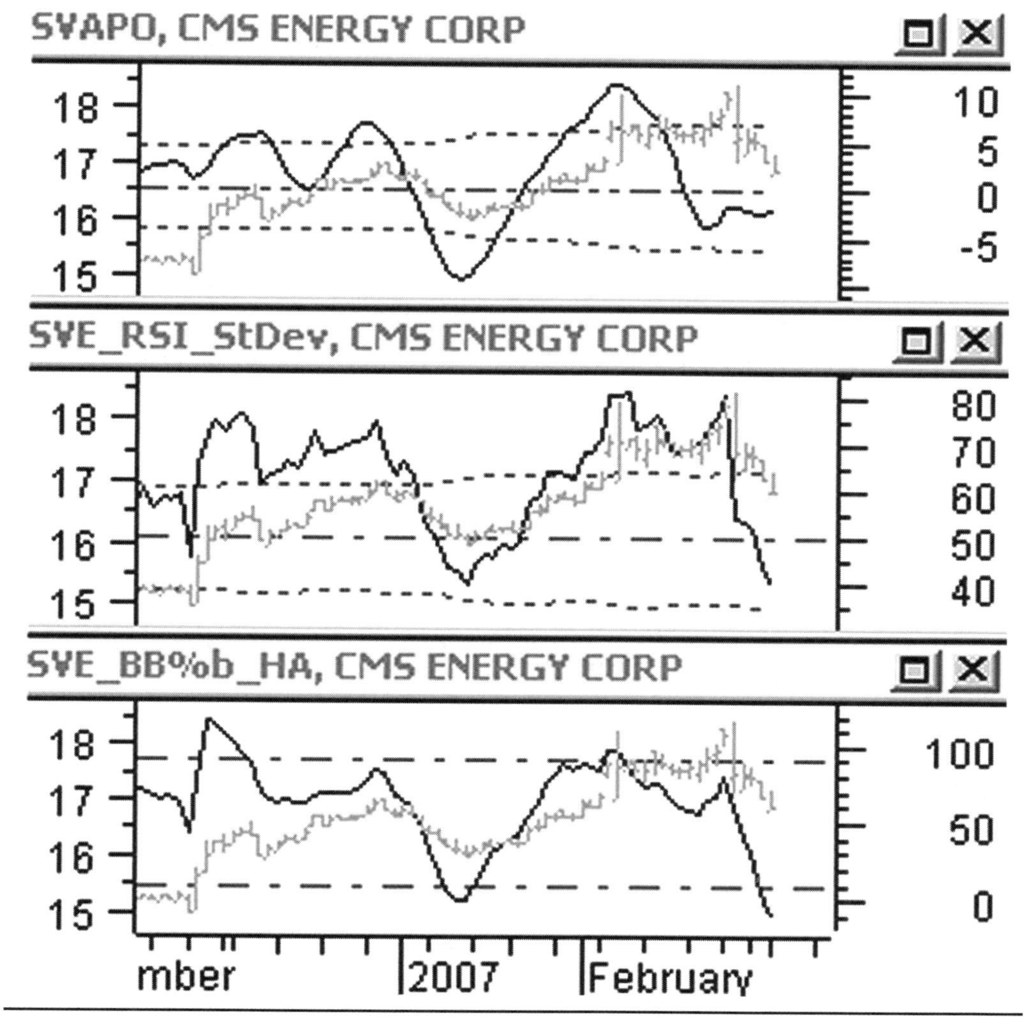

Source - MetaStock® charts courtesy of Equis International.

average, and close to the lower side of the longer-term, up-moving pitchfork. There also were three dojis in the last four days.

These are enough reasons to believe in a short-term reaction and maybe even in the start of a new medium-term up-move on the way to a new top.

In figure 8.17, SVAPO is turning up again, and the RSI and SVE_BB%b have the room for turning up. It still seems early for trading, but to be on the safe side, we take profit and close the short position.

Figure 8.18: CMS daily, initial stop holds, price moving up

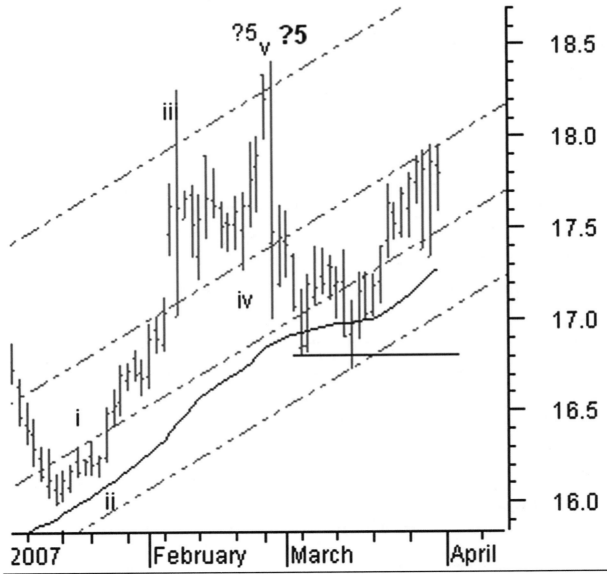

We buy back CMS at $16.86. The profit is $18.21-$16.86=$1.35, for a total of $1.35*96=$129. We have now a capital of $1,755+$129=$1,884 available for the next trade.

There is a lot of support at the actual price level and, with an initial stop at the lower side of the doji, we again have an ideal risk-to-reward ratio. There is no doubt about opening a new long position here. We buy CMS at a closing price of $16.86, or a total of ($1,884/16.86) 111 shares.

Figure 8.19: CMS daily, room in indicators for a farther move up

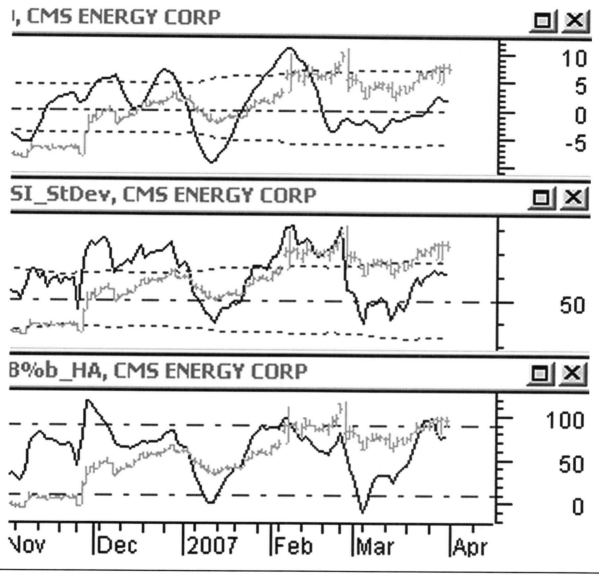

Looking at figure 8.18 (03/30/2007), there was no problem with the initial stop; the price turned around and is now moving up again.

Figure 8.19 also shows that the indicators still have room for a farther up–move.

This means that there is a good chance that we are going for a higher top than the previous one. If this is the case, our long-term Elliott count is not correct.

Figure 8.20: CMS daily, adapted wave count, higher top expected

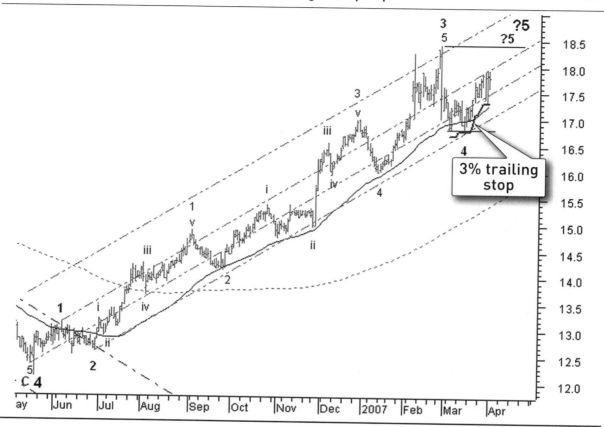

Source - MetaStock® charts courtesy of Equis International.

The new wave count in figure 8.20 assumes a new top above $18.50; this will be our first target price.

Because we do not really believe in a much higher top for the moment and we want to hold on to as much profit as possible, we now set a closer trailing stop at 3%, which looks okay for the short term.

Figure 8.21: CMS daily, multiple price targets reached

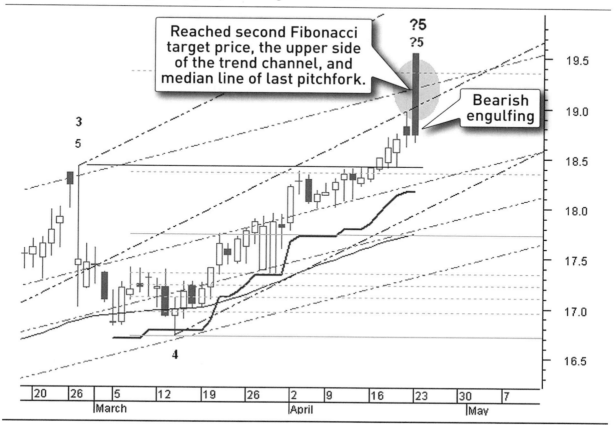

Reached second Fibonacci target price, the upper side of the trend channel, and median line of last pitchfork.

Bearish engulfing

Closing the Long Position

The price up-move continues (04/23/2007), and there is no problem with the small trailing stop.

But wait! In figure 8.21, the price went through the resistance of the previous top and the first Fibonacci target.

We have a big black candle forming a bearish engulfing reversal pattern and we have reached the second Fibonacci target, the upper side of the long-term pitchfork, and the median line of a shorter-term pitchfork.

These are a lot of valid indications pointing to a possible reversal.

Figure 8.22: CMS daily, topping and possible diverging indicators; closing long position

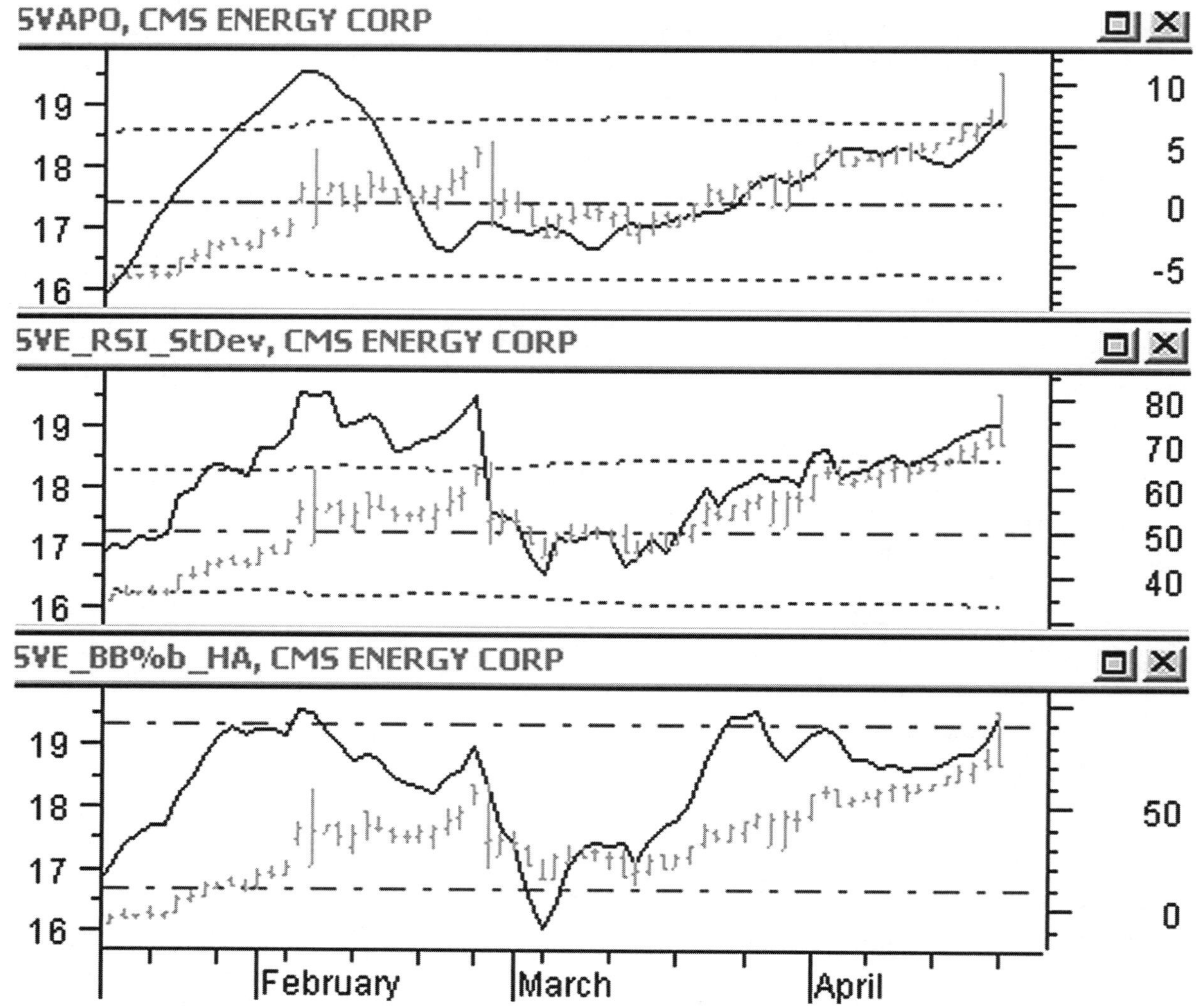

Source - MetaStock® charts courtesy of Equis International.

Figure 8.22 shows that the indicators are topping and that there are signs of a prospective divergence with the price.

Let's recap our LOCKIT trading so far:

- We close the long position and sell the shares at a closing price of $18.73.

- This gives us a profit of $18.73-16.86 = $1.87.

- Total profit is: 111 shares*$1.87=$207.

- The total available capital for this stock is now: $1,884+207 = $2,091, or a gain of 67% on the starting capital.

Is This the Top of Long-term Wave 5?

Let's look at the complete move on a weekly chart in figure 8.23.

We reach a second Fibonacci target based on a projection where the first target also would have been a perfect match. Taking wave 1 as a reference would slightly pass this target.

Because we are using a linear price scale with a rather big move in price, we use logarithmic trend lines. Here you can see clearly how correction waves 2 and 4 are near or touching this uptrend line. The same is valid for the upper trend line for waves 1 and 3.

Figure 8.23: CMS weekly, longer-term wave 5 top reached?

It is quite normal for wave 5 not to reach the upper trend line. Often, the size of wave 5 is 61.8% of the size of wave 3.

Once again, the price reaches the median line of the pitchfork, fitting perfectly well between the logarithmic trend lines.

The price distance to the 50- and 200-day simple moving averages has become large.

Looking at the weekly chart indicators in figure 8.24, we have divergences between the higher top 5 in price and the lower tops in the indicators.

Figure 8.24: CMS weekly, converging and diverging indicators

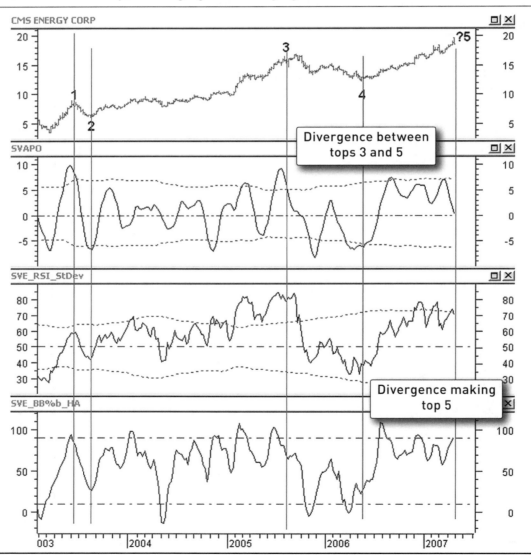

Source - MetaStock® charts courtesy of Equis International.

Top 3 in price was made with converging tops in the indicators, while top 5 in price was made with diverging indicators. It is very likely that we have reached the top of wave 5.

Note how all the indicators normally converge at the start of wave 3, with higher bottoms in price and in the indicators. The start of wave 5 often is with diverging indicators, or lower bottoms in price with higher bottoms in the indicators.

Top 5 Reached

Let's examine the weekly chart of figure 8.25 to follow up on what came next.

Figure 8.25: CMS weekly, a big correction followed

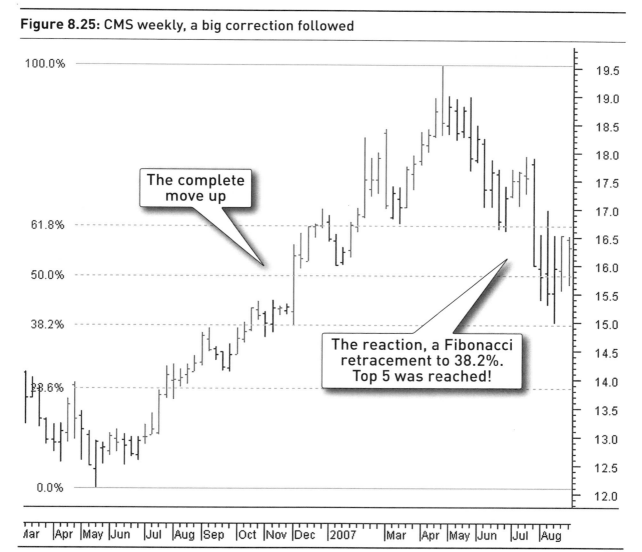

Source - MetaStock® charts courtesy of Equis International.

On 04/23/2007, we actually reached the top of wave 5. There was a big correction with a Fibonacci retracement to 38.2% of the complete up-wave.

That means that until the middle of August 2007, 61.8% of the up-move profit was lost. A buy-and-hold strategy would have resulted in only a small profit!

Applying the *LOCKIT* system, on the other hand, was very profitable!

LOCKIT

> Next, we will review some additional useful techniques that complement LOCKIT, for an above-average success rate to enter and exit trades.

 For a closer look at the charts in this chapter, go to www.traderslibrary.com/TLEcorner.

Chapter 9

LOCKIT Complementary Techniques

It's possible to open a position with a higher probability for making a profit if you trade after a trend reversal or after a trend continuation confirmation.

TREND REVERSAL TRADING

First, we will have a look at a trade after a trend reversal confirmation. What's most important, of course, is accurately finding a medium-term price reversal point.

Abaxis Example

Look at figure 9.1 on page 274 for an example with Abaxis Inc.

The price closed above the downtrend line (8/07/2007). From the top, in April, the price fell back with an Elliott ABC zigzag correction. Wave A broke through the 50- and 100-day simple moving averages (dashed line); the price reacted and formed wave B. There was some resistance from the 100-day moving average; the price turned down, bouncing against the resistance of the 50-day moving average.

Are we now reaching the end of correction wave C? Should we open a long position here?

Figure 9.1: Abaxis daily, looking for medium term-trend reversal

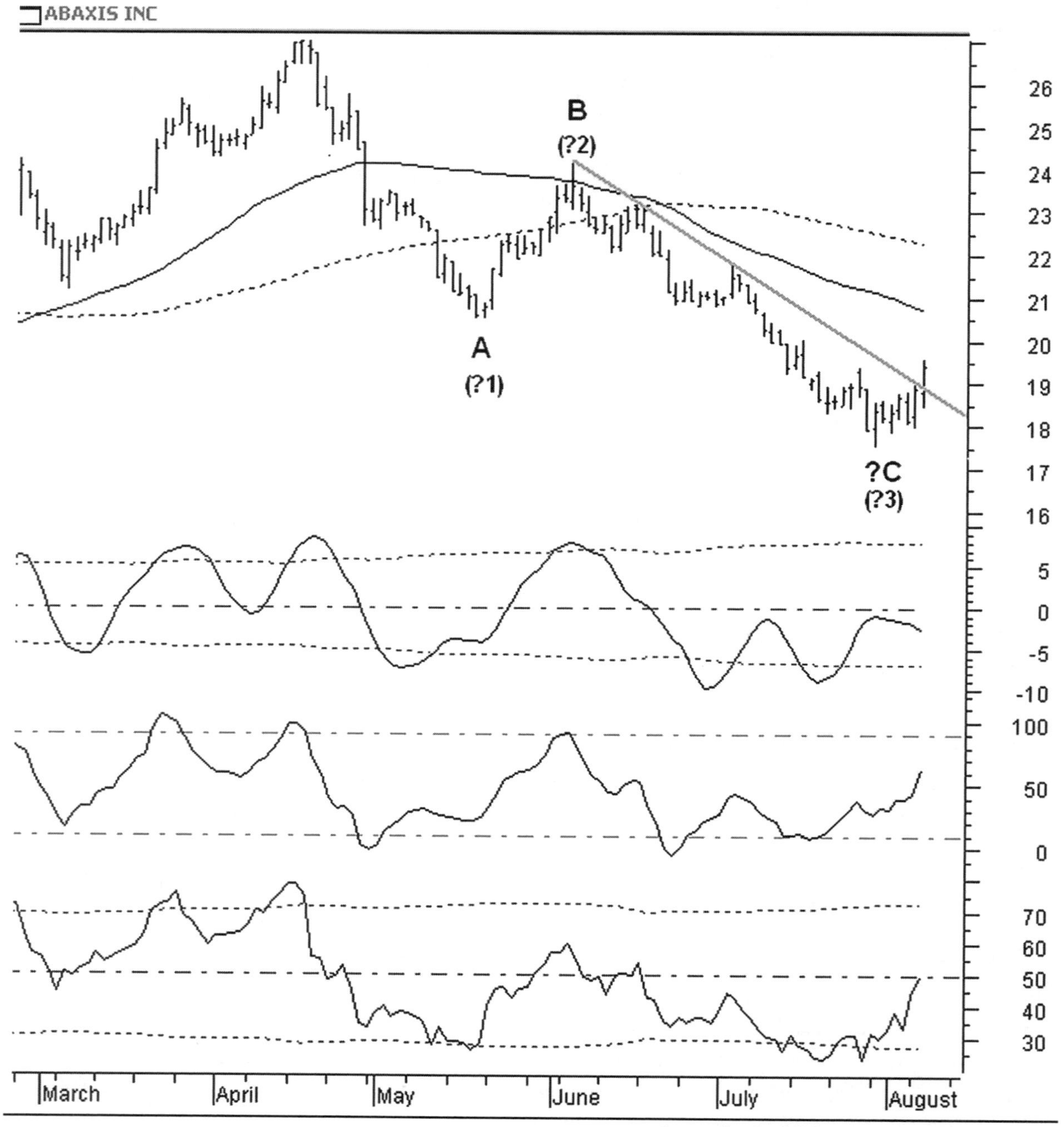

ABAXIS INC

Source - MetaStock® charts courtesy of Equis International.

Arguments for Buying

In figure 9.1, the first indicator below the price bar, SVAPO(8,1), made a double bottom with divergence; this is an indicator for a medium–term reversal. The second indicator has a double bottom with divergence in the SVE_ BB%b_HA(18) now moving up. Finally, in the last indicator, the RSI(14), we are moving out of the oversold area.

The closing price crossed above the downtrend line.

We may have a completed ABC Elliott correction wave.

Arguments against Buying

It's strange that the price up-move of the last few days goes with a declining SVAPO. This would mean that the price up-move is not confirmed with higher volume.

The 50- and 100-day moving averages are nearby and will present resistance very soon.

The risk-to-reward ratio is not good. There is a lot of resistance very close by, and with a buying price of $19.44 and an initial stop at the previous turning point at $17.54, this would mean a stop at the rather high level of 11%.

After the correction wave, we would be starting a new impulse wave 1. Impulse wave 1 is followed by correction wave 2, which takes back a big part of wave 1 most of the time.

Finally, we have no idea if wave C is complete or if we have reached the lowest point already. It is possible that we still are in the first correction wave (A) down, with an impulse wave 1 to 5. We then would get wave 4 now, followed by lower prices for wave 5 later on.

A More Certain Bottom Reversal

Correction wave C is an impulse wave; however, it is not always easily recognized in an individual stock. But, there often will be a number of waves down, each time with a lower low in price.

We most certainly are in a bottom reversal when there is no lower bottom anymore, which is why it is best to wait for the medium-term downtrend to make a higher low before opening a position.

In the daily chart shown in figure 9.2, the closing price moves above the short-term descending trend line on September 11, 2007. It seems that wave C was already completed. The short-term bottoms of waves 2 and (2) have higher lows and are probably the start of a longer-term wave 3. The price also is breaking out of a triangle pattern.

All of the indicators now converge with the price move.

Figure 9.2: Abaxis daily, a more certain bottom reversal

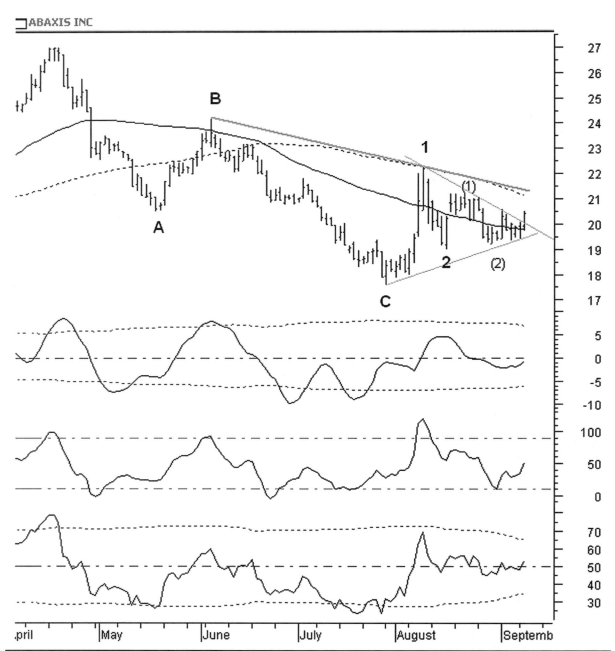

Source - MetaStock® charts courtesy of Equis International.

If the price remains above the uptrend line of the rare triangle reversal pattern, we can use a close stop value of less than 5%, thereby limiting the risk.

The 100-day simple moving average provides close resistance against buying now. We could wait to break this resistance, but there is the disadvantage of a possibly worse risk-to-reward ratio. I opt for opening a long position now at a closing price of $20.41, keeping a stop above the uptrend line and a trailing stop of 10%.

Figure 9.3: Abaxis daily, sell now or hold on to the long position?

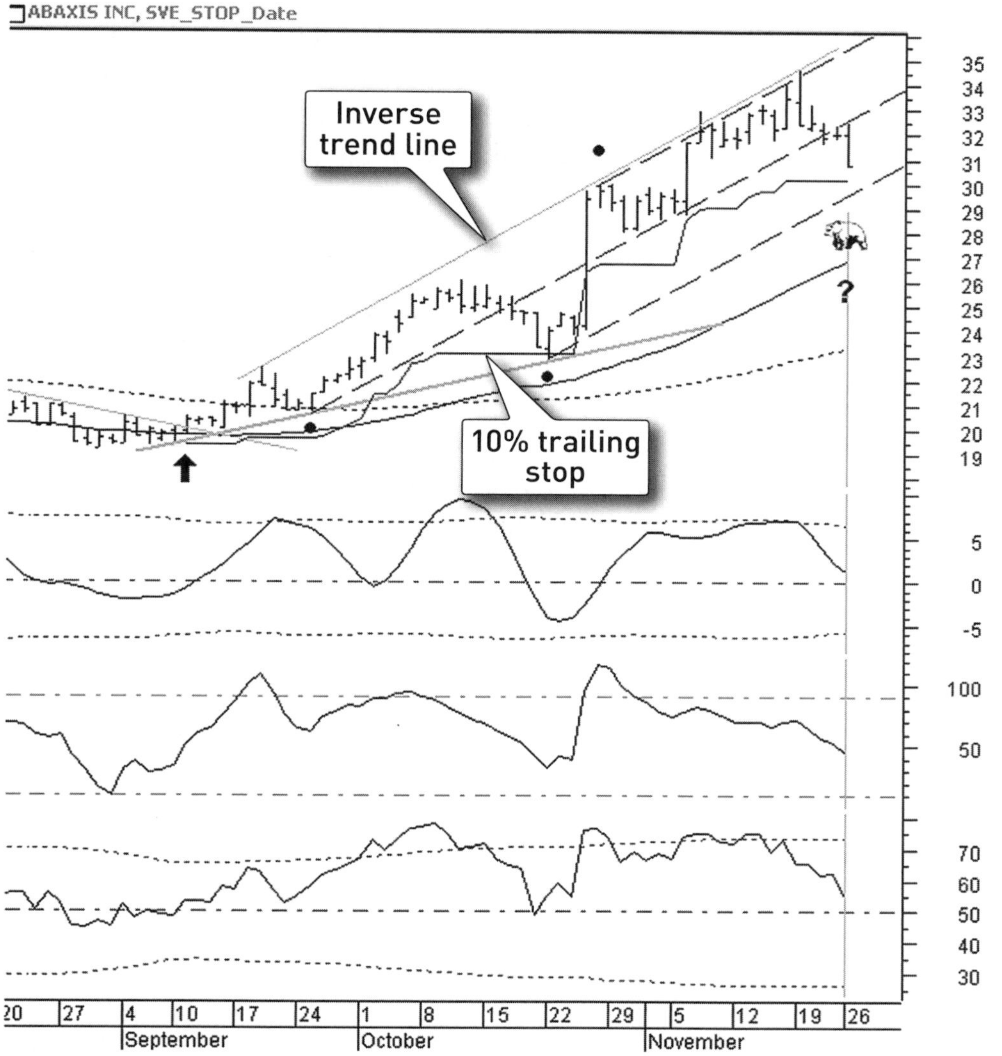

Source - MetaStock® charts courtesy of Equis International.

In figure 9.3 (11/26/2007), look at how the price moved up slowly; then, from the beginning of October, it fell back to the uptrend line, while the closing price remained above the 10% trailing stop. There was no divergence visible in the indicators. Next, the price accelerated, continuing the uptrend.

Looking at the indicators, we are now at a point where we can ask ourselves if this would be a good time to sell. All three indicators are diverging and a move down to the 50-day moving average is likely.

On the other hand, looking at all the available support, it is probably worthwhile and justifiable to hold onto the position for the moment.

The lower side of the pitchfork, based on the turning points indicated by the three dots, is close and will give support. We can draw an inverse trend line through a number of previous price tops. A parallel line with this inverse trend line through the October low point, gives an uptrend line that falls

Figure 9.4: Abaxis daily, reversal signals; closing the long position

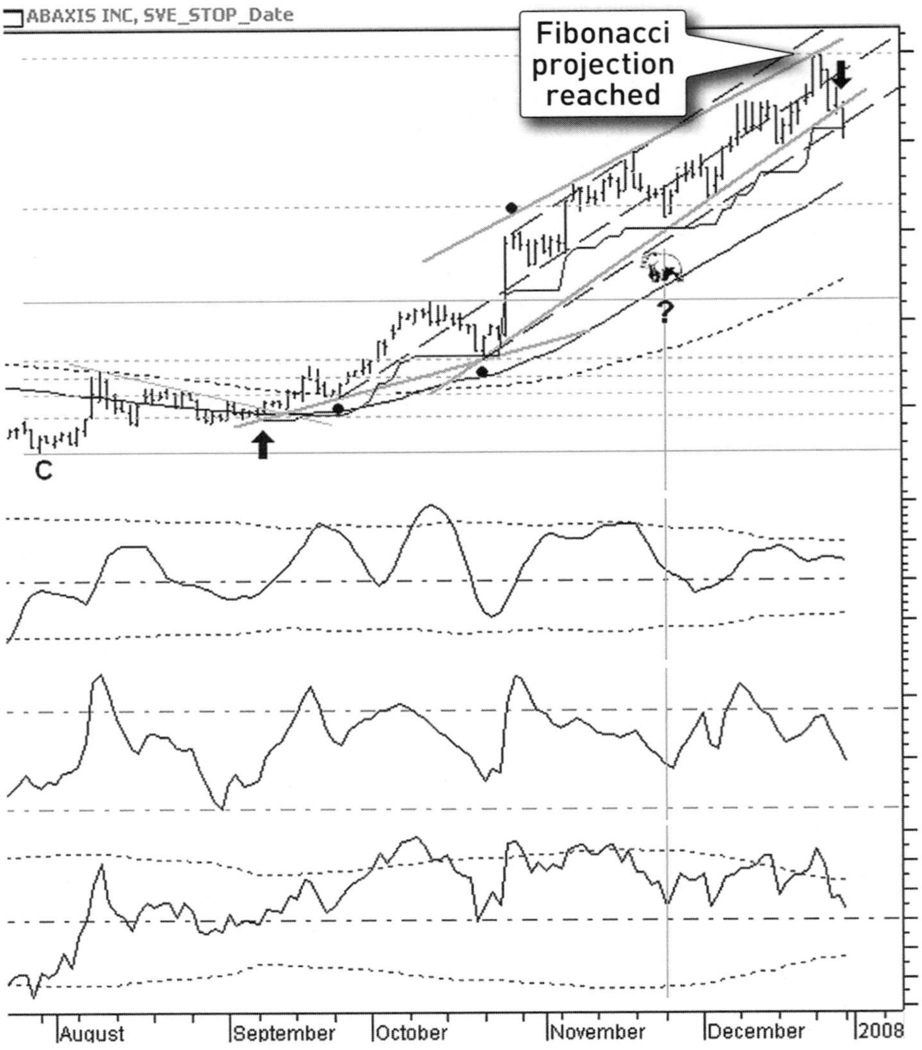

Source - MetaStock® charts courtesy of Equis International.

exactly together with the lower line of the pitchfork channel. These trend lines comprise a trend channel; the lower side of this channel gives support. You also can see that these trend lines are perfectly in line with the 50-day moving average slope. The price is just a fraction away from the 10% trailing stop level. These are enough good reasons to hold onto the position and forget about the indicators for the moment.

And yes, looking at figure 9.4, we see that the price keeps moving up!

On 12/31/2007:

- We have short- and medium-term divergences in the indicators.

- The last top is made at the level of a Fibonacci target.

- The price falls through the uptrend line.

- The price falls out of an up-moving wedge pattern and, possibly, creating a top reversal pattern; it probably is an Elliott-ending wedge impulse wave.

- The price falls out of the up-moving pitchfork.

- The price is very close to the trailing stop.

- Opening the position at $20.41 with a closing price now of $35.86, gives a 75% profit. Certainly, this is another solid reason to close the position now.

We close the long position. Should we open a short position now?

No, not if we want to be more certain that we really are at a medium-term top level. We can never rule out the possibility that the price will continue the up-move after the correction.

A More Certain Top Reversal

Look at figure 9.5 and notice how the price falls through the 50-day simple moving average and down to the 61.8% Fibonacci retracement level of the complete last up-move.

Next, look at the price reaction up, followed by the price turning down again. This is the first time we have a lower top: the first sign of a possible trend reversal. The uptrend might be broken now.

The SVAPO oscillator makes a higher top and will be diverging. Both of the other indicators are turning down and converging with the price. A further move down holds the best cards.

Figure 9.5: Abaxis daily, a more certain top reversal

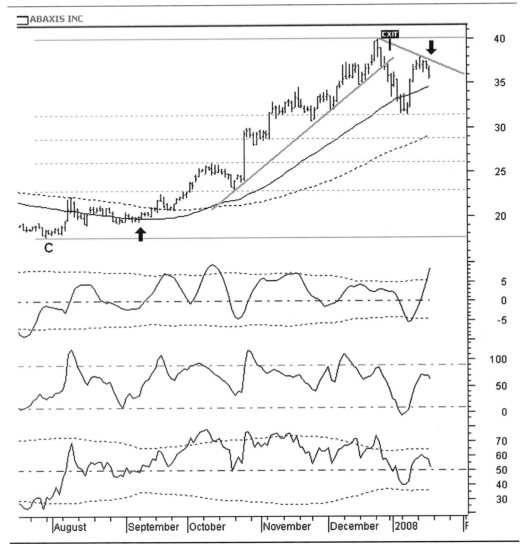

Source - MetaStock® charts courtesy of Equis International.

Opening a short position at a closing price of $35.79 allows us to keep a short stop because the price should not move above the descending trend line. Keeping an initial stop at $37.50 gives a good risk-to-reward ratio; the initial risk is limited to just about 2.5%.

We expect a fall back to the very common retracement level of 50%, at $29.

The price continues the move down (figure 9.6), allowing us to draw an ever steeper downtrend line. The breaking of the last steepest trend line is the right moment to close the short position with a nice profit. Indicators are now oversold, and SVE_BB%b_HA is making a divergence with the price.

Figure 9.6: Abaxis daily, breaking the last steepest downtrend line

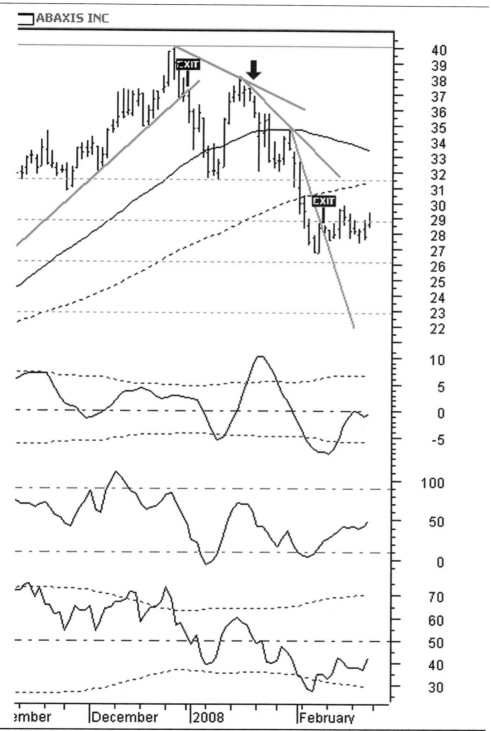

LOCKIT

> This trend reversal technique demonstrates that waiting for a trend reversal confirmation increases the chance to make a profitable trade. This is good use of our LOCKIT methodology.

TREND CONTINUATION AFTER A CORRECTION

Continuation in a Rising Trend

You have a great chance for success when entering a trade after a price correction. Again, it is important to find as much confirmation as possible that

Figure 9.7: AMR Corp. daily, rising trend continuation

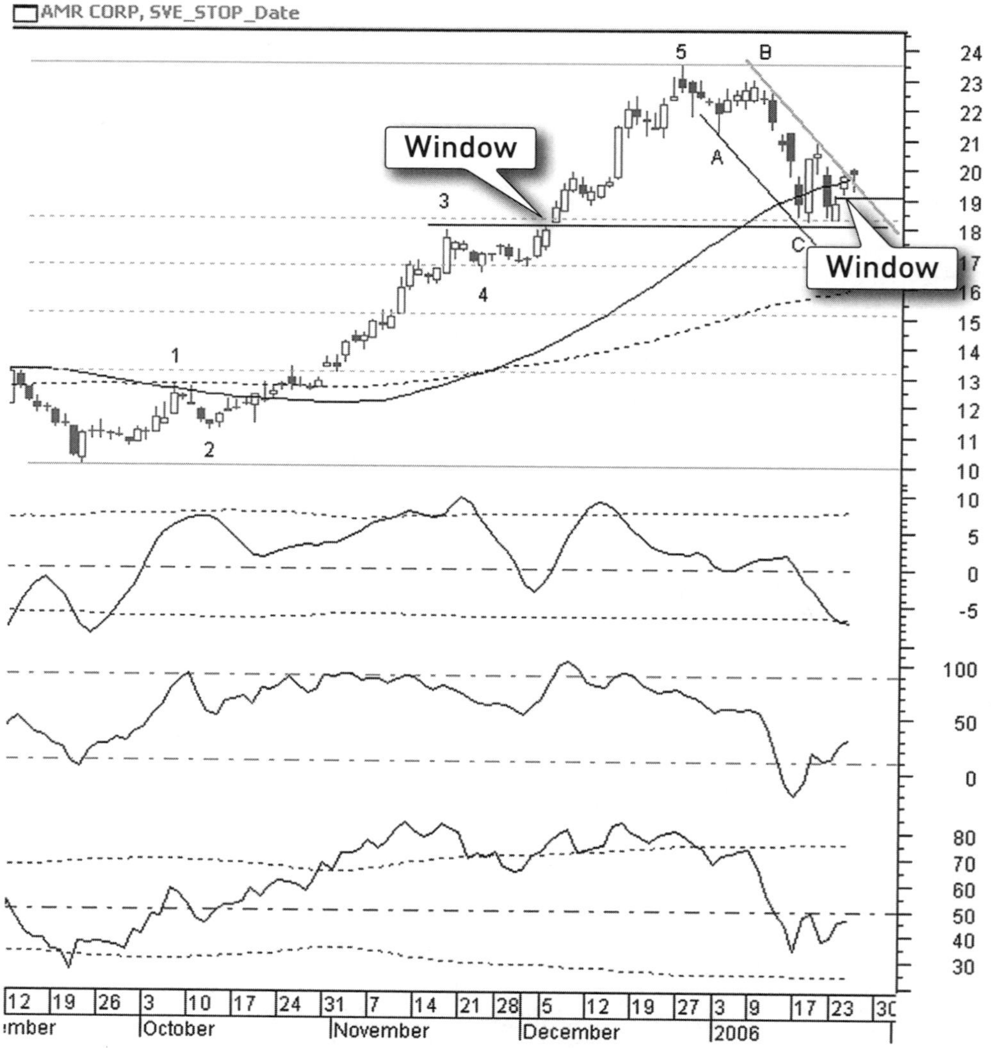

Source - MetaStock® charts courtesy of Equis International.

the trend will continue after the correction. This is where your LOCKIT strategy will come into play. Let's look at AMR Corp. as an example.

In figure 9.7, let's assume you missed the start of the up-move in the second half of September 2005 and that you did not open a position after the correction half of October.

The price moved far away from the 50-day simple moving average, but you hesitated to open a position because you expected a reaction to occur anytime.

On 1/25/2006 – Time to Buy?

The price makes a nice Elliott impulse wave 5 up, followed by a zigzag ABC correction wave. This correction brings the price back to the level of the 50-day simple moving average and to the support of the 61.8% Fibonacci retracement. At this level, there is additional support from a window in the December rise. A parallel line with the last descending trend line makes up a short-term descending trend channel. The price also finds support at the lower side of this channel.

There is a rising window in the up-move of the last days that we can use as a support level. The price is now breaking out of the downtrend channel. If this is the end of the correction move, we have the opportunity to open a trade with a very good risk-to-reward ratio.

We buy at a closing price of $19.88 and keep an initial stop at the lower side of the window at $19.14; this is an initial risk of less than 4%. We expect, on the other hand, for the price to move above the previous top at $23.53, which would yield a profit of more than 20%.

Looking at the volatility of this stock in the recent past, we decide on an 8% trailing stop level.

SVAPO, the first graph below the price chart, is in the oversold area; SVE_BB%b_HA, the indicator in the middle, is turning up from below; and the last indicator, the RSI, is turning up with a small W-figure. There is an inverse divergence in all indicators, with a higher bottom in price and a lower bottom in the indicators.

These are a lot of indications that support our decision to open a long position.

Figure 9.8: AMR Corp, daily, reversal signals

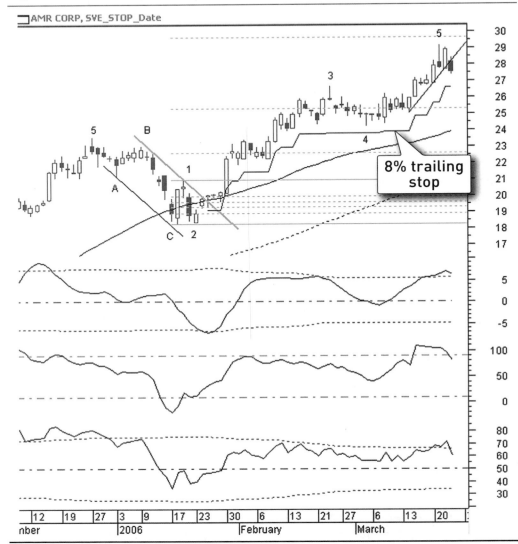

Source - MetaStock® charts courtesy of Equis International.

On 3/23/2006 – Time to Close?

In figure 9.8, the price stays above the initial and trailing stop levels.

Taking into consideration the previous, larger up-move, the rising prices since January are probably an Elliott wave 5 with an extension impulse wave; but, this seems to be ending now.

A Fibonacci projection from wave 1 shows that we now are reaching the third projection level.

Figure 9.9: AMR Corp. daily, a big correction followed

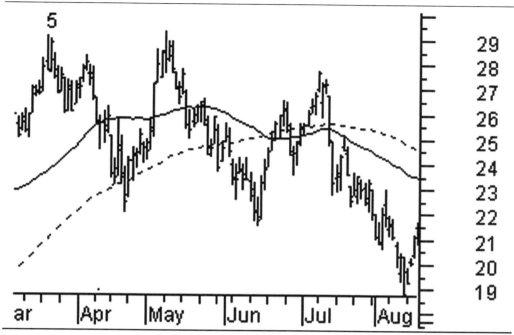

Source - MetaStock® charts courtesy of Equis International.

The last short-term uptrend line is now broken to the downside, and the price is at a bigger distance from the 50-day simple moving average.

All indicators are turning down from the overbought levels. There is no short-term divergence between the tops 3 and 5, but there is a divergence on the medium term between the top 5 of December 2006 and the top 5 now.

We could wait for the trailing stop to be broken, but with what we see now in the chart, there is a big chance that we have reached a top and that a bigger correction is on the way. So, it is sensible to close the position now at a closing price of $27.47, minus the buying price of $19.88, which gives us a profit of 35%.

And the future price move (figure 9.9) was indeed a bigger correction after the price still made a double top, but then fell back to a price level of $19.

> **Entering a trade after a correction phase, where a continuation of the trend is expected, can be very profitable.**

LOCKIT

Figure 9.10: GT daily, falling trend continuation

Source - MetaStock® charts courtesy of Equis International.

Continuation in a Falling Trend

Continuation in a falling trend mostly will be visible after an Elliott correction wave B.

We use GT (Goodyear Tire & Rubber Co.) in figure 9.10 as an example.

Let's Look at 4/06/2006

After a longer-term up-move, there is a bigger correction at the beginning of 2006. This is probably the first correction wave A. In the beginning of March, the price makes an up-move but turns at the 50-day simple moving average. The price also finds resistance against the 61.8% Fibonacci retracement level.

The indicators are turning down without making high levels. This is because we just had a correction in the downtrend and not a new up-move. The price now drops below the short-term uptrend line.

Is this the top of correction wave B? Are we going to continue the downtrend below the bottom of wave A to finish wave C?

With a stop at the top of wave B and the actual closing price, we have a good risk-to-reward ratio; and, there is a fair chance that wave C has started. So we open a short position at the closing price of $14.08.

What Happens in May?

As you can see in figure 9.11 on the next page, we kept an initial stop at the last top "a." This top, the previous turning point A, and the first low point before A are the three reference points of a downward pitchfork (5/02/2006).

In the first instance, the price drops but does not reach the median line of the pitchfork. The price turns up to the resistance of the 50-day moving average and the upper side of the pitchfork. After a small correction, the price then moves above the 50-day moving average, above the pitchfork channel, and the downtrend line.

Because we did not reach the median line of the pitchfork, the price should, theoretically, move above the previous top "a." It looks like the price is making an extension for wave B.

Closing the position now will give a small loss; however, the loss will be bigger if the price continues to move up toward the direction of the 61.8% Fibonacci retracement, above the previous top, and if it breaks the initial stop. On the other hand, we cannot be a one-hundred percent certain that we are making an extension of wave B. We may be at the start of a new impulse wave up. It is best to take the small loss now; then wait and see what is going to happen.

As expected, the price continues to move up and bounces back against the 100-day simple moving average (figure 9.12 on page 289). Additionally, there is the resistance of the 61.8% Fibonacci retracement level and the resistance from the upper side of an up pitchfork. At the turning point, we have a dark cloud cover in the candle chart, confirmed with a spinning top and a lower closing price. The indicators are topping; this is probably the top of wave B.

The risk-to-reward ratio is ok. We open a new short position May 9 at a closing price of $14.91.

Figure 9.11: GT daily, closing position for minimum loss

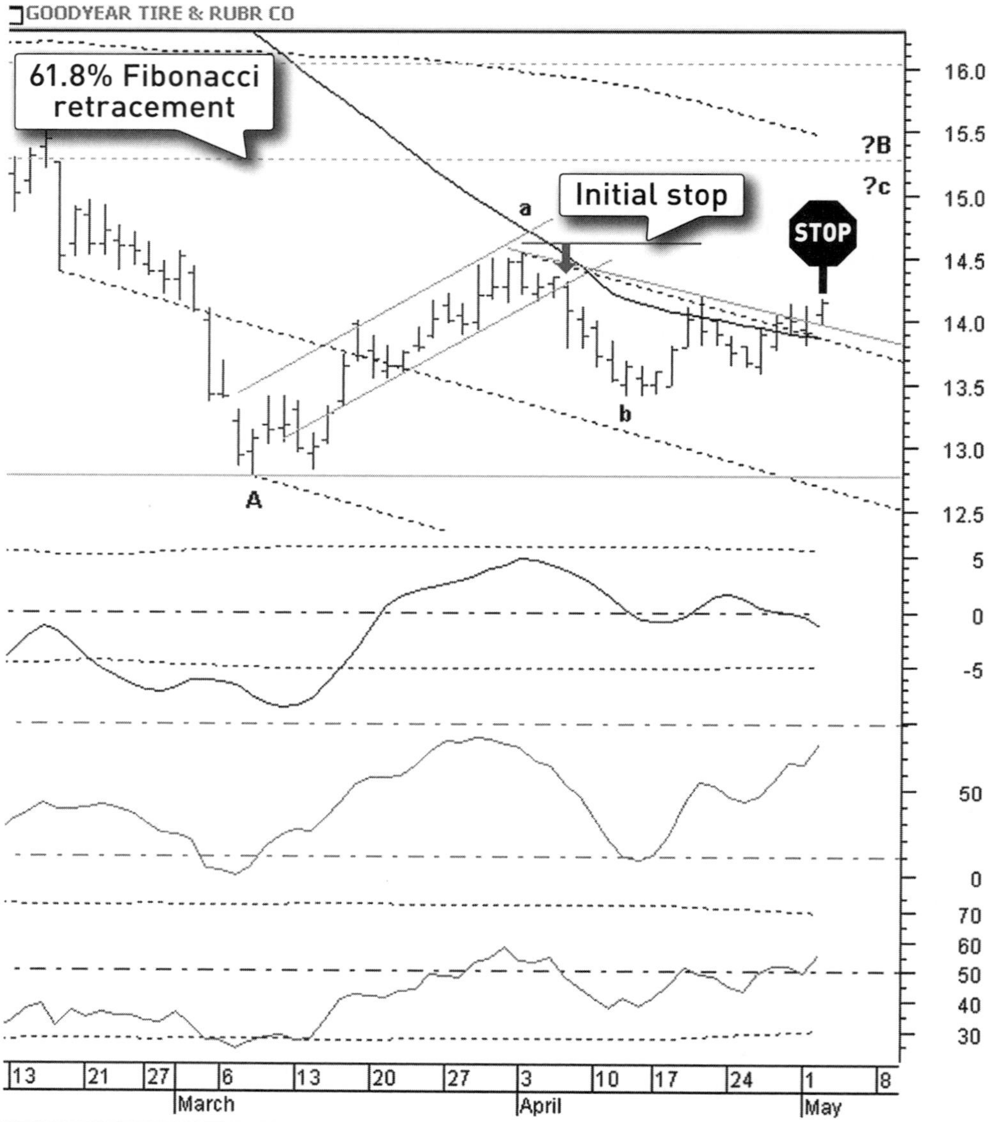

Source - MetaStock® charts courtesy of Equis International.

Figure 9.12: GT daily, end of wave B reached

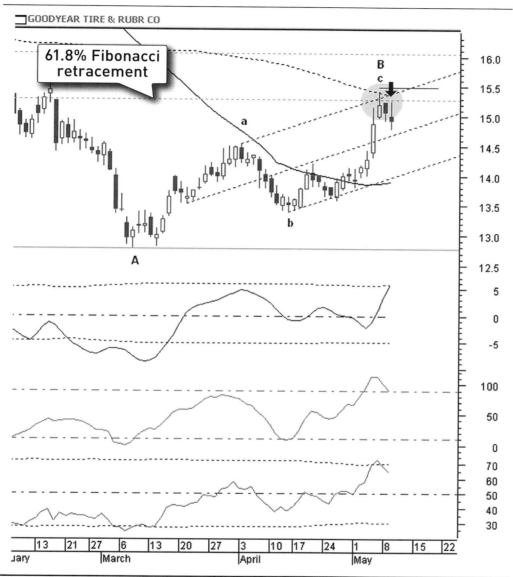

GOODYEAR TIRE & RUBR CO

61.8% Fibonacci retracement

Figure 9.13: GT daily, projecting price and time targets

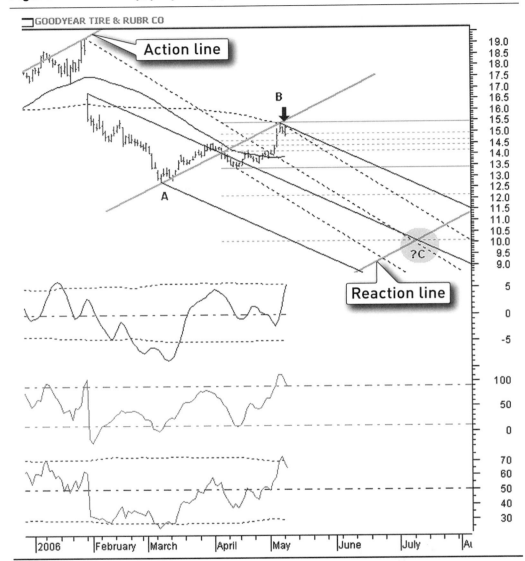

Source - MetaStock® charts courtesy of Equis International.

Target Price

If the price is indeed turning down to create correction wave C, we can try to estimate a price target and a time period.

For this, we draw a center line through the turning points of waves A and B, with a parallel action line through a previous top and a reaction line at the same distance into the future.

A Fibonacci projection to the future is only possible using a previous historical turning point.

Figure 9.14: GT daily, closing short position

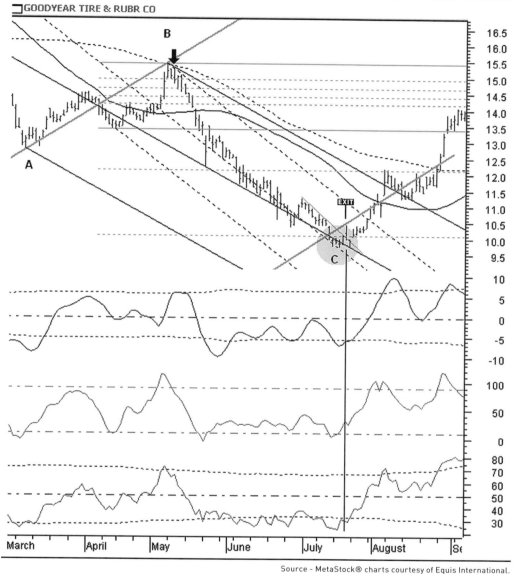

Source - MetaStock® charts courtesy of Equis International.

We also can create two descending pitchforks.

We can see how, by mid-July, all of the projections are coming together. This projection also shows that in an ABC correction, waves A and C tend toward equality. This certainly is the case here in time and in price. We expect a price target of $10, around the middle of July.

And, yes, we get a smooth move down to our target (figure 9.14). We close the short position with a very nice profit on July 20, 2006. We had reached our price target, and the price had moved up above the short-term descending trend line with all indicators turning up from their low levels.

Clearly, estimating a price target makes the decision to close an open position much easier.

Trading after a reaction in a downtrend offers a better chance for a successful trade!

THE QUEST FOR PROFITABLE MOVING AVERAGE CROSSOVERS

The use of moving average crossovers is a traditional way of finding buying and selling points in technical analysis.

In most circumstances, trading based on traditional crossovers, such as simple, exponential, or weighted averages, does not create a profitable business. Here, within LOCKIT, we are looking for an alternative that will give us a better and a more reliable end result.

Smoothing Closing Prices

Generally, it's a contradiction to have a smooth, reliable moving average crossover on one side, while having a fast reaction to price turning points on the other. Faster normally refers to shorter moving averages, but that, in turn, will result in more choppy moves and create more false buy and sell signals.

So, if you want to create fast and reliable crossovers, the first thing you have to look for is a way to smooth closing prices with as little lag as possible.

In figure 9.15, we compare three different 10-day averages on the daily price bars:

- The thin line represents the 10-day exponential moving average (EA). The main disadvantage is that this average lags too much; it takes a couple of weeks for it to signal a new uptrend.

- The dotted line represents the 10-day TEMA (triple exponential moving average). This average responds quickly, but there is not enough smoothing; it is almost as choppy as the closing prices.

- The thick line is a 10-day TEMA based on the re-calculated OHLC heikin ashi closing prices. It looks good; it's fast, and the smoothing is excellent.

Figure 9.15: Smoothing closing prices with 3 different averages

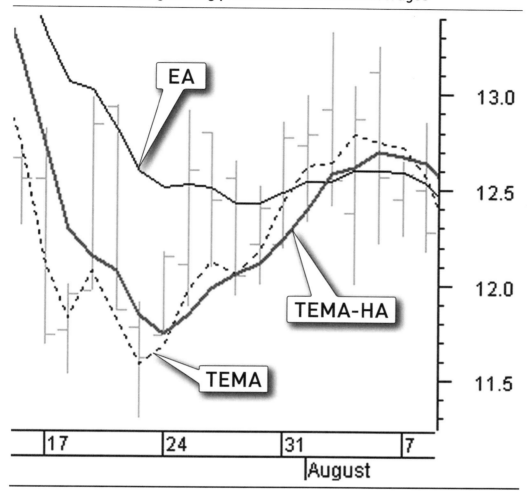

Source - MetaStock® charts courtesy of Equis International.

Faster with Zero-lagging!

In the next step, shown in figure 9.16, we will limit the lag of the TEMA-HA average compared to the faster TEMA average on closing prices.

The TEMA average is very fast at the turning points. The disadvantage is that bigger short-term moves will create too many false crossing signals in combination with any other average.

The use of the TEMA-HA average gives better smoothing and, as a result, fewer false signals. The disadvantage here is an extra delay at the turning points, compared to the TEMA average straight on the closing prices.

Figure 9.16: Limiting the lag with the zero-lagging heikin ashi TEMA average

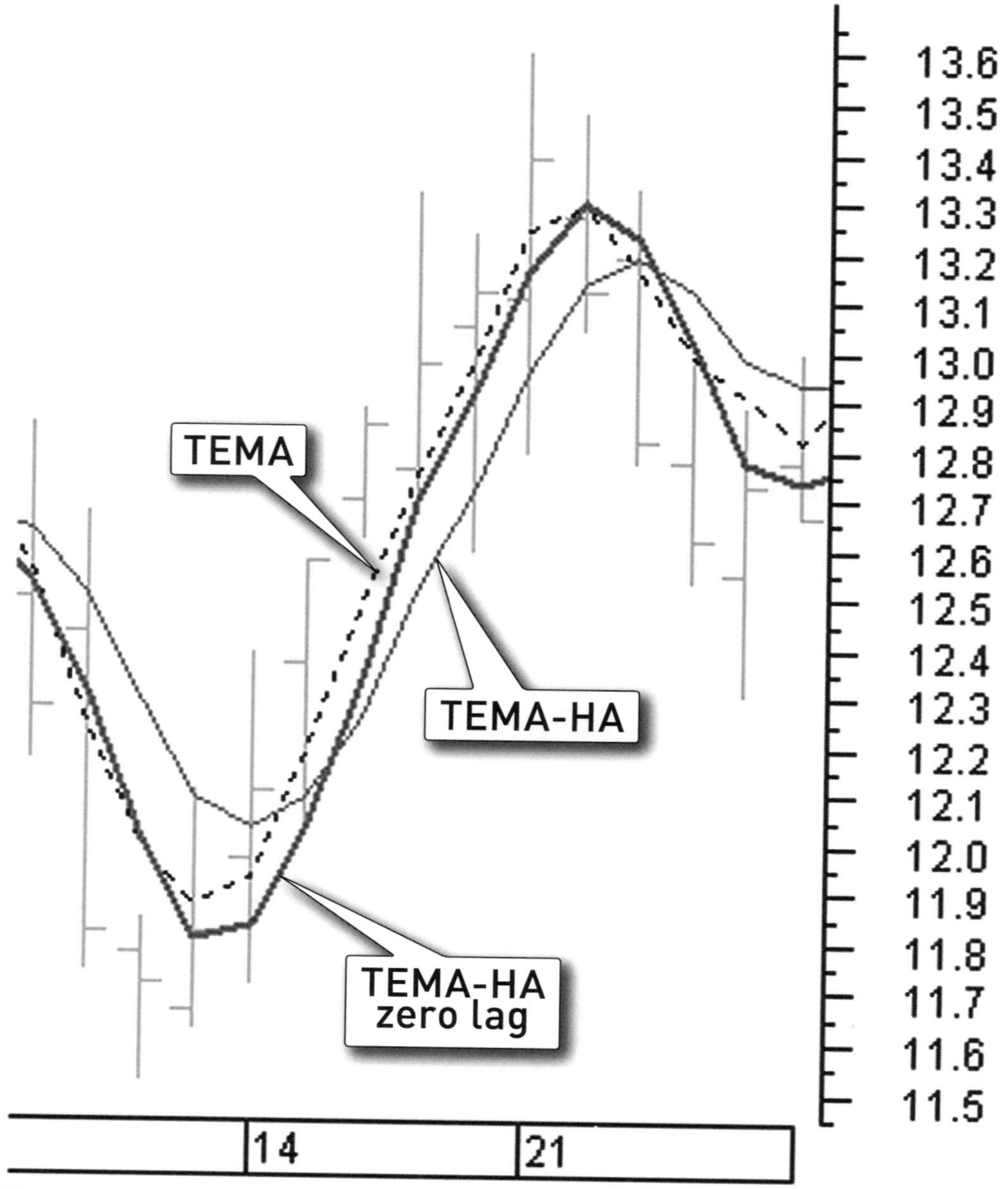

With a TEMA-HA zero-lag average, we can compensate for this delay while keeping almost the same smoothing.

In MetaStock® formula language, you can create a zero-lag heikin ashi TEMA average as follows:

> avg := Input("TEMA average? ",1,100,55);
>
> haOpen:=(Ref((O+H+L+C)/4,-1) + PREV)/2;
>
> haC:=((O+H+L+C)/4+haOpen+Max(H,haOpen)+Min(L,haOpen))/4;
>
> TMA1:= Tema(haC,avg);
>
> TMA2:= Tema(TMA1,avg);
>
> Diff:= TMA1 - TMA2;
>
> ZeroLagHA:= TMA1 + Diff;
>
> ZeroLagHA

 Please utilize the disc in the back of the book for instant access to these codes. You may also download them from www.traderslibrary.com/tlecorner.

One of the crossing averages we are going to use is this zero-lag TEMA average on heikin ashi prices; it has good smoothing and almost no lagging.

Fast, Reliable Crossovers

The referencing average we are going to use is also a zero-lag TEMA average, but now on the typical price. This average price consists of the high price, plus the low price, plus the closing price divided by three. It is smoothed with the same average that was used for the heikin ashi zero-lag TEMA average. We use 55 bars as the default TEMA average.

The MetaStock® formula for a zero-lag typical price TEMA average is as follows:

> period := Input("TEMA period? ",1,100,55);
>
> TMA1:= Tema(Typ(),period);
>
> TMA2:= Tema(TMA1,period);
>
> Difference:= TMA1 - TMA2;
>
> ZeroLagCl:= TMA1 + Difference;
>
> ZeroLagCl

 Please utilize the disc in the back of the book for instant access to these codes. You may also download them from www.traderslibrary.com/tlecorner.

Figure 9.17: Bankrate daily snapshot of longer-term crossover testing

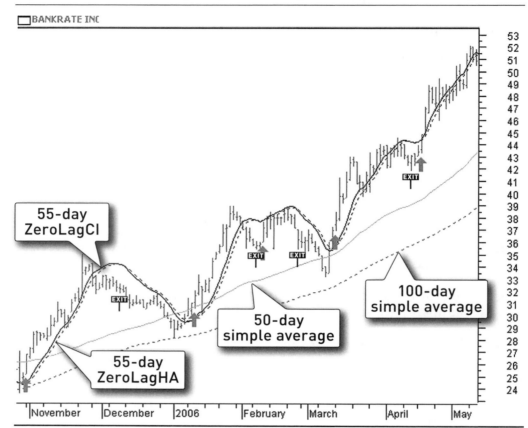

Source - MetaStock® charts courtesy of Equis International.

Results in a Trending Market

We tested for longer-term results by buying Bankrate Inc. stock in a longer-term up-move for a three-year period from October 2004 until October 2007. The end result was a profit of 250%, with a total of 28 trades.

In figure 9.17, we are looking at an example of a trending market out of that test period, from October 2005 until May 2006, which shows an up-move with a few retracements to the 50-day and 100-day simple moving averages.

The up arrow is a buying signal when the ZeroLagCl average crosses above the ZeroLagHA average. The exit signal is the selling signal when the ZeroLagCl average crosses below the ZeroLagHA average.

> Short-term flat moves will create losing trades most of the time, as was the case during February 2006. Applying more technical analysis techniques, as outlined in your LOCKIT methodology, during periods like these can prevent entering these losing trades and can yield even more positive results at the end.

Results in a Flat-moving Market

There is no doubt that in a flat-moving market, almost all positions opened based on average crossings will be losing trades.

This is why it makes sense that every signal is checked with other technical analysis techniques to avoid losing trades as much as possible.

In figure 9.18, we can see Bankrate Inc. after a larger down-move. There is a buying signal based on the crossing averages. Should you buy here?

Figure 9.18: Bankrate daily, ignore the buying signal from the averages crossover

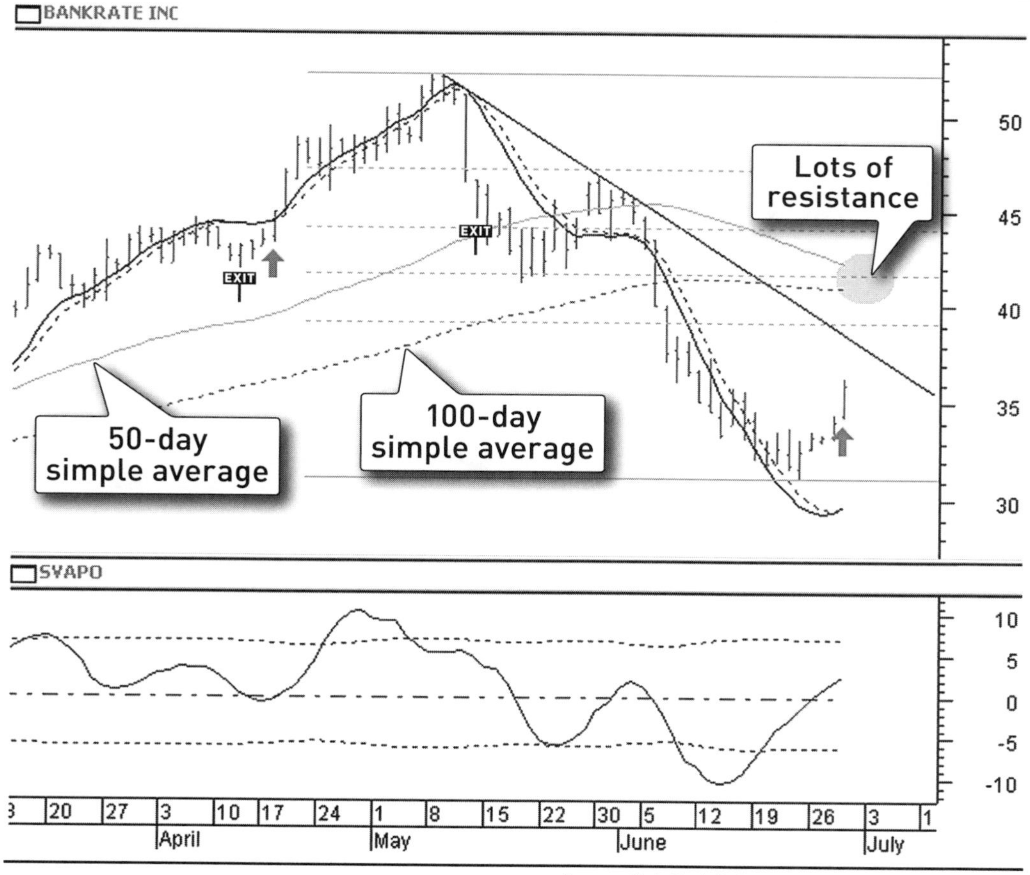

Source - MetaStock® charts courtesy of Equis International.

After the bigger correction down, the price is now moving back up to the 50-day and 100-day moving averages. This target also is close to the 50% retracement of the complete down-move. Between the actual price and this target, there is resistance from a downtrend line. There are no divergences between the lower bottoms in price and the bottoms in the indicators. This is probably an indication that the down move is not yet finished. We must also remember that, after a bigger down move, it usually takes time to consolidate before a new price direction is chosen.

You could take this trade, but you will need to be alert for a small profit. After our additional analysis, it looks better to skip this trade and wait.

In figure 9.19, we see how the price moves up just one more day, reaching the resistance of the 100-day moving average and the downtrend line; then continues its way down.

Figure 9.19: Bankrate daily, price breaks above trend line and new crossover buying signal

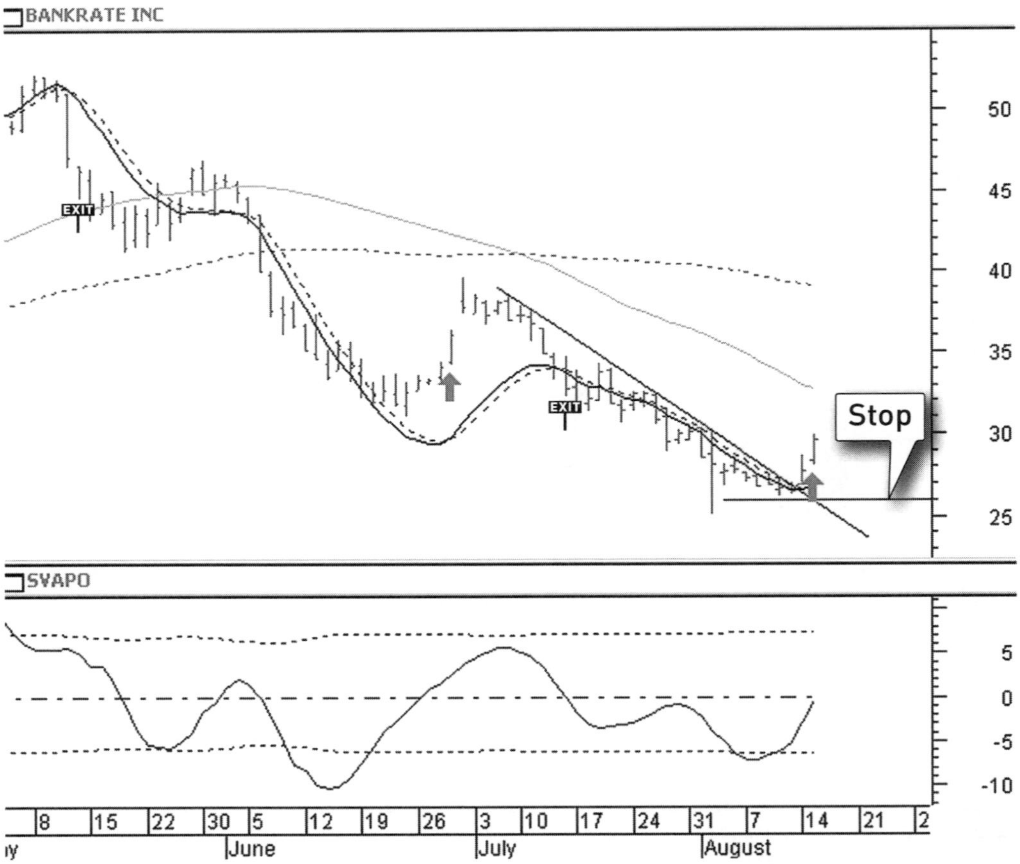

Not taking this position saved us a losing trade.

Now, the price breaks above the last downtrend line, and we have a new buying signal from the crossing averages. There is a divergence between the bottoms in price during June and August and the bottoms in the SVAPO oscillator.

After a 50% correction in price, it seems obvious that the price needs some time to consolidate. On the other hand, we do not like the idea of missing the beginning if this is indeed a new longer-term up-move.

The best alternative is to take this long trade and then set a stop at the last turning point. Eventually, we should keep a stop $1 lower, at the most recent low point.

Notice in figure 9.20 how the price reaches the resistance of the 50-day simple moving average in just two days and turns back down. A couple of weeks

Figure 9.20: Bankrate daily, ignoring crossover signals

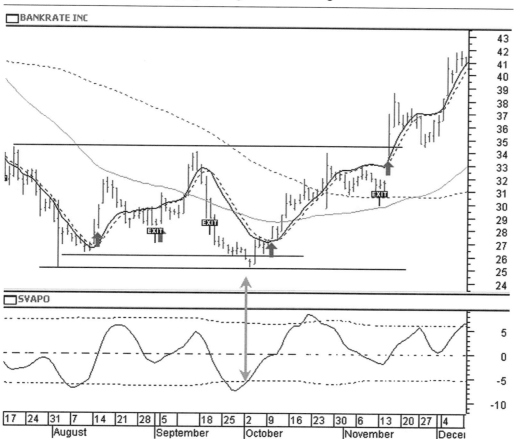

later, we get a selling signal from the crossing averages; however, the price bottom is still higher than the previous bottom and still dollars away from the initial stop level. So there is no reason to close the position yet; "wait and see" is the message here.

The price is moving up again the next day. The 50-day moving average is broken, but the 100-day moving average resistance is too strong and forces the price to turn down again.

We get a new selling signal; however, the price is still above the last price bottom and far away from our initial stop. The message, again, is "wait and see."

But the price keeps moving down slowly. It reaches the stop level, moves through it, and then holds on at the lowest point since the start of the flat move. Generally, we should sell here; but, it is clear that as long as we stay above the low point, we could risk this extra dollar, especially because the SVAPO has already turned up again from below the lower reference level. This should give us the confidence that we are at the end of the correction and that it is better to wait one more day.

The price does turn up, and we now can see it moving in a rectangular pattern. Most of the time, this is a continuation pattern, but it also can be a reversal pattern. So we will have to watch to see which side it will break.

The price moves up until the resistance of the upper side of the rectangle. Next, the price drops back to the support of the 100-day simple moving average.

We receive a selling signal from the crossing averages.

We ignore this signal because the price is clearly finding support on the 100- and the nearby 50-day simple moving averages, and the price makes equal-to-higher bottoms. The trend remains positive, and we still have some profit left in our trade.

Finally, the price breaks the upper side of the rectangle.

Remember, *always* keep some ultimate stop loss level; otherwise, you run the risk that you will continue to postpone closing the trade, making your loss bigger than you intended.

You could have increased your long position at the price bottom at the beginning of October. There was a big chance for the price to move up at least to the upper side of the rectangle.

The up arrow (figure 9.20) is a buying signal when the ZeroLagCl average crosses above the ZeroLagHA average. The EXIT signal is the selling signal when the ZeroLagCl average crosses below the average.

Trading based on crossing averages ZeroLagCl and ZeroLagHA can be profitable and applying different technical analysis and risk management techniques can help you avoid some losing trades.

AUTOMATIC TRADING

Let's find out if using this crossover system can be profitable on its own.

First, we have to create the buy and sell conditions (using Metastock).

Buy condition:

```
avg:= 65;

EMA1:= Tema((H+L+C)/3,avg);

EMA2:= Tema(EMA1,avg);

Difference:= EMA1 - EMA2;

ZlCl:= EMA1 + Difference;

haOpen:=(Ref((O+H+L+C)/4,-1) + PREV)/2;

haC:=((O+H+L+C)/4+haOpen+Max(H,haOpen)+Min(L,haOpen))/4;

EMA1:= Tema(haC,avg);

EMA2:= Tema(EMA1,avg);

Difference:= EMA1 - EMA2;

ZlHa:= EMA1 + Difference;

Cross(ZlCl,ZlHa)
```

 Please utilize the disc in the back of the book for instant access to these codes. You may also download them from www.traderslibrary.com/tlecorner.

Sell condition is completely the same except that for the last statement the crossing would be the other way around with: Cross(ZlHa,ZlCl)

Trading Conditions

We will use 25 volatile stocks within the time period 01/16/2003 to 11/09/2007. Because of the long period for the TEMA average, the first buy signals will only appear for half of 2004. So, for this example, we are talking about real trading for approximately three years.

The 25 stocks we will use are: AIRM, AKAM, AMD, ANF, ATI, AYE, BGC, BRCM, CRDN, CVO, EBAY, FTO, ILMN, INTC, MED, MIND, NCR, NVDA, SNDK, SPNC, TRE, TWTC, VPHM, WFR, X.

The general test conditions will be $1,000 capital per stock with no profit or loss sharing between the stocks and a 0.1% broker entry cost and 0.1% exit cost. Only long positions will be traded at the closing price the day we have a buy or sell signal.

Results

With the $25,000 starting capital ($1,000 per stock) and using the stocks and rules mentioned before, we gain a profit of $36.994, or a 148% profit, with an average of 29 trades per stock in the period 01/16/2003 to 11/09/2007.

Figure 9.21 shows individual results for all the stocks. The last column is the count of the winning/losing trades per stock.

Since this crossover system is profitable on its own, it can be used to help you with your decision-making.

LOCKIT

> This concludes PART IV where we looked at the basic strategy of the LOCKIT system with the buying and selling rules, an application example, and some complementary techniques for even better results.

→ **For a closer look at the charts in this chapter, go to www.traderslibrary.com/TLEcorner.**

Figure 9.21: Crossover system individual trading results for all the stocks

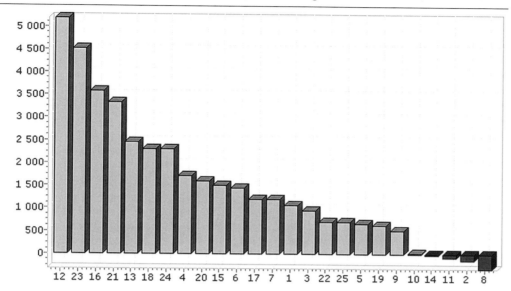

ID	Security	Symbol	Date Range	Net Profit	% Gain	Trades	Trade...
12	FRONTIER OIL C...	FTO	01/16/2003 - 11/09/2007	$5182.90	518.29 %	23	14/9
23	VIROPHARMA INC	VPHM	01/16/2003 - 11/09/2007	$4523.27	452.33 %	26	10/16
16	MITCHAM INDS INC	MIND	01/16/2003 - 11/09/2007	$3572.85	357.29 %	27	15/12
21	TANZANIAN ROY...	TRE	01/16/2003 - 11/09/2007	$3341.57	334.16 %	28	9/19
13	ILLUMINA INC	ILMN	01/16/2003 - 11/09/2007	$2453.98	245.40 %	31	12/19
18	NVIDIA CORP	NVDA	01/16/2003 - 11/09/2007	$2310.23	231.02 %	30	15/15
24	MEMC ELECTR M...	WFR	01/16/2003 - 11/09/2007	$2297.56	229.76 %	28	16/12
4	ABERCROMBIE &...	ANF	01/16/2003 - 11/09/2007	$1709.26	170.93 %	27	11/16
20	SPECTRANETICS...	SPNC	01/16/2003 - 11/09/2007	$1606.34	160.63 %	27	12/15
15	MEDIFAST INC	MED	01/16/2003 - 11/09/2007	$1500.21	150.02 %	27	11/16
6	ALLEGHENY ENE...	AYE	01/16/2003 - 11/09/2007	$1454.14	145.41 %	27	13/14
17	NCR CORP NEW	NCR	01/16/2003 - 11/09/2007	$1199.30	119.93 %	23	12/11
7	GENERAL CABLE ...	BGC	01/16/2003 - 11/09/2007	$1194.95	119.50 %	37	15/22
1	Air Methods Corp...	AIRM	01/16/2003 - 11/09/2007	$1061.00	106.10 %	32	12/20
3	ADVANCED MICR...	AMD	01/16/2003 - 11/09/2007	$955.81	95.58 %	28	10/18
22	TIME WARNER T...	TWTC	01/16/2003 - 11/09/2007	$700.00	70.00 %	33	13/20
25	UNITED STATES ...	X	01/16/2003 - 11/09/2007	$694.62	69.46 %	35	13/22
5	ALLEGHENY TEC...	ATI	01/16/2003 - 11/09/2007	$666.70	66.67 %	37	13/24
19	SANDISK CORP	SNDK	01/16/2003 - 11/09/2007	$624.68	62.47 %	34	10/24
9	CERADYNE INC	CRDN	01/16/2003 - 11/09/2007	$512.27	51.23 %	30	13/17
10	CENVEO INC	CVO	05/17/2004 - 11/09/2007	$14.71	1.47 %	18	6/12
14	INTEL CORP	INTC	01/16/2003 - 11/09/2007	$-28.52	-2.85 %	32	10/22
11	EBAY INC	EBAY	01/16/2003 - 11/09/2007	$-87.12	-8.71 %	29	13/16
2	AKAMAI TECHNO...	AKAM	01/16/2003 - 11/09/2007	$-140.04	-14.00 %	37	13/24
8	BROADCOM CORP	BRCM	01/16/2003 - 11/09/2007	$-327.15	-32.71 %	36	10/26

Source - MetaStock® charts courtesy of Equis International.

TEST YOUR CHAPTER 9 KNOWLEDGE

1. What is a good sign of a medium-term bottom reversal?

_____

_____

_____

_____

2. What is a good sign of a medium-term top reversal?

_____

_____

_____

_____

3. What are reliable indications for a trend continuation after a correction?

_____

_____

_____

_____

4. The heikin ashi TEMA average cross-over system is a profitable system. How would you make this system even more profitable?

_____

_____

_____

_____

Q&A For answers, please visit the Traders' Library Education Corner at www.traderslibrary.com/tlecorner.

PART V
LOCKIT MONEY AND RISK MANAGEMENT

Chapter 10

Money and Risk Management

In LOCKIT, maintaining good money- and risk-management habits is more important than correctly applying technical analysis! Good money-management habits ensure that you'll survive in the stock market, even with a number of trading failures in a row. Good risk-management habits ensure that the risk-to-reward ratio is in your favor, with at least a ratio of one to three.

Practicing good money and risk management helps limit losses in losing trades and helps create profits in winning trades. Let's assume that you are trading based on daily charts; you would buy a stock and then sell it when the stock drops more than 3% below the buying price. Unfortunately, however, limiting losses is not that easy. In this example, the outcome most likely will be too many losing trades that result in losing all of your money at the end.

How much loss you're willing to accept will be proportional to how much profit you want to make in a certain period of time. While it's likely that you'll only suffer a 2% loss when using hourly charts, your profit target will be in the order of 5%. Using daily charts will result in losses in the range of 10%, but with a profit target in the order of 25%.

Also, do not forget that behind every stock is a company that can go broke! So, you may lose all of your money by investing it in only one stock.

GOOD MONEY-MANAGEMENT PRACTICES

- Only use money that you do not need for living expenses.

- Do not put more money at risk than what you have.

- Investing and using a credit line or leverage (e.g., futures, options) should only be done with money you can afford to lose in full.

- Depending on the amount of starting capital, you must spread the money among several stocks.

- You must limit the loss in a single trade to 1% up to a maximum of 2% of your portfolio's total value.

- You must limit the loss in one trade to no more than a 15% maximum of the trade value.

- If your starting capital is too low to invest in more stocks, you can use an Exchange Traded Fund (ETF) tracker of a stock index. The index takes care of the necessary stock risk spread.

GOOD RISK-MANAGEMENT PRACTICES

Keep an initial stop based on:

- The maximum allowed loss in a trade.

- The maximum allowed loss in relation to the total portfolio value.

- The use of an initial stop based on technical analysis.

- A risk-to-reward ratio of a minimum of one to three.

Keep a trailing stop for maximum profit based on:

- The volatility of the stock.

- Applying a method for distributing profits or losses between stocks in your portfolio.

AN ARBITRARY NUMBER OF STOCKS

A first money-management method would be to trade in a limited number of stocks out of an unlimited list of stocks. A second method, which we will discuss later on, would be to trade a fixed, limited number of stocks.

A \$25,000 starting capital could be used to invest in 10 stocks at any moment in time, limiting the capital per stock to \$2,500. Keeping an average loss per stock of 10%, or \$250, would only constitute a 1% loss in relation to the total capital.

Of course, you would have to calculate your buying power with each purchase in relation to your cash value and the value of the stocks in the portfolio. You could use the following spreadsheet for this.

Calculation of the Maximum Buying Power for a Single Stock		
		Available cash
Total buying power	25000	=RC[-1]-(SUM(R[1]C[-1]:R[10]C[-1]))
Buying value_1	0	=RC[-1]-(RC[-1]*0.1)
Buying value_2	0	=RC[-1]-(RC[-1]*0.1)
Buying value_3	0	=RC[-1]-(RC[-1]*0.1)
Buying value_4	0	=RC[-1]-(RC[-1]*0.1)
Buying value_5	0	=RC[-1]-(RC[-1]*0.1)
Buying value_6	0	=RC[-1]-(RC[-1]*0.1)
Buying value_7	0	=RC[-1]-(RC[-1]*0.1)
Buying value_8	0	=RC[-1]-(RC[-1]*0.1)
Buying value_9	0	=RC[-1]-(RC[-1]*0.1)
Buying value_10	0	=RC[-1]-(RC[-1]*0.1)
Allowed buying value		=IF(R[-12]C<R[-2]C,0,SUM(R[-12]C:R[-2]C)/10)
	=SUM(R[-12]C:R[-3]C)	=SUM(R[-12]C:R[-3]C)
	Total investment	**Remainder**

One-hundred percent of the cash value above \$25,000 will be available for new investments.

The *actual* value of the 10 contracts in the portfolio will be reduced by 10% (the average stop value) as an extra precaution when calculating the new contract value.

The maximum buying value for one new contract will then be the available cash and the value of the open contracts divided by 10 (10% of the total capital).

Calculation of the Maximum Buying Power for a Single Stock		
		Available cash
Total buying power	25000	25000
Buying value_1	0	0
Buying value_2	0	0
Buying value_3	0	0
Buying value_4	0	0
Buying value_5	0	0
Buying value_6	0	0
Buying value_7	0	0
Buying value_8	0	0
Buying value_9	0	0
Buying value_10	0	0
Allowed buying value		**2500**
	0	0
	Total investment	**Remainder**

We will get the following result with $25,000 starting capital and consecutively buying 10 stocks.

Calculation of the Maximum Buying Power for a Single Stock		
		Available cash
Total buying power	25000	1096
Buying value_1	2500	2250
Buying value_2	2475	2228
Buying value_3	2450	2205
Buying value_4	2426	2183
Buying value_5	2401	2161
Buying value_6	2377	2139
Buying value_7	2354	2119
Buying value_8	2330	2097
Buying value_9	2307	2076
Buying value_10	2284	2056
Allowed buying value		**0**
	23904	21514
	Total investment	**Remainder**

As an example, let's close trades 1 and 4 with a 30% profit, while all of the other contracts remain open. Adding this profit to the capital gives a new allowed buying value of $2,458.

Calculation of the Maximum Buying Power for a Single Stock		
		Available cash
Total buying power	26477	7499
Buying value_1	0	0
Buying value_2	2475	2228
Buying value_3	2450	2205
Buying value_4	0	0
Buying value_5	2401	2161
Buying value_6	2377	2139
Buying value_7	2354	2119
Buying value_8	2330	2097
Buying value_9	2307	2076
Buying value_10	2284	2056
Allowed buying value		2458
	18978	17080
	Total investment	Remainder

You can always see the total invested value and the remaining value when all trades would suffer a 10% loss.

Is this Setup Sufficiently Crash Resistant?

Let's apply this system and calculate the maximum allowed buying value for each contract. Next, let's assume the most negative scenario: Each of the 10 contracts ends up as a losing trade with a 10% loss. This happens 10 times in a row for a total of 100 consecutive losing trades.

Crash resistant?	10 contracts, investment	10 contracts, losing trades	Remaining amount
Starting value	25000		
Trade_1	23904	2390	22610
Trade_2	21618	2162	20448
Trade_3	19552	1955	18493
Trade_4	17682	1768	16725
Trade_5	15994	1599	15126
Trade_6	14464	1446	13680
Trade_7	13080	1308	12372
Trade_8	11830	1183	11189
Trade_9	10699	1070	10119
Trade_10	9676	968	9151

There still is a remaining capital of $9,151. It looks like good money management; you survive for quite a while, and it's possible that the following trades will make up for all of the losses!

In the table, you can see the remaining capital after each 10-stock trade.

A LIMITED STOCK SELECTION

A second money-management possibility is to select a limited number of stocks for trading. I prefer this method because it is much easier to follow-up on a limited number of stocks with technical analysis techniques.

With a fixed, limited number of stocks, it is possible to keep individual charts with specific notes over longer periods of time.

We can start with a fixed capital per stock. Assuming a starting capital of $25,000, we could divide this money over 20 stocks, each of which gets a starting capital of $1,250. Each of the 20 stocks is traded individually, with no profit or loss sharing. All profits or losses are attributed to the individual stock. This means, of course, that each stock must be followed individually because it can only use its own private capital.

Applying this kind of money management is effective and has a number of advantages:

- With a starting capital of $25,000 and a spread between 20 stocks, each with $1,250, the total loss of one stock only represents a loss of 5% in the total portfolio.

- A stock doing well will generate maximum profits, thereby re-investing all profits.

- A stock producing bad results will have less capital to spend, thereby limiting losses when things continue to go the wrong way.

- The profits of a stock doing well are not lost when they are invested in stocks not doing that well.

Poorly performing stocks will be recognized more quickly, which means that they can be replaced much faster. In the worst case scenario, the stocks will not be in the race anymore because there will be no more capital left.

Spreading the capital among a sufficient number of stocks will improve the end result because some stocks will be doing much better than the average.

To find the results using a portfolio with or without profit and loss sharing, we can run a test with the same stocks over the same period and with the same buying, selling, and cost of trade conditions.

In figure 10.1 on the next page, we are using a list of stocks with daily prices over a six-year period dating back from the end of September 2008.

I used one of my automatic expert buy-and-sell test systems. Although the system used is not necessarily important, it is imperative to use the same system test under the same circumstances and during the same time period. In this example, we only took long positions. For the first test, we have a starting capital of $25,000 to be divided between the 20 stocks. But there is profit and loss sharing, so each stock will get 5% of the portfolio value at any moment in time.

The Result with Profit and Loss Sharing

There was an average of 25 trades per stock in the total time period. The total profit is $128,872.

Please note, the %Gain indication in the result table (figure 10.2 on page 315) is the profit percentage compared to the total capital!

Figure 10.1: List of stocks used for testing

Symbol	Name
ABAX	ABAXIS INC
AIRM	Air Methods Corporation
AMR	AMR CORP
AOB	AMERICAN ORIENTAL BIOENGR IN
ATI	ALLEGHENY TECHNOLOGIES INC
BOOM	DYNAMIC MATLS CORP
CELG	CELGENE CORP
CMCO	COLUMBUS MCKINNON CORP N Y
CRDN	CERADYNE INC
DXPE	DXP ENTERPRISES INC NEW
FTK	FLOTEK INDS INC DEL
GIGM	GIGAMEDIA LTD
KNOT	KNOT INC
NTRI	NUTRI SYS INC NEW
POZN	POZEN INC
QDEL	QUIDEL CORP
RATE	BANKRATE INC
TIE	TITANIUM METALS CORP
USG	U S G CORP
VPHM	VIROPHARMA INC

Source - MetaStock® charts courtesy of Equis International.

Figure 10.2: Test result with profit and loss sharing

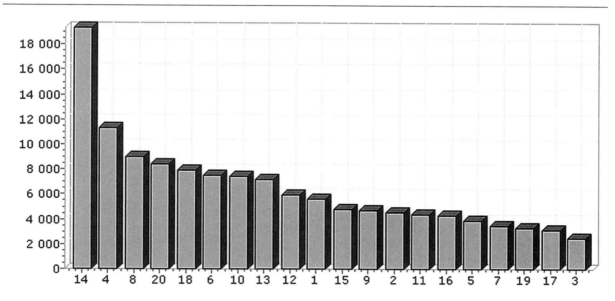

ID	Symbol	Per...	Date Range	Net Profit	% Gain	Trades	Trade Profit/Loss
14	NTRI	Daily	03/21/2002 - 09/29/2008	$19334.21	77.34 %	28	12/16
4	AOB	Daily	02/13/2002 - 09/29/2008	$11331.48	45.33 %	31	10/21
8	CMCO	Daily	10/15/2002 - 09/29/2008	$9045.30	36.18 %	21	10/11
20	VPHM	Daily	10/15/2002 - 09/29/2008	$8460.82	33.84 %	29	9/20
18	TIE	Daily	10/15/2002 - 09/29/2008	$7915.11	31.66 %	26	10/16
6	BOOM	Daily	10/15/2002 - 09/29/2008	$7494.10	29.98 %	25	14/11
10	DXPE	Daily	10/07/2002 - 09/29/2008	$7433.73	29.73 %	23	17/6
13	KNOT	Daily	08/02/2002 - 09/29/2008	$7171.19	28.68 %	23	10/13
12	GIGM	Daily	10/15/2002 - 09/29/2008	$5984.02	23.94 %	27	12/15
1	ABAX	Daily	10/15/2002 - 09/29/2008	$5649.98	22.60 %	26	10/16
15	POZN	Daily	10/15/2002 - 09/29/2008	$4796.84	19.19 %	23	12/11
9	CRDN	Daily	10/15/2002 - 09/29/2008	$4738.94	18.96 %	24	12/12
2	AIRM	Daily	10/15/2002 - 09/29/2008	$4518.83	18.08 %	23	11/12
11	FTK	Daily	01/03/2003 - 09/29/2008	$4416.26	17.67 %	15	8/7
16	QDEL	Daily	10/15/2002 - 09/29/2008	$4286.12	17.14 %	24	10/14
5	ATI	Daily	10/15/2002 - 09/29/2008	$3879.90	15.52 %	30	13/17
7	CELG	Daily	10/15/2002 - 09/29/2008	$3466.64	13.87 %	18	12/6
19	USG	Daily	10/15/2002 - 09/29/2008	$3312.93	13.25 %	34	11/23
17	RATE	Daily	10/15/2002 - 09/29/2008	$3160.10	12.64 %	32	19/13
3	AMR	Daily	10/15/2002 - 09/29/2008	$2474.51	9.90 %	32	13/19

Figure 10.3: Test result without profit and loss sharing

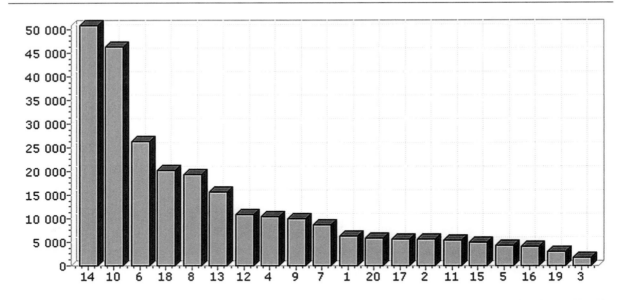

ID	Symbol	Per...	Date Range	Net Profit	% Gain	Trades	Trade Profit/Loss
14	NTRI	Daily	03/21/2002 - 09/29/2008	$50856.97	4068.56 %	28	12/16
10	DXPE	Daily	10/07/2002 - 09/29/2008	$46184.46	3694.76 %	23	17/6
6	BOOM	Daily	10/15/2002 - 09/29/2008	$26269.74	2101.58 %	25	14/11
18	TIE	Daily	10/15/2002 - 09/29/2008	$20194.68	1615.57 %	26	10/16
8	CMCO	Daily	10/15/2002 - 09/29/2008	$19259.47	1540.76 %	21	10/11
13	KNOT	Daily	08/02/2002 - 09/29/2008	$15626.01	1250.08 %	23	10/13
12	GIGM	Daily	10/15/2002 - 09/29/2008	$10968.48	877.48 %	27	12/15
4	AOB	Daily	02/13/2002 - 09/29/2008	$10536.45	842.92 %	31	10/21
9	CRDN	Daily	10/15/2002 - 09/29/2008	$9977.79	798.22 %	24	12/12
7	CELG	Daily	10/15/2002 - 09/29/2008	$8656.93	692.55 %	18	12/6
1	ABAX	Daily	10/15/2002 - 09/29/2008	$6215.61	497.25 %	26	10/16
20	VPHM	Daily	10/15/2002 - 09/29/2008	$5793.77	463.50 %	29	9/20
17	RATE	Daily	10/15/2002 - 09/29/2008	$5754.53	460.36 %	32	19/13
2	AIRM	Daily	10/15/2002 - 09/29/2008	$5655.35	452.43 %	23	11/12
11	FTK	Daily	01/03/2003 - 09/29/2008	$5463.40	437.07 %	15	8/7
15	POZN	Daily	10/15/2002 - 09/29/2008	$4953.82	396.31 %	23	12/11
5	ATI	Daily	10/15/2002 - 09/29/2008	$4306.04	344.48 %	30	13/17
16	QDEL	Daily	10/15/2002 - 09/29/2008	$4079.51	326.36 %	24	10/14
19	USG	Daily	10/15/2002 - 09/29/2008	$2937.72	235.02 %	34	11/23
3	AMR	Daily	10/15/2002 - 09/29/2008	$1665.31	133.23 %	32	13/19

Source - MetaStock® charts courtesy of Equis International.

The Result without Profit and Loss Sharing

There were, on average, 25 trades per stock during the entire period. The total profit is $265,356.

Please note, the %Gain indication in the results table (figure 10.3) is in relation to the starting capital of each stock ($1,250).

The final profit has more than doubled. Trading a selected, limited number of stocks and not sharing profits or losses is the better choice!

> For trading stocks with LOCKIT, I strongly advise you to divide your capital between a limited, fixed number of stocks and to not share any individual loss or profit between these stocks. You will have to do an individual follow-up of profit and loss for each stock.

LOCKIT

RISK MANAGEMENT

Once a buying order is executed, you must limit the risk by keeping an initial stop. The initial stop itself is variable from trade to trade because it will be based on different technical analysis techniques. On the other hand, you must use a trailing stop as the ultimate selling signal to avoid losing too much profit. And, of course, you must apply the money-management technique as explained in the previous paragraph.

Initial Stop

Fixing the level of the initial stop is based on LOCKIT technical analysis techniques.

The following MetaStock® formula "SVE_Stop_Trail%_Date" creates an initial and percentage trailing stop on the price chart from an entry date:

{SVE_Stop_Trail%_Date - Fixed percentage trailing stop from date}

InpMonth:=Input("Month",1,12,1);

InpDay:=Input("Day",1,31,1);

InpYear:=Input("Year",1800,2050,2009);

LongShort:=Input("1=Long or 2=Short? ",1,2,1);

InitStop:=Input("Initial Stop Price",0.1,10000,10);

Perc:=Input("Trailing Stop Percentage",1,30,12);

Loss:=C*Perc/100;

Entry:= InpYear=Year() AND InpMonth=Month() AND InpDay=DayOfMonth();

EntryLock:=If(Ref(Entry,-1)=0 AND Entry=1,1,PREV);

support:=If(LongShort=1,C-loss,C+loss);

StopLong:= If(EntryLock=0 OR Entry=1,InitStop,

If(support>Ref(Support,-1),Max(support,PREV),PREV));

StopShort:= If(EntryLock=0 OR Entry=1,InitStop,

If(support>Ref(Support,-1),Min(support,PREV),PREV));

Trail:=If(LongShort=1,Stoplong,Stopshort);

Trail

 Please utilize the disc in the back of the book for instant access to these codes. You may also download them from www.traderslibrary.com/tlecorner.

Initial Stop Application

Let's assume we bought the stock in figure 10.4 on January 6, 2003, based on the fact that the closing price was breaking the downtrend line.

With an initial stop at $6.10, we are at the support of a previously low pivot point. With a closing price below this stop, there is a good chance that the correction phase is not finished and that it will be better to close the trade with a loss. This stop gives a possible 13% loss and keeps the trade more or less within the limits of an acceptable loss on a single trade.

Figure 10.4: Buying the stock on January 6, 2003

Source - MetaStock® charts courtesy of Equis International.

Opening the formula "SVE_Stop_Trail%_Date", we enter the date (figure 10.5) in this trailing stop date function; we select 1 for a long position and we set an initial stop value of $6.10. Finally, we set the trailing stop at 7%, but we

Figure 10.5: Entering the stop properties

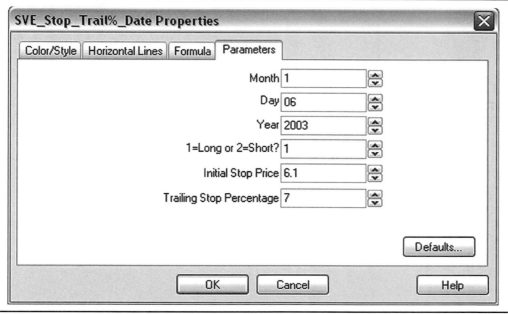

Source - MetaStock® charts courtesy of Equis International.

can change this value once the price begins moving in the right direction. We will close this long position at the latest when the closing price falls through the initial or trailing stop.

Figure 10.6: Stop broken right from the start

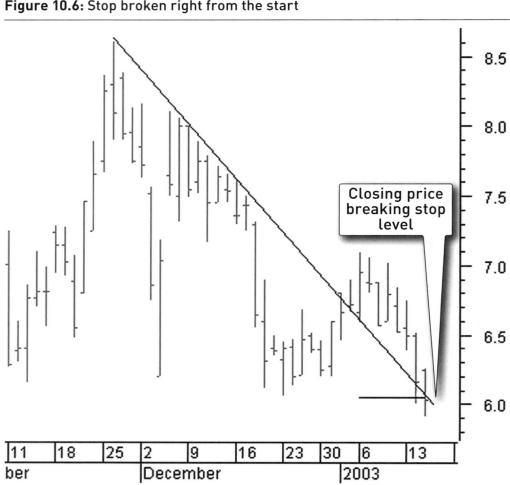

Source - MetaStock® charts courtesy of Equis International.

Unfortunately, right from the buying moment, the price starts falling and passes the initial stop (figure 10.6). When the closing price drops through the initial stop, the transaction is closed.

Figure 10.7: Disastrous trade without a proper stop

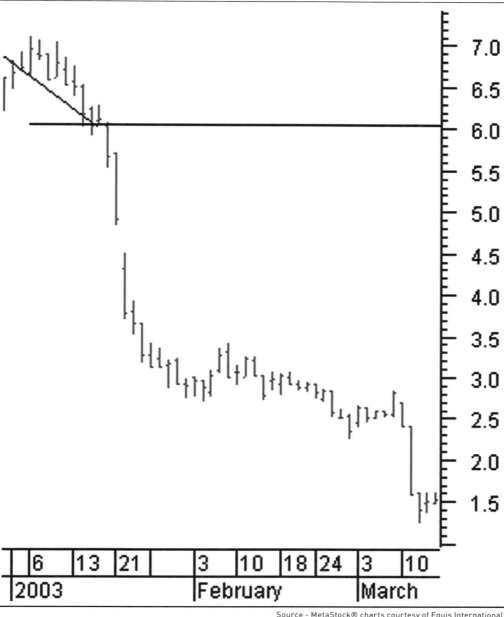

Source - MetaStock® charts courtesy of Equis International.

But, as you can see in figure 10.7, it is a consolation to know that without this stop, this trade could have ended in catastrophe. That's why keeping an initial stop is so important: to limit the loss after opening a position.

This initial stop is the last warning to sell! It is bad practice not to obey this last warning!

Trailing Stop

With a long position and a price that has continued to move up after opening the trade, a trailing stop will track the up-move and will signal if price falls back more than by its allowed value. After a sufficient up-move, the trailing stop will prevent all of the profit from being lost.

The initial stop will always remain the ultimate warning for closing the trade.

Figure 10.8: Buying signal when the closing price breaks above the last descending trend line

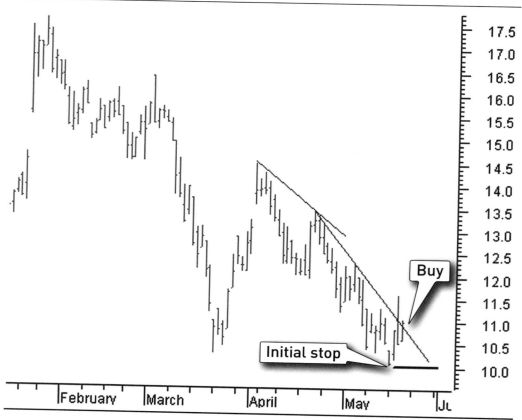

Source - MetaStock® charts courtesy of Equis International.

In figure 10.8, we have a buying signal when the closing price breaks above the last descending trend line. With an initial stop at $10.00, or about 9% below the buying price, we are just below the last lowest turning point.

Choosing a trailing stop value is contingent on the desired outcome of the trade. Are you a short-term swing trader, or do you like to catch the bigger moves on the medium- to longer-term trends?

Figure 10.9: Small trailing stop broken

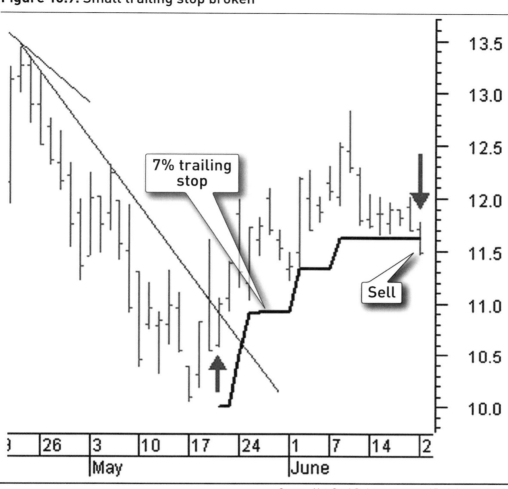

Source - MetaStock® charts courtesy of Equis International.

Let's first have a look at the short-term trend. Looking at the average daily price movement for this stock, it looks like we have to allow price reactions in the order of 7%. We, therefore, keep for our shorter-term example a trailing stop of 7%.

On June 21 (figure 10.9), this trailing stop is broken; the position can be closed with a small profit.

Trying to catch bigger moves, usually related to longer time periods, will require you to use a bigger trailing stop percentage; this will allow bigger intermediate price reactions to keep you in the trade. Looking at the past volatility of this stock, 12% seems to be a good choice as a medium- to longer-term trailing stop.

Figure 10.10: Longer-term stop broken

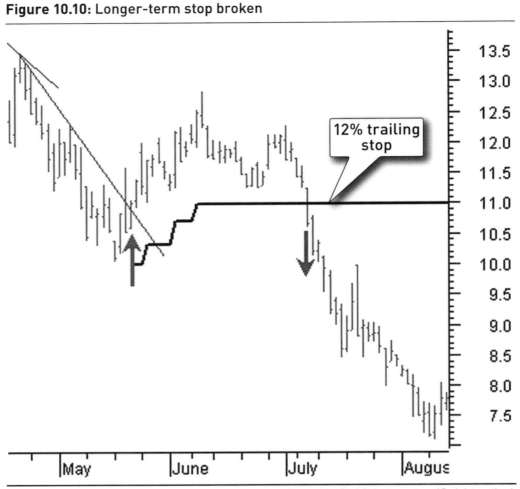

Source - MetaStock® charts courtesy of Equis International.

Apparently, the up-move in June was just a short-term reaction in a longer-term down-move, as we can see in figure 10.10. On July 8, the closing price falls through the 12% trailing stop. We close the position with a small loss.

Again, it is clear that not executing a stop is a bad practice and may subsequently leave you with very big losses.

Figure 10.11: Trailing stop performing well in medium-term uptrend

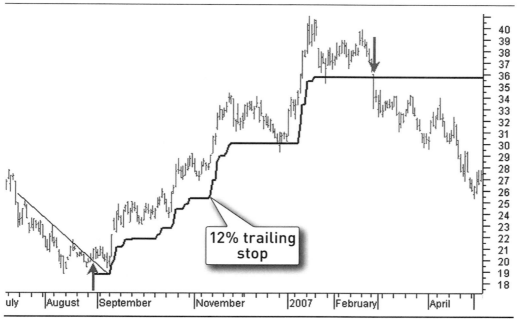

Source - MetaStock® charts courtesy of Equis International.

In figure 10.11, we see that in a medium-term uptrend, the trailing stop does a good job as a last warning signal. It tells us to take profit before losing any more profits, while keeping us in the trade for the kind of price moves and time period we want.

> **In LOCKIT you must always use an initial stop and a trailing stop as a last warning signal to close a position. Remember, you can also use the ATR-based trailing stop I presented in chapter 5.**

LOCKIT

Risk-to-Reward Ratio

The K-ratio within LOCKIT includes the money-management method and manages risk by using an initial and trailing stop. The initial stop should be such that we always, at a minimum, have a risk-to-reward ratio of 1 to 3.

Limiting the possible loss in a trade is probably the most important factor when considering a new position. Assume that of all trades, 50% are winning trades and 50% are losing trades. With an average loss of 15%, we would have to make an average profit of 25% on winning trades to end up with a final profit of only 10%. Don't forget that a 25% up-move in a stock is already a big move. It will not be easy to make profits!

If, on the other hand, we suffer a loss of only 5% on a losing trade, we would have to make a limited 15% profit on winning trades to end up with a 10% profit. This is much easier, since smaller moves are more common. At the opening of a position, the risk-to-reward ratio should be a minimum of one to three.

Figure 10.12: Centerpoint Energy Inc. breaking out of triangle correction pattern

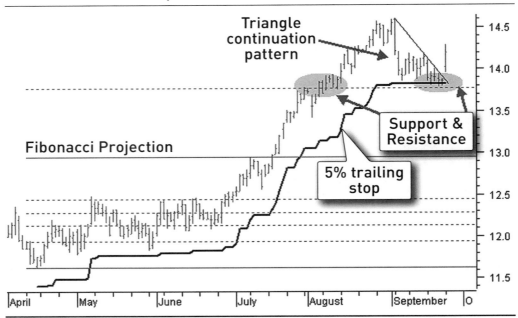

Source - MetaStock® charts courtesy of Equis International.

The up-move in the Centerpoint Energy Inc. chart (in figure 10.12) is slowing down during the month of September. The correction makes a triangle continuation chart pattern, with a breakout to the upper side. At the same time, the price finds support at the level of the first Fibonacci target projection (161.8%) and at a 5% trailing stop level, in use since the beginning of the up-move.

The detailed candlestick chart in figure 10.13 confirms the support of a doji at the beginning of September and is further confirmed with a number of dojis and the support of a window.

Now buying Centerpoint at a closing price of $14.20 allows us to keep a close stop at $13.90 at the low of the window support, followed by a lot more support just a fraction lower.

Figure 10.13: Centerpoint Energy Inc. detailed candlestick view

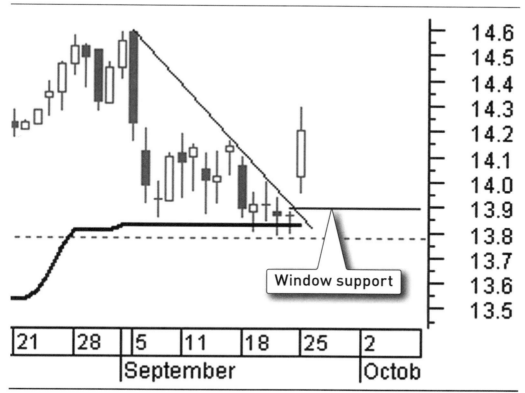

Source - MetaStock® charts courtesy of Equis International.

What are the Price Targets?

The next Fibonacci price target (see chapter 6 "Price Projections") is at 261.8%, or $15.10. This also is the level of a previous top in the price chart (not shown). This target is sufficient to comply with the one to three risk-to-reward ratio.

If the window we have now is a continuation window in the uptrend, it would mean that we are only about halfway through the up-move, which means that the target will still be a lot higher.

Finally, there is the third Fibonacci target at 423.6%, or $17.20, that we should not exclude: It is a window out of the past (not shown) that has not yet been closed.

We can, therefore, consider this a favorable risk-to-reward ratio. We buy the stock with an initial stop at $13.80 or about 3% below our buying price, just below the last turning point, and we continue using the 5% trailing stop.

Figure 10.14: Centerpoint Energy Inc., a very positive result

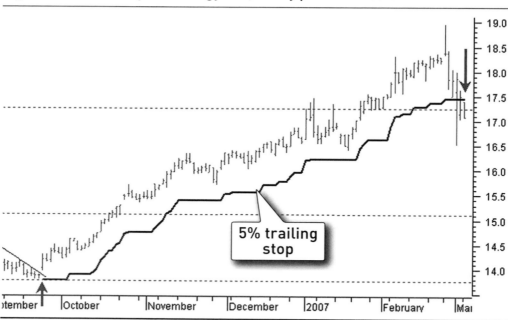

Source - MetaStock® charts courtesy of Equis International.

If the move up continues, as is the case here (figure 10.14), we have an enormously positive risk-to-reward ratio. And, had the move turned out wrong, the risk would have been limited to a loss of about 3%.

Even with just 40% winning trades and 60% losing trades, the end result will still be positive. This is why it is very important to apply good money- and risk-management techniques with every trade.

Gammon Lake Res Inc.: Buy Here?

In figure 10.15, the price has made a bigger correction and is now turning up and breaking the last steeper downtrend line. There is some support from a previous window, even if it has been broken recently. There is also support from a last and a previous turning point and from a hammer pattern in the candlestick chart at the same level as the window support. All of these are good technical reasons to open a trade.

What about the Risk-to-Reward Ratio?

Buying at a price of about $11, we find a first support level at around $10, some 10% lower. The trailing 10% stop that was used in the last down move appears to be a sensible stop with the actual price volatility. This stop is not yet broken by the new uptrend. The first price target is at $12, the last previous high. Next, there is the resistance of two windows at $12.50 and $13.

Figure 10.15: Gammon Lake Res Inc., buy here or not?

Source - MetaStock® charts courtesy of Equis International.

This rather high initial stop of 10% and the three resistance levels very close by give us a bad risk-to-reward ratio.

The decision to take is not to buy!

Three days later (figure 10.16) Gammon Lake Res Inc. is still moving up.

We now have a window between the price of yesterday and today. This window gives support, together with a previous small bottom from the end of September. Buying now allows us to set a very close initial stop at 3%.

A Fibonacci projection from the low point and the start of the window, which is also the small previous low point in price that we can use to create a historical Fibonacci projection, gives price targets at $12.50 and $14.50. Buying here gives us a very good risk-to-reward ratio.

We should buy now!

Buying with the first signal would have given a fraction more profit. But the risk-to-reward ratio was really bad that moment in time! We now have almost the same profit, but with an initial risk of only a 3% loss.

Figure 10.16: Gammon Lake Res Inc. three days later, a better buying moment

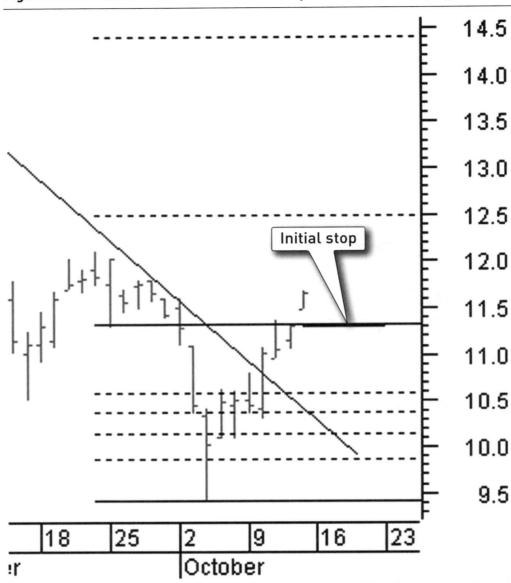

Initial stop

18   25   2   9   16   23

ᴉr   October

Source - MetaStock® charts courtesy of Equis International.

In figure 10.17, we reach the Fibonacci targets at $12.50 and $14.50. Even the next Fibonacci target at $17.50 came very close.

In the beginning of September, you could have made the decision to buy this stock when the price started moving up with a window. Even the risk-to-reward ratio would have been acceptable. Unfortunately, though, this would have been a losing trade.

Figure 10.17: Gammon Lake Res Inc. reaching the Fibonacci targets

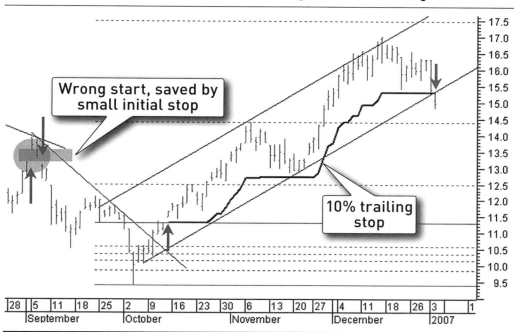

Source - MetaStock® charts courtesy of Equis International.

Thanks to the close stop at the lower side of the window, you would have gotten out of the trade with only a small loss. Of course, it makes no sense to systematically use a small initial stop of, for example, 3%. The stop level used must be supported by technical analysis.

Adapting the Buying Capital?

Could we make more profit by adapting the buying capital in some circumstances?

When analyzing buying signals, you will notice that some trades have a higher probability for success than others. Some buying signals are supported and confirmed by Fibonacci levels, some when the price makes a move after a longer consolidation period or breaks out of a price pattern, and so on. This is especially true when more of these confirmations act together.

Opening a position with a high probability for success can be made more profitable by risking some extra capital. You could, for example, use 75% for buying with some doubts and a not-that-great risk-to-reward ratio; 100% for a standard buy; and 150% for a trade with high probability for success.

STOCK INSURANCE POLICY

Besides using, as proposed by LOCKIT, money management, trailing stops, and initial stops with a good risk-to-reward ratio, you could use stock options to limit losses right from the start.

If you really want to know beforehand your maximum loss when trading stocks, you can have an insurance policy using stock options. This is a rather lengthy topic, which I will only briefly cover here. If you have a large interest in options, I would suggest you check out material by the Options Industry Council (OIC) at http://www.optionseducation.org. There are also many great books available at www.traderslibrary.com.

LOCKIT

> In LOCKIT, our main concern is to analyze each trade for the proper risk-to-reward ratio and to use our stops appropriately.

General Tire & Rubber Co.

Let's use GT as an example. And let's assume a total capital of $30,000, investing in a minimum of 10 different stocks to spread the risk.

Figure 10.18: Stock insurance policy example with GT

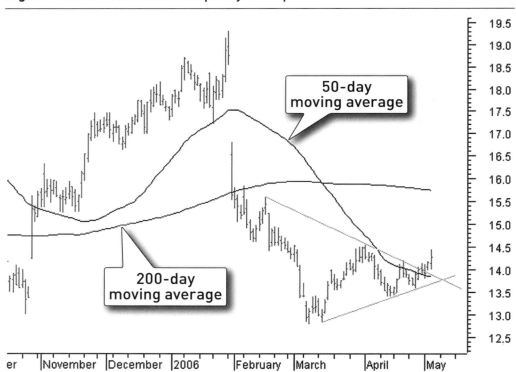

Source - MetaStock® charts courtesy of Equis International.

We then have a starting amount of $3,000 per stock. We allow a 10% loss from the start, or as a trailing stop, because we want to catch the bigger moves of this stock. This means a loss of $300 in one trade. This limits the loss to 1% in relation to the total investment capital, complying with good money management.

Buying the Stock

On May 4, 2006, GT moves above a descending trend line in figure 10.18 after a bottom is reached. The price makes a new up-move with higher bottoms. The stock price is also above the 50-day simple moving average. We buy GT at the opening price the next day (figure 10.19).

Figure 10.19: Buying GT at the next day opening price

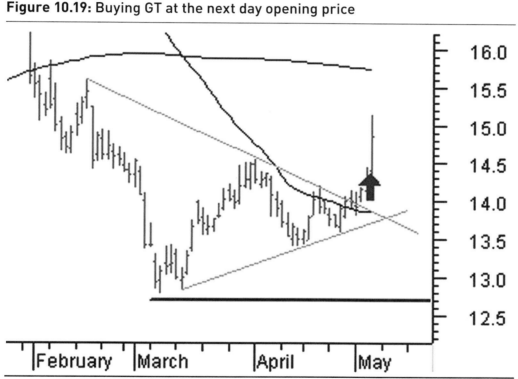

Source - MetaStock® charts courtesy of Equis International.

First, let's look at the scenario without options. We invested $2,890 buying 200 pieces of GT on May 4 at the opening price of $14.45. We allowed a maximum loss from the start until just below the lowest point from the beginning of March. This was a stop at $12.70, for a possible loss of $1.75, or 12%.

Insurance with Put Options

In this scenario, we will not use a stop loss, but we will limit the possible loss by covering the position with a put option. A put option is a contract that gives the owner the right, but not the obligation, to sell a stock at the strike price before the expiration date. One option contract gives the right to control 100 shares of stock until expiration, unless the contract otherwise specifies.

For all theoretical option calculations using the Black–Scholes model, let's assume a volatility of 25%, an interest rate of 5%, and an expiration date of January 2007. With an exercise price of $14, we will pay $0.80 for this option. We will buy two contracts to cover the 200 shares of GT that we bought. The total cost for these two put contracts is $160.

We now own the right to sell 200 shares of GT at a price of $14 until the third Friday in January 2007. At worst, the total possible loss will be 14.45 -14 = 0.45 + 0.80 = $1.25, or a 9% loss. Our total investment is $3,050.

Price Drops below Support

The stock price hits resistance and fails to break the 200-day simple moving average (figure 10.20); it drops below the ascending trend line out of the ascending price channel and below the 50-day simple moving average.

Looking at the short term, there is a big chance that the stock price will move down farther.

Writing Covered Call Options

This is an opportunity to win back part of our insurance money.

Let's write a couple of covered call options. Writing a call option is a contract that obliges the owner to deliver the stock at the strike price before the expiration date. As is the case with puts, the option contract controls 100 shares of the underlying stock until expiration unless the contract otherwise specifies.

At the stock price of $13.74 on May 17, we write two call options with an expiration of July 2006 and with an exercise price of $14. This brings in $110 and pays back part of the cost of the put options we bought as insurance, at least if all goes as expected.

Possible Result

The bad scenario: The stock price rises short term to $15 (for example). We may be exercised and have to deliver the stock. Closing this transaction will give the following result: stock value ($3,000) plus the actual value of the put option ($120) minus the actual value of the written call options ($280) for a

Figure 10.20: Price hits resistance and fails to break the moving average

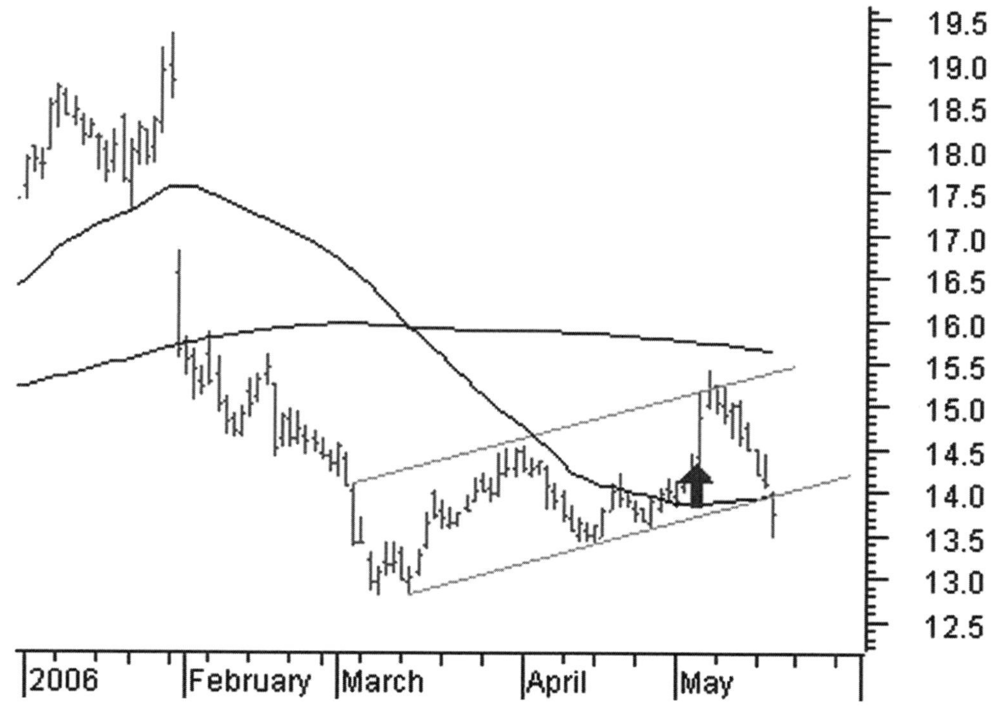

total of $2,840, or a loss of $210. If the stock price moves above the exercise price of the written calls, it clearly is better to close the position or, in any case, buy back the calls; otherwise, if the stock price keeps moving up, the invested capital is blocked.

The good scenario: The stock price drops to $12.50 (for example). Your protection with the put options at 14 is unchanged. The written call options now have a value of only $0.30. You can buy them back and make a net profit of $80.

Writing these call options is an opportunity, but you do not have to do it. It generally will not change the final result all that much.

Figure 10.21: Price drops below the stop loss

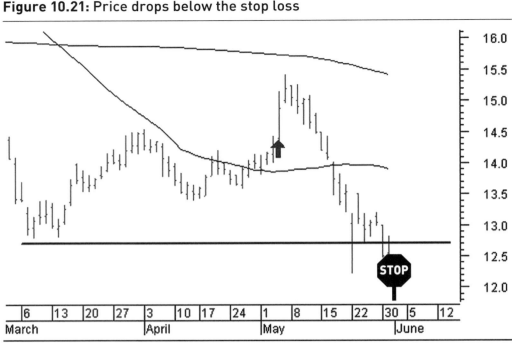

Source - MetaStock® charts courtesy of Equis International.

Price Drops below the Stop Loss

Without the put options insurance, you must sell GT at a value of $12.54 on May 31 (figure 10.21).

The stock price drops below the stop loss; this would create a loss: the buying cost (-$2,890) plus the sell ($2,508) for a total of -$382, or a loss of 13.2%.

Forced to Sell After a Big Move Down?

When using put options as insurance, what is the result when you have to close the trade after a big move down because you need the money?

On July 28, the stock price is at $10.57 in figure 10.22. The price is close to the lowest low point. If, for any reason, you had to close the position now, what would the result be?

Be warned that without the put options, holding your position because you don't like to take losses or because you believe that what comes down must go up again will create a very unhealthy situation.

You are looking at a loss: buying cost (-$2,890) plus the sell ($1,943) equals -$947, or a loss of 32.7%. This is very bad money and risk management; something you cannot permit very often!

Figure 10.22: Forced to sell after a big move down?

Source - MetaStock® charts courtesy of Equis International.

Things look a lot better when covered by the put options insurance. In this case, your loss is minimized: buying cost (-$2,890) minus the cost of the put options (-$160) plus the selling of the stock ($2,114) plus the selling the put options ($640) equals -$296, or a loss of 10.2%.

If you had made $80 writing calls, your loss would be further limited to -$216, or -7.4%. That is a big difference compared to the loss of -32.7%, which was caused by not having the options insurance policy.

Figure 10.23: Making extra profit buying call options

Source - MetaStock® charts courtesy of Equis International.

Making Extra Profit Buying Call Options

On August 28, the stock price moves above a resistance line and is already moving for some time above the 50-day simple moving average.

In figure 10.23, you can see how the price breaks out of an ascending triangle. This is a continuation pattern for a further price upmove. It looks like a new uptrend is on the way some three months later than first imagined when the stock was bought.

Taking a small, additional risk can add to our profits… if the price keeps going up. We buy an extra pair of out-of-the-money call options.

At a stock price of $12.60, we buy two call contracts with an expiration date of January 2007 (the same expiration date as the put options we bought as insurance) and an exercise price of $14. This costs us just $80.

Closing the Position, November 30

After a price top of around $19 (figure 10.24), the price falls back and we decide to take profit.

Figure 10.24: Taking profit, closing the position

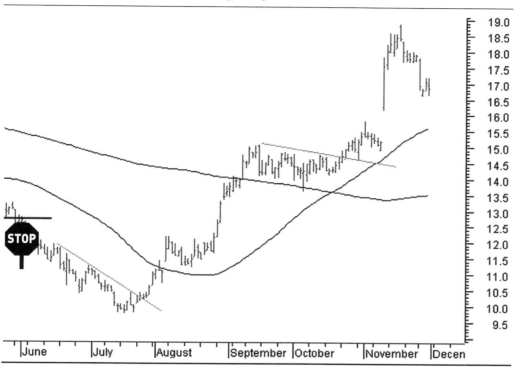

On November 30, the stock price is at $16.85. Without the extra call options the profit is the sell of the stock ($3,370) plus the buying cost (-$2,890) plus the cost of the put options (-$160) equaling $320, or an 11% gain. Do not forget that we had more than a 30% drawback in between.

With the extra call options, the profit is the sell of the stock ($3,370) plus the sell of the call options ($600) plus the buying cost of the stock (-$2,890) plus the cost of the put options (-$160) plus the cost of the call options (-$80) equaling $840 in profit, or 29%.

The Result at Expiration Date

With the put options, you are covered until January 19, 2007. The call options expire on the same date. If the price remains above support and above the 50-day simple moving average, it could be worth waiting for more profit.

Another possibility would be to fix the profit, close the positions, and invest part of the profit in new longer-term call options. That way, you continue to profit if the price continues its way up.

Figure 10.25: The result at expiration date

On January 19, in figure 10.25, the stock price is at $24.22. The result without the extra call options is $4,844 minus $160 equaling $4,684, or a 53% profit.

The result with the extra call options is better: we sold the stock for $4,844 plus the call options ($2,000) minus the cost of the put options ($160) minus the cost of the call options ($80) equaling $6,604, or a profit of 117%.

Remarks

Combining stocks and options can be very profitable. Big drawbacks that normally force you out of the position with big losses are no problem with an options insurance policy. What is most important about the insurance setup is to buy the put options at the same moment that you buy the stock. This fixes the maximum possible loss.

Once you are convinced that the stock is moving the right way, you can buy some call options to boost possible profits. To allow sufficient time for the stock to make the move, you should buy options with an expiration time from six to, preferably, nine months out.

Making an immediate decision is no longer urgent because whatever happens with the stock, the worst possible loss is already known. No more stress; sleeping like a baby is guaranteed.

> This concludes PART V. We looked at crash resistant money-management and risk-management LOCKIT techniques that use initial and trailing stop loss settings and carefully calculated risk-to-reward ratios. We also briefly covered the use of a put option insurance technique.

LOCKIT

 For a closer look at the charts in this chapter,
go to www.traderslibrary.com/TLEcorner.

TEST YOUR CHAPTER 10 KNOWLEDGE

1. I would not open a new long trade here. Can you tell me why?

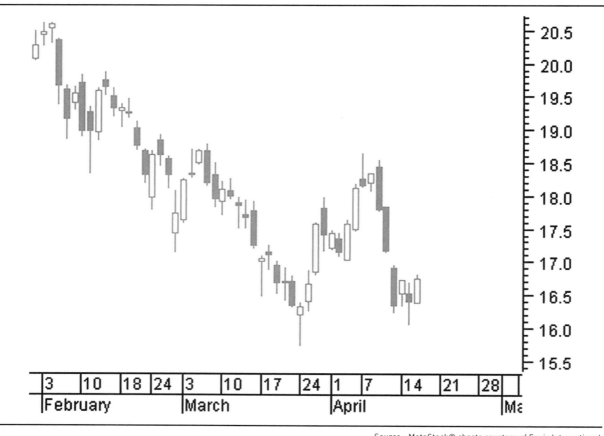

Source - MetaStock® charts courtesy of Equis International.

2. You missed the entry at the start of the new uptrend, but your friend tells you that this stock is going to move much higher; should you buy?

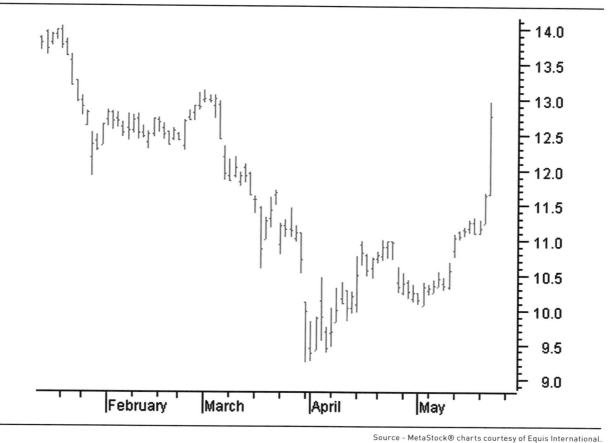

3. Would you close an open long trade or would you risk a short trade here?

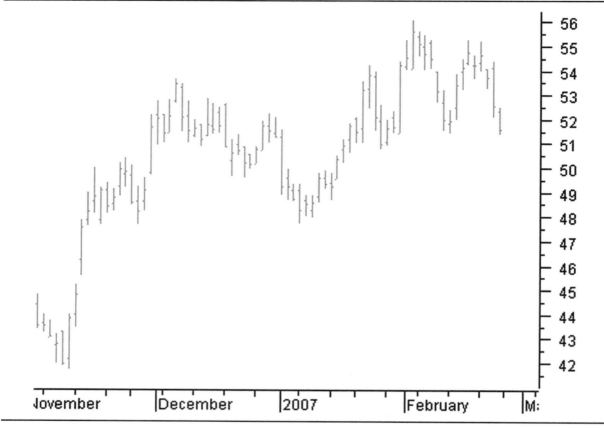

_____

_____

_____

_____

_____

_____

_____

_____

Q&A For answers, please visit the Traders' Library Education Corner at
www.traderslibrary.com/tlecorner.

CONCLUSION

LOCKIT is all about applying the broad field of technical analysis and money- and risk-management techniques for better trading results. Let's summarize what we've learned.

L

With **"L"** you are not only looking at the **long-term trend**, but you are also looking at the recent past. This will help you to decide if a longer or shorter price turnaround can be expected. You can imagine that after a 100% price up move, it will be extremely rare for a correction to end in just a couple of days or weeks or with only a small 10% correction.

O

"O" looks at **opening a trade** using basic technical analysis like support and resistance lines, trend lines or indicators, and more complex techniques like candle chart pattern recognition and Elliott wave analysis. Let's not forget that we discussed some complementary tools that will help you find entries with a high probability for success and my own SVAPO oscillator.

C

"C" stands for **closing the trade** using exactly the same techniques that we used for opening a trade. However, since an open trade is involved, closing a trade will always be additionally protected by an initial and a trailing stop. Furthermore, price moves that reach their price projection targets will carry more weight in our decision-making process.

K

With "K" for **k-ratio,** we look at money management and risk management. The most profitable money-management method I could find is using a fixed quantity of stocks. Stocks are given the same amount of money from the start, and we will not distribute any profit or loss between these stocks. Risk management is split in applying an initial stop loss and a trailing stop loss setting.

I

"I" stands for an **initial stop loss setting**. Initial stops are based mainly on support or resistance levels. It is clear that the smaller the initial stop level, the better the risk-to-reward ratio will be. Avoid entering trades with too high a risk level. There will be plenty of opportunities that will allow you to use just a small initial stop.

T

Finally, "T" makes sure that you use a **trailing stop setting**. With the initial stop and the trailing stop, there will be an ultimate selling signal if our decision-making based on normal technical analysis fails.

I hope that the **LOCKIT** system and all of the technical analysis techniques explained therein, plus our money-management and risk-management techniques and my SVAPO oscillator, will boost your own technical analysis trading… and that it will make you a lot of **money**.

I wish you successful and happy trading!

Sylvain Vervoort

APPENDIX

Special indicators in this book are written in MetaStock® formula programming language. In this appendix you will find all LOCKIT special indicator formulas. I've also included a list of other technical analysis programs which make available most of the formulas here.

Contact your program provider to find the available formulas.

LIST OF OTHER TECHNICAL ANALYSIS PROGRAM PROVIDERS

These providers have most of the special LOCKIT formulas available.

Program	Company	Website
TradeStation	Tradestation securities Inc	www.TradeStation.com
eSignal	Interactive Data Corp.	www.esignalcentral.com
WealthLab	WealthLab.com	www.wealth-lab.com
AmiBroker	AmiBroker	www.amibroker.com
Neuroshell Trader	Ward Systems Group	www.neuroshell.com
Ameritrade	TD Ameritrade Holding Corp.	www.tdameritrade.com
Blocks	Worden Brothers Inc.	www.Blocks.com
AIQ	AIQ Systems	www.aiqsystems.com
TradersStudio	TradersStudio Inc.	www.TradersStudio.com
NeoTicker	TickQuest Inc.	www.tickquest.com
StrataSearch	Avarin Systems Inc.	www.StrataSearch.com
Aspen Graphics	Aspen Research Group Ltd.	www.Aspenres.com
OmniTrader Pro	Nirvana Systems Inc.	www.omnitrader.com
Ninja Trader	Ninja Trader LLC	www.ninjatrader.com
MetaTrader 4	MistigriFX	www.mistigrifx.com
VT Trader	CMS Forex	www.cmsfx.com

SPECIAL METASTOCK® FORMULAS USED IN LOCKIT

 Please utilize the disc in the back of the book for instant access to these codes. You may also download them from www.traderslibrary.com/tlecorner.

ZeroLagSMA - zero-lag simple moving average on the closing prices

> Period:= Input("Which period?",1,250,10);
>
> SMA1:= Mov(CLOSE,Period,S);
>
> SMA2:= Mov(SMA1,Period,S);
>
> Difference:= SMA1 - SMA2;
>
> ZeroLagSMA:= SMA1 + Difference;
>
> ZeroLagSMA

ZeroLagEMA - zero-lag exponential moving average on the closing prices

> Period:= Input("Which period?"1,250,10);
>
> EMA1:= Mov(CLOSE,Period,E);
>
> EMA2:= Mov(EMA1,Period,E);
>
> Difference:= EMA1 - EMA2;
>
> ZeroLagEMA:= EMA1 + Difference;
>
> ZeroLagEMA

ZeroLagTMA Cl (ZLTMACL) – zero-lag TEMA average on the closing prices

> Period:= Input("Zero-lagging CL TEMA Average ",1,100,60);
>
> TMA1:= Tema(CLOSE,Period);
>
> TMA2:= Tema(TMA1,Period);
>
> Difference:= TMA1 - TMA2;
>
> ZeroLagTMACL:= TMA1 + Difference;
>
> ZeroLagTMACL

ZeroLagTMATyp – zero-lag TEMA average on the typical prices

```
period := Input("TEMA period? ",1,100,55);
TMA1:= Tema(Typ(),period);
TMA2:= Tema(TMA1,period);
Difference:= TMA1 - TMA2;
ZeroLagTMATyp:= TMA1 + Difference;
ZeroLagTMATyp
```

haC - Average heikin ashi closing price

```
haOpen:=(Ref((O+H+L+C)/4,-1) + PREV)/2;
haC:=((O+H+L+C)/4+haOpen+Max(H,haOpen)+Min(L,haOpen))/4;
haC
```

ZeroLagTMAHA (ZLTMAHA) - zero-lag heikin ashi TEMA average

```
avg := Input("TEMA average? ",1,100,55);
haOpen:=(Ref((O+H+L+C)/4,-1) + PREV)/2;
haC:=((O+H+L+C)/4+haOpen+Max(H,haOpen)+Min(L,haOpen))/4;
TMA1:= Tema(haC,avg);
TMA2:= Tema(TMA1,avg);
Diff:= TMA1 - TMA2;
ZeroLagTMAHA:= TMA1 + Diff;
ZeroLagTMAHA
```

Automatic trading system with zero-lag TEMA crossovers
Buying condition:

```
avg:= 65;
EMA1:= Tema((H+L+C)/3,avg);
EMA2:= Tema(EMA1,avg);
Difference:= EMA1 - EMA2;
ZlCl:= EMA1 + Difference;
haOpen:=(Ref((O+H+L+C)/4,-1) + PREV)/2;
haC:=((O+H+L+C)/4+haOpen+Max(H,haOpen)+Min(L,haOpen))/4;
EMA1:= Tema(haC,avg);
EMA2:= Tema(EMA1,avg);
Difference:= EMA1 - EMA2;
ZlHa:= EMA1 + Difference;
Cross(ZlCl,ZlHa)
```

Selling condition:

```
avg:= 65;
EMA1:= Tema((H+L+C)/3,avg);
EMA2:= Tema(EMA1,avg);
Difference:= EMA1 - EMA2;
ZlCl:= EMA1 + Difference;
haOpen:=(Ref((O+H+L+C)/4,-1) + PREV)/2;
haC:=((O+H+L+C)/4+haOpen+Max(H,haOpen)+Min(L,haOpen))/4;
EMA1:= Tema(haC,avg);
EMA2:= Tema(EMA1,avg);
Difference:= EMA1 - EMA2;
ZlHa:= EMA1 + Difference;
Cross(ZlHa,ZlCl)
```

ATRCustom – ATR basic calculation

MetaStock® has a predefined ATR() function. If you need to calculate it on something other than the closing price, you can use the following formula (replace the "C" for closing price by what you want to use.

```
{Get the required ATR period;}
period:=Input("ATR Period :",1,100,5);
{Calculate the biggest difference based on the true range concept;}
diff1:=Max(H-L,Abs(H-Ref(C,-1)));
diff2:=Max(diff1,Abs(L-Ref(C,-1)));
{Use Wilders' moving average method to calculate the Average
True Range;}
ATRCustom:=Mov(diff2,period*2-1,E);
ATRCustom
```

SVE_RSI_StDev - RSI custom formula with variable standard deviation lines:

```
{SVE_RSI_StDev}
period:= Input("RSI period?",1,100,14);
afwh:= Input("Standard deviation high side",0.1,5,1.5);
afwl:= Input("Standard deviation Low side",0.1,5,1.5);
afwper:= Input("Standard deviation lookback",1,200,100);
SVERSIStDev:=RSI(C,period);
50+afwh*Stdev(SVERSIStDev,afwper);
50-afwl*Stdev(SVERSIStDev,afwper);
SVERSIStDev
```

SVE_BB%b_HA - heikin ashi Bollinger Bands %b indicator:

```
{SVE_BB%b_HA}
peri:=Input("Average period: ",2,100,18);
haOpen:=(Ref((O+H+L+C)/4,-1) + PREV)/2;
haC:=((O+H+L+C)/4+haOpen+Max(H,haOpen)+Min(L,haOpen))/4;
SVEBB%bHA:=((haC+2*Stdev(haC,peri)-Mov(haC,peri,W))/
(4*Stdev(haC,peri)))*100;
SVEBB%bHA
```

SVAPO – Short Term Volume And Price Oscillator

```
{calculate the heikin ashi closing average haCl and get the input
variables}
haOpen:=(Ref((O+H+L+C)/4,-1) + PREV)/2;
haCl:=((O+H+L+C)/4+haOpen+Max(H,haOpen)+Min(L,haOpen))/4;
period:= Input("SVAPO period :", 2, 20, 8);
cutoff:= Input("Minimum %o price change :",0,10,1);
{Inputs for standard deviation bands}
devH:= Input("Standard Deviation High :", 0.1, 5, 1.5);
devL:= Input("Standard Deviation Low :", 0.1, 5, 1.3);
stdevper:= Input("Standard Deviation Period :", 1, 200, 100);
{Smooth HaCl closing price}
haC:=Tema(haCl,period/1.6);
{Medium term MA of Volume to limit extremes and division factor}
vave:=Ref(Mov(V,period*5,S),-1);
vmax:=vave*2;
vc:=If(V<vmax,V,vmax);
{Basic volume trend}
vtr:=Tema(LinRegSlope(V,period),period);
{SVAPO result of price and volume}
SVAPO:=Tema(Sum(If(haC>(Ref(haC,-1)*(1+cutoff/1000)) AND
Alert(vtr>=Ref(vtr,-1),2), vc, If(haC<(Ref(haC,-1)*(1-cutoff/1000))
AND Alert(vtr>Ref(vtr,-1),2),-vc,0)),period)/(vave+1),period);
devH*Stdev(SVAPO,stdevper);
-devL*Stdev(SVAPO,stdevper);
zeroref:=0;
zeroref;
SVAPO
```

SVAPO_NoVol – SVAPO for data that has no volume component

```
{calculate heikin ashi closing average haCl and get the input vari-
ables}

haOpen:=(Ref((O+H+L+C)/4,-1) + PREV)/2;

haCl:=((O+H+L+C)/4+haOpen+Max(H,haOpen)+Min(L,haOpen))/4;

{input SVAPO period}

period:= Input("SVAPO period :", 2, 20, 8);

{input minimum per thousand price change}

cutoff:= Input("Minimum %o price change :",0.0,10,1);

{Inputs for standard deviation bands}

devH:= Input("Standard Deviation High :", 0.1, 5, 1.5);

devL:= Input("Standard Deviation Low :", 0.1, 5, 1.3);

stdevper:= Input("Standard Deviation Period :", 1, 200, 100);

{Smooth HaCl closing price}

haC:=Tema(haCl,period/1.6);

{MA of closing price to limit extremes}

vave:=Ref(Mov(C,period*5,S),-1);

vmax:=vave*2;

vc:=If(C<vmax,C,vmax);

{Basic price trend}

vtr:=Tema(LinRegSlope(C,period),period);

{SVAPO result of price, extremes and basic trend}

SVAPONoVol:=Tema(Sum(If(haC>(Ref(haC,-1)*(1+cutoff/1000)) AND
Alert(vtr>=Ref(vtr,-1),2), vc, If(haC<(Ref(haC,-1)*(1-cutoff/1000))
AND Alert(vtr>Ref(vtr,-1),2),-vc,0)),period)/(vave+1),period);

devH*Stdev(SVAPONoVol,stdevper);

-devL*Stdev(SVAPONoVol,stdevper);

zeroref:=0;

zeroref;

SVAPONoVol
```

SVE_Elliott_Count – help indicator for Elliott wave counts

```
{SVE_Elliott_Count}
Proc:= Input("ZigZag %?",.01,50,2.4);
haOpen:=(Ref((O+H+L+C)/4,-1) + PREV)/2;
haC:=((O+H+L+C)/4+haOpen+Max(H,haOpen)+Min(L,haOpen))/4;
SVEElliottCount:=Zig(haC,Proc,%);
SVEElliottCount
```

SVE_Stop_Trail% - auto reversing trailing stop on closing price percentage change

```
{SVE_Stop_Trail%}
perc:=Input("Trailing Loss % :",0,100,14);
loss:=C*perc/100;
trail:=
If(C>PREV AND Ref(C,-1)>PREV,
Max(PREV,C-loss),
If(C<PREV AND Ref(C,-1)<PREV,
Min(PREV,C+loss),
If(C>PREV,C-loss,C+loss)));
Trail
```

SVE_Stop_Trail%_Date - initial and percentage trailing stop from an entry date

```
{SVE_Stop_Trail%_Date - Fixed percentage trailing stop from date}
InpMonth:=Input("Month",1,12,1);
InpDay:=Input("Day",1,31,1);
InpYear:=Input("Year",1800,2050,2009);
LongShort:=Input("1=Long or 2=Short? ",1,2,1);
InitStop:=Input("Initial Stop Price",0.1,10000,10);
Perc:=Input("Trailing Stop Percentage",1,30,12);
Loss:=C*Perc/100;
Entry:= InpYear=Year() AND InpMonth=Month() AND
InpDay=DayOfMonth();
EntryLock:=If(Ref(Entry,-1)=0 AND Entry=1,1,PREV);
support:=If(LongShort=1,C-loss,C+loss);
StopLong:= If(EntryLock=0 OR Entry=1,InitStop,
If(support>Ref(Support,-1),Max(support,PREV),PREV));
StopShort:= If(EntryLock=0 OR Entry=1,InitStop,
If(support>Ref(Support,-1),Min(support,PREV),PREV));
Trail:=If(LongShort=1,Stoplong,Stopshort);
Trail
```

SVE_StopLong_Trail_ATR_Date –
Long position initial and ATR trailing stop from an entry date

```
{SVE_StopLong_Trail_ATR_Date- ATR trailing stop long from date}
InpMonth:=Input("Month",1,12,1);
InpDay:=Input("Day",1,31,2);
InpYear:=Input("Year",1800,2050,2009);
InitStop:=Input("Initial Stop Price",0.1,10000,10);
atrper:=Input("ATR period :",1,100,5);
atrfact:=Input("ATR multiplication :",1,10,3.5);
loss:=atrfact*ATR(atrper);
EntryLong:= InpYear=Year() AND InpMonth=Month() AND
```

```
InpDay=DayOfMonth();
EntryLock:=If(Ref(EntryLong,-1)=0 AND EntryLong=1,1,PREV);
support:=C-loss;
TrailStopLong:= If(EntryLock=0 OR EntryLong=1,InitStop,
If(support>Ref(Support,-1),Max(support,PREV),PREV));
TrailStopLong
```

SVE_StopShort_Trail_ATR_Date –
Short position initial and ATR trailing stop from an entry date

```
{SVE_StopShort_Trail_ATR_Date- ATR trailing stop Short from
date}
InpMonth:=Input("Month",1,12,1);
InpDay:=Input("Day",1,31,2);
InpYear:=Input("Year",1800,2050,2009);
InitStop:=Input("Initial Stop Price",0.1,10000,10);
atrper:=Input("ATR period :",1,100,5);
atrfact:=Input("ATR multiplication :",1,10,3.5);
loss:=atrfact*ATR(atrper);
EntryLong:= InpYear=Year() AND InpMonth=Month() AND
InpDay=DayOfMonth();
EntryLock:=If(Ref(EntryLong,-1)=0 AND EntryLong=1,1,PREV);
support:=C+loss;
TrailStopShort:= If(EntryLock=0 OR EntryLong=1,InitStop,
If(support>Ref(Support,-1),Min(support,PREV),PREV));
TrailStopShort
```

Please utilize the disc in the back of the book for instant access to these codes. You may also download them from www.traderslibrary.com/tlecorner.

INDEX

Note: Figures are indicated by "f" following the page number.

I

impulse waves
longer-term rising, description of, 97–99
overview of, 94–96
as part of a cycle, 102
patterns, ending wedge wave, 110–112
patterns, recognizing, 103–107
patterns, starting wedge wave, 107–109
price targets for, 119–124
and trend channels, 119
indicators
overview of, 139–140
and price relation, 140–140
See also RSI (Relative Strength Index); SVAPO (Short Term Volume And
Price Oscillator); SVE_BB%b_HA
initial stop loss setting, 213, 346
in-neck line patterns, 88
inverse trend line, 16–17
inverted hammer patterns, 80

J

Japanese Candlestick Charting Techniques (Nison), 6, 66

K

K-ratio. *See* risk-to-reward ratio (K-ratio)

L

Liber Abaci (Fibonacci), 180
linear scaling, 7–9, 269
line charts, definition of, 5
LOCKIT acronym definitions, 345–346
logarithmic scaling, 7–9, 20, 204, 269–270
long-legged doji, 67, 73
long-term trend, 202–205, 345

M

marubozu candles, 67, 70
mat hold patterns, 87

T

WORKS CITED
& DISCLAIMERS

WORKS CITED

Bollinger, John. *Bollinger on Bollinger Bands.* New York: McGraw-Hill, 2001.

Frost, A. J., and Robert Prechter. *Elliott Wave Principle: Key to Market Behavior.* New York: John Wiley and Sons, 1978.

Mulloy, Patrick."Tema or Triple Exponential Moving Average." *Technical Analysis of Stocks & Commodities* 12, no. 2 (February 1994).

Nison, Steve. *Japanese Candlestick Charting Techniques.* New York: New York Institute of Finance, 1991.

Valcu, Dan. "Using the Heikin-Ashi Technique." *Technical Analysis of Stocks & Commodities* 22, no. 2 (February 2004): 16-28.

Wilder, J. Welles. *New Concepts in Technical Trading Systems.* Trend Research, June 1978.

Articles from *Technical Analysis of STOCKS & COMMODITIES*™ Magazine

Vervoort, Sylvain. "Trading Trend line Breaks, Part 1," *Technical Analysis of Stocks & Commodities* 25, no. 7 (July 2007): 56-58.

———. "Trading Trend line Breaks, Part 2," *Technical Analysis of Stocks & Commodities* 25, no. 9 (September 2007): 20-28.

———. "Trading Trend line Breaks, Part 3," *Technical Analysis of Stocks & Commodities* 25, no. 10 (October 2007): 40-46.

———. "Short-Term Volume and Price Oscillator," *Technical Analysis of Stocks & Commodities* 25, no. 11 (November 2007): 20-26.

———. "Short Term Trading with SVAPO," *Technical Analysis of Stocks & Commodities* 25, no. 13 (December 2007): 34-42.

———. "The Quest for Reliable Crossovers." *Technical Analysis of Stocks & Commodities* 26, no. 5 (May 2008): 20-25.

———. "Stock Insurance Policy." *Technical Analysis of Stocks & Commodities* 26, no. 8 (August 2008): 42-47.

These can be found at http://www.traders.com/. ©2008 Technical Analysis, Inc. All are used with permission.

DISCLAIMERS
Liability

Trading financial products involves risk. The information contained in this book is not comprehensive. Despite all efforts, it may not be accurate, up-to-date, or applicable to the circumstances of any particular case. We cannot accept any liability for any inaccuracies or omissions in this book, and any decisions you make based on information contained in this book are your sole responsibility. The publisher and author do not accept liability for any direct, indirect, special, consequential, or other losses or damages of whatsoever kind arising out of access to, or the use of this book or any information contained in it.

Copyright and Trademarks

The information available in this book is protected by the copyright laws. Copying, reproducing, publishing, or distributing the content of this book, in whole or in part, is strictly forbidden. Owners of this book are entitled to copy information contained in this book for non-commercial personal use. The prior written authorization of the publisher is required for any other use.

Risk Disclosure

CFTC RULE 4.41 Hypothetical or simulated performance results have certain inherent limitations unlike actual performance records: simulated results do not represent actual trading. Also, since the trades have not actually been executed, the results may have under- or overcompensated the impact, if any, of certain market factors, such as lack of liquidity. Simulated trading programs in general are also subject to the fact that they are designed with the benefit of hindsight. No presentation is being made that any account will or is likely to achieve profits or losses similar to those predicted or shown.

MetaStock® Charts

MetaStock® charts and used formula language courtesy of Equis International.

ABOUT
THE AUTHOR

After earning a degree in electronics, Sylvain Vervoort started his professional career with a Belgian ITT telecommunications company. As a technical support engineer to export sales, he was training people in many parts of the world. He spent the second half of his career in the security business with Siemens. He has been studying and using technical analysis since 1978 with the birth of the European Option Exchange (EOE) in Amsterdam. After completing two years of evening classes to become an investment and credit advisor, he has conducted many courses and presentations about technical analysis. His first book (Dutch only) on technical analysis was published in 2000. Since his retirement he has been publishing articles in *Technical Analysis of Stocks & Commodities* magazine, trading short-term on stocks, E-mini futures, and Forex, and maintaining a website (http://stocata. org/) about trading based on the application of technical analysis.

Marketplace Books is the preeminent publisher of trading, investing, and finance educational material. We produce professional books, DVDs, courses, and electronic books (ebooks) that showcase the exceptional talent working in the investment world today. Started in 1993, Marketplace Books grew out of the realization that mainstream publishers were not meeting the demand of the trading and investment community. Capitalizing on the access we had through our distribution partner Traders' Library, Marketplace Books was launched, and today publishes the top authors in the industry—household names like Jack Schwager, Oliver Velez, Larry McMillan, Sheldon Natenberg, Jim Bittman, Martin Pring, and Jeff Cooper are just the beginning. We are actively acquiring some of the brightest new minds in the industry including technician Jeff Greenblatt and programmers Jean Folger and Lee Leibfarth.

From the beginning student to the professional trader, our goal is to continually provide the highest quality resources for those who want an active role in the world of finance. Our products focus on strategic information and cutting edge research to give our readers the best education possible. We are at the forefront of digital publishing and are actively pursuing innovative ways to deliver content. At our Traders' Forum events, our readers get the chance to learn and mingle with our top authors in a way unprecedented in the industry. Our titles have been translated in most major world languages and can be shipped all over the globe thanks to our preferred online bookstore, TradersLibrary.com.

Visit us today at:

www.marketplacebooks.com & www.traderslibrary.com

SOFTWARE AND INFORMATION LICENSE

The software and information on this diskette (collectively referred to as the "Product") are the property of Marketplace Books, and are protected by both United States copyright law and international copyright treaty provision. You must treat this Product just like a book, except that you may copy it into a computer to be used and you may make archival copies of the Products for the sole purpose of backing up our software and protecting your investment from loss.

By saying "just like a book," Marketplace Books means, for example, that the Product may be used by any number of people and may be freely moved from one computer location to another, so long as there is no possibility of the Product (or any part of the Product) being used at one location or on one computer while it is being used at another. Just as a book cannot be read by two different people in two different places at the same time, neither can the Product be used by two different people in two different places at the same time (unless, of course, Marketplace Books' rights are being violated).

Marketplace Books reserves the right to alter or modify the contents of the Product at any time.

This agreement is effective until terminated. The Agreement will terminate automatically without notice if you fail to comply with any provisions of this Agreement. In the event of termination by reason of your breach, you will destroy or erase all copies of the Product installed on any computer system or made for backup purposes and shall expunge the Product from your data storage facilities.

LIMITED WARRANTY

Marketplace Books warrants the physical diskette(s) enclosed herein to be free of defects in materials and workmanship for a period of sixty days from the purchase date. If Marketplace Books receives written notification within the warranty period of defects in materials or workmanship, and such notification is determined by Marketplace Books to be correct, Marketplace Books will replace the defective diskette(s). Send request to:

Customer Service
Marketplace Books
3881 Ten Oaks Rd.
Glenelg, MD 21737

The entire and exclusive liability and remedy for breach of this Limited Warranty shall be limited to replacement of defective diskette(s) and shall not include or extend any claim for or right to cover any other damages, including but not limited to, loss of profit, data, or use of the software, or special, incidental, or consequential damages or other similar claims, even if Marketplace Books has been specifically advised as to the possibility of such damages. In no event will Marketplace Books's liability for any damages to you or any other person ever exceed the lower of suggested list price or actual price paid for the license to use the Product, regardless of any form of the claim.

Marketplace Books SPECIFICALLY DISCLAIMS ALL OTHER WARRANTIES, EXPRESS OR IMPLIED, INCLUDING BUT NOT LIMITED TO, ANY IMPLIED WARRANTY OF MERCHANTABILITY OR FITNESS FOR A PARTICULAR PURPOSE. Specifically, Marketplace Books makes no representation or warranty that the Product is fit for any particular purpose and any implied warranty of merchantability is limited to the sixty day duration of the Limited Warranty covering the physical diskette(s) only (and not the software or information) and is otherwise expressly and specifically disclaimed.

This Limited Warranty gives you specific legal rights; you may have others which may vary from state to state. Some states do not allow the exclusion of incidental or consequential damages, or the limitation on how long an implied warranty lasts, so some of the above may not apply to you.

This Agreement constitutes the entire agreement between the parties relating to use of the Product. The terms of any purchase order shall have no effect on the terms of this Agreement. Failure of Marketplace Books to insist at any time on strict compliance with this Agreement shall not constitute a waiver of any rights under this Agreement. This Agreement shall be construed and governed in accordance with the laws of Maryland. If any provision of this Agreement is held to be contrary to law, that provision will be enforced to the maximum extent permissible and the remaining provisions will remain in force and effect.

Installation Instructions

This CD has an Autorun feature. Insert the CD into the CD-ROM drive and it will start automatically. Please allow sufficient time for loading.

If the Autorun feature does not work, insert the CD, open your CD-ROM drive and double-click on the MetaStock_Demo_CD.exe icon. From here you can access introductions to the MetaStock program. These are denoted by "MetaStock Power Tools" and "MetaStock A-Z." To view the videos, simply click on the subject heading. To receive a special offer on the MetaStock program, click on the "Special Offer" subject heading or call 1-800-252-9901 and mention code "Capturing Profit." This will ensure you receive your discount. This CD also contains bonus indicators meant as a follow up to the book. These indicators will not work unless you have installed MetaStock previous to installing the indicators. To install the indicators, click on the "Capturing Profit with Technical Analysis" subject heading.

1. We recommend not changing the default installation settings.

2. This program is best viewed using small fonts.

3. This CD is best viewed in 800 X 600 pixels and 256 colors.

4. For additional support, please go to Support at www.equis.com.

Learn more about MetaStock at www.equis.com/capturingprofit/.

EQUIS INTERNATIONAL

90 S. 400 W. Ste. 620, Salt Lake City, UT 84101

800-252-9901

Web Site: www.equis.com